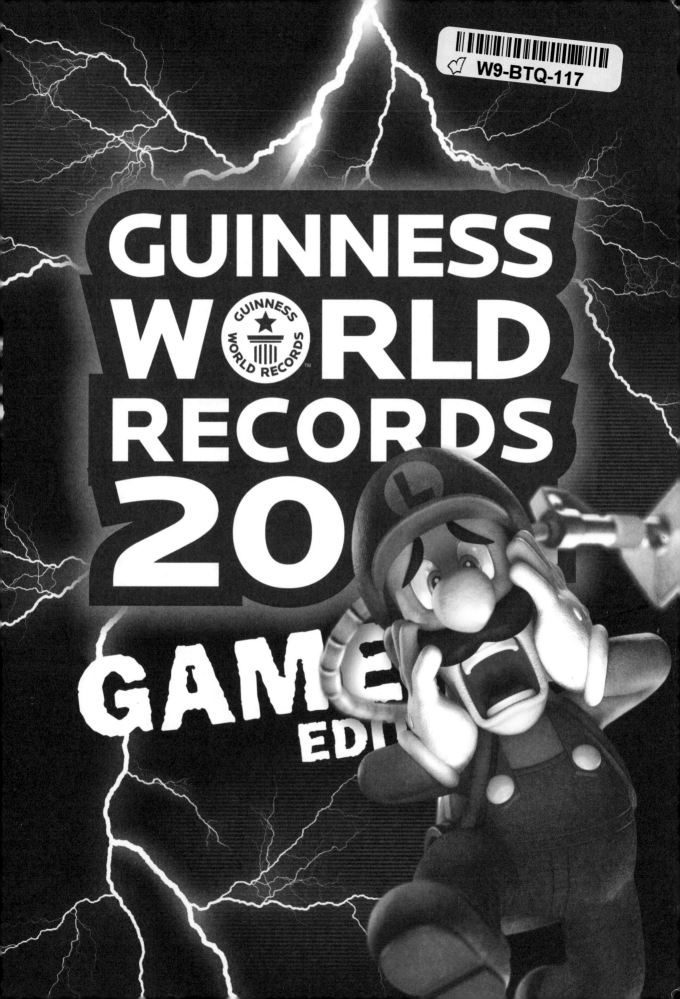

GUINNESS WORLD RECORDS

GUINNESS WORLD RECORDS™

RECORDS
20
GAMER
EDI

British Library Cataloguing-in-Publication Data: a catalogue record for this book is available from the British Library.

ISBN-13: 978-1-908843-07-4
ISBN-10: 1-908843-07-1

Check the official **GWR GAMER'S EDITION** website at: **guinnessworld records.com/ gamers**.

ACCREDITATION:
Guinness World Records Limited has a very thorough accreditation system for record verification. However, while every effort is made to ensure accuracy, Guinness World Records Limited cannot be held responsible for any errors contained in this work. Feedback from our readers on any point of accuracy is also welcomed.

GAMER'S EDITION 2014

SENIOR MANAGING EDITOR
Stephen Fall

LAYOUT EDITORS
Eddie de Oliveira
Lucian Randall

ASSISTANT EDITOR
Roxanne Mackey

EDITORIAL CONSULTANTS
Rob Cave
Eddie de Oliveira

PROOFREADING
Matthew White

INDEX
Chris Bernstein

PICTURE EDITOR
Michael Whitty

DEPUTY PICTURE EDITORS
Fran Morales
Laura Nieberg

TALENT RESEARCHER
Jenny Langridge

ORIGINAL PHOTOGRAPHY
Paul Michael Hughes
Ranald Mackechnie
Kevin Scott Ramos
Ryan Schude

DESIGN
Ryan Gale

VP PUBLISHING
Frank Chambers

EDITOR-IN-CHIEF
Craig Glenday

DIRECTOR OF PROCUREMENT
Patricia Magill

PUBLISHING MANAGER
Jane Boatfield

PUBLISHING EXECUTIVE
Charlie Peacock

PRINTING
Courier Corporation, USA

CONTRIBUTORS
Louise Blain
Matthew Bradford
Martyn Carroll
Rob Cave
David Crookes
Andy Davidson
Paul Dean
Matthew Edwards
Rachael Finn
Ellie Gibson
Ben Griffin
David Hawksett
Phil Iwaniuk
Dan Morgan
James Newman
Iain Simons
Philippa Warr
Dan Whitehead

GUINNESS WORLD RECORDS

President: Alistair Richards

SVP Global Business Development: Frank Foley

SVP Americas: Peter Harper

President (Greater China): Rowan Simons

Country Manager (Japan): Erika Ogawa

Country Manager (UAE): Talal Omar

VP Creative: Paul O'Neill

PROFESSIONAL SERVICES
EVP Finance, Legal, HR & IT: Alison Ozanne

Financial Controller: Scott Paterson

Management Accountants: Dan Artman, Shabana Zaffar

Accounts Payable Manager: Kimberley Dennis

Accounts Payable Assistant: Victoria Aweh

Accounts Receivable Manager: Lisa Gibbs

Head of Legal & Business Affairs: Raymond Marshall

Legal & Business Affairs Manager: Michael Goulbourn

Legal & Business Affairs Executive: Xiangyun Rablen

Director of IT: Rob Howe

Senior Developer: Philip Raeburn

Web Applications Developer: Anurag Jha

Desktop Support: Ainul Ahmed

Head of HR: Jane Atkins

Office Manager (UK): Jacqueline Angus

HR & Office Manager (US): Morgan Wilber

Office Manager (Japan): Michiyo Uehara

Office Manager (Greater China): Tina Shi

Office Assistant (Greater China): Daisy Xie

TELEVISION
SVP Programming & TV Sales: Christopher Skala

Director of Television: Rob Molloy

TV Distribution Manager: Denise Carter Steel

GLOBAL MARKETING
SVP Global Marketing: Samantha Fay

Marketing Director (US): Stuart Claxton

Marketing Director (Greater China): Sharon Yang

PR Manager (US): Jamie Panas

PR & Marketing Executive (US): Sara Wilcox

Marketing Manager: Justine Tommey

Marketing Executive: Christelle BeTrong

PR Director (UK): Jaime Strang, Amarilis Whitty

PR & Marketing Manager (UK): Claire Burgess

PR & Marketing Manager (Japan): Kazami Kamioka

Senior PR Executive: Damian Field

PR Executive: Jamie Clarke

Marcomms Co-ordinator: Anne-Lise Rouse

Director of Digital Media: Katie Forde

Video Content Manager: Adam Moore

Community Manager: Dan Barrett

Online Editor: Kevin Lynch

Designer: Neil Fitter

Design Executive: Jon Addison

Creative & Brand Executive (Japan): Momoko Cunneen

Content Manager (US): Mike Janela

Content Manager (Japan): Takafumi Suzuki

Digital Manager (Greater China): Jacky Yuan

COMMERCIAL SALES
SVP Sales UK & EMEA: Nadine Causey

VP Commercial: Andrew Brown

Publishing, Sales & Product Director (US): Jennifer Gilmour

Content Director (Greater China): Angela Wu

Senior National Accounts Manager (UK & international): John Pilley

Sales & Distribution Executive (UK & international): Richard Stenning

Licensing Manager, Products & Promotions: Samantha Prosser

Licensing Manager, Publishing: Emma Davies

Commercial Director (Greater China): Blythe Fitzwiliam

Business Development Manager (US): Amanda Mochan

Business Development Manager (Japan): Kaoru Ishikawa

Account Managers: Dong Cheng (China), Ralph Hannah (UK/Paraguay), Annabel Lawday (UK), Takuro Maruyama (Japan), Nicole Pando (USA), Terje Purga (Estonia), Nikhil Shukla (India), Lucia Sinigagliesi (Italy), Şeyda Subaşı-Gemici (Turkey), Charlie Weisman (USA)

Account Co-ordinator (Japan): Asumi Funatsu

Commercial Assistant (Greater China): Catherine Gao

Project Manager (UAE): Samer Khallouf

RECORDS MANAGEMENT
SVP Records: Marco Frigatti

Director of RMT: Turath Alsaraf

Head of Records Management (US): Kimberly Partrick

Head of Records Management (Japan): Carlos Martínez

Database Manager: Carim Valerio

RMT Operations: Alex Angert (USA), Anatole Baboukhian (France), Benjamin Backhouse (UK), Kirsty Bennett (Australia), Jack Brockbank (UK), Fortuna Burke (UK), Shantha Chinniah (UK), Michael Empric (USA), Jacqueline Fitt (UK), Kirsti Gorringe (UK), Johanna Hessling (USA), Lisa Hoffman (Canada), Tom Ibison (UK), Sam Mason (UK), Aya McMillan (Japan), Deborah Mrongowius (Germany), Annie Nguyen (USA), Eva Norroy (UK), Anna Orford (France), Pravin Patel (UK), Philip Robertson (USA), Chris Sheedy (Australia), Athena Simpson (USA), Elizabeth Smith (UK), Louise Toms (UK), Gulnaz Ukassova (Kazakhstan), Lorenzo Veltri (Italy), Charles Wharton (UK)

GUINNESS WORLD RECORDS 2014

GAMER'S EDITION

CONTENTS

116

INTRODUCTION

Welcome to *Guinness World Records Gamer's Edition 2014*. We are delighted to bring you the seventh edition of the world's greatest gaming almanac.

You'll find hundreds of new and updated records here, with awesome images of your favourite games. Our picture team has been out and about, too, and photographed some of our Officially Amazing record holders.

Meet instant gamer Stephen Kish, who has set records on both *Angry Birds* (see pp.72–73) and *PAC-Man* (pp.174–75).

Then there's Caped Crusader fan Sean "DarthKnight" Grayson, who took on the dangers of both *Batman: Arkham Asylum* and *Arkham City* and came out victorious. Read about his record on pp.28–29.

James Evans and Bruce Ashton set gaming records through mind-boggling physical extremes – read about their ice hockey endurance feat on pp.60–61, which helped them raise money for the Canadian Cancer Society.

Meet Carrie Swidecki, who believes that fitness games are a fun way to get healthy. She proved it with an astonishing marathon on *Just Dance 4* (see pp.162–63).

ON THE PAGE

Look out for the Boost and Bo:om! boxes. Boost brings you records on a particular theme, such as speed-runs, while Bo:om! serves up the tastiest nuggets of gaming trivia. And for a gaming tip or hint, check out our Tip-Offs.

BOOST
SPACE INNOVATORS

In 1981, legendary arcade release *Space Invaders* (Taito, 1978) became the **first arcade game** debated in British Parliament when the UK's Labour Party MP George Foulkes tabled a bill to have it banned for what he described as a connection to child "deviancy". It was also the **first game to feature animated aliens**. Decades after its heyday during the Golden Age of arcades, *Space Invaders* finally altered its basic, famous gameplay function: the **first *Space Invaders* game with vertical movement** was Taito's

BO:OM!

If imitation is the sincerest form of flattery, Mario Kart 64's (Nintendo, 1996) track designers must be delighted by the most-played track in *LittleBigPlanet Karting* (Sony, 2012). The level named "MooMoo Farm – MKART 64", created by gamer MooJoolt, is a recreation of the Moo Moo Farm farmyard track from the N64 game. It has been played 184,620 times and received 22,904 "hearts".

TIP-OFF
Are you considering selling an item? It's always a good idea to check the item's price history to see whether it has the potential to make you more gold at a later date or whether now is the right time to try to shift it.

MARIO

LOWDOWN

PUBLISHER: Nintendo
DEVELOPER: Nintendo
DEBUT: 1983

The **longest-running gaming character**, Mario was originally a carpenter named Jumpman when he made his debut in *Donkey Kong* (Nintendo, 1981), the **first platform game**. He got his big solo break in the arcade game *Mario Bros.* (1983), and has evaded bad guy Bowser ever since.

NAME THE GAME
Wife of Mortimer Goth, the dark-haired Bella's favourite colour is red.

MOST CRITICALLY ACCLAIMED GAME
Super Mario Galaxy (2007) is the most acclaimed game of all time, with a GameRankings score of 97.64% as of 31 July 2013. Sequel *Super Mario Galaxy 2* (2010) is third, on 97.35%, with Nintendo's The *Legend of Zelda: Ocarina of Time* (1998) sandwiched between them on 97.54%. *Super Mario Galaxy*'s score makes it the **most critically acclaimed Wii game** and the **most critically acclaimed Mario game**.

TIP-OFF
Before you step through the door in each boss battle of *New Super Mario Bros. U* (2012), hit the hidden "?" block to get a power-up. Stand next to the nearby wall and jump to reveal the block and get a helping hand.

THIS YEAR'S RECORDS

In terms of records, our focus this time is on the most fundamental achievements. Which games of each genre have earned the highest (and the lowest!) ratings? Which games have sold the most? What are the highest scores on your favourite games? How long can you play them for? Look out for the Lowdown box on the left-hand side of each records spread. This will give you a brief guide to the most essential information on each game or, if it's on one of our Best of the Rest round-ups, to the gaming genre. There's also our Name the Game quiz, which starts on p.18. Before you check the answers on p.206, how many can you get right?

007

As usual, we also have news, charts and a panoramic range of features to round up what's been happening in gaming. These features cover everything from *Star Trek* to arcade games, superheroes to the great gaming crash of 1983.

FEATURE
HEROES

These are the ultimate gaming heroes – the super-men and women achieving the impossible in the name of all things good. Eddie de Oliveira checks out some of the games behind the flowing capes.

SPIDER-MAN
BATMAN
THOR

XBOX ONE

LOWDOWN

INSIDE OUT

THE GAMES

NAME THE GAME

We always like to hear from readers, so please tell us what you think of the book: follow us on Twitter @GWRGamers or visit our website at the address below. And if you think you can set a record of your own, turn to p.8 to find out how.

And finally, we hope you enjoy the exciting new look of the book. Our designer Ryan Gale shares our passion for gaming and it shows in his fresh and dynamic pages.

BE A RECORD-BREAKER!

Anyone can be a record-breaker. You might have developed a pioneering game, be a master at speed-running and setting high scores, or have a considerable collection – if so, we want to hear from you.

Record-breaking is free and open to everyone, so if you're keen to get your hands on an official Guinness World Records certificate, find us online at **guinnessworldrecords.com**. Just click on "Set a record" and tell us about your idea. If it meets the criteria for a record, we'll send you the guidelines explaining what evidence we need to assess your claim.

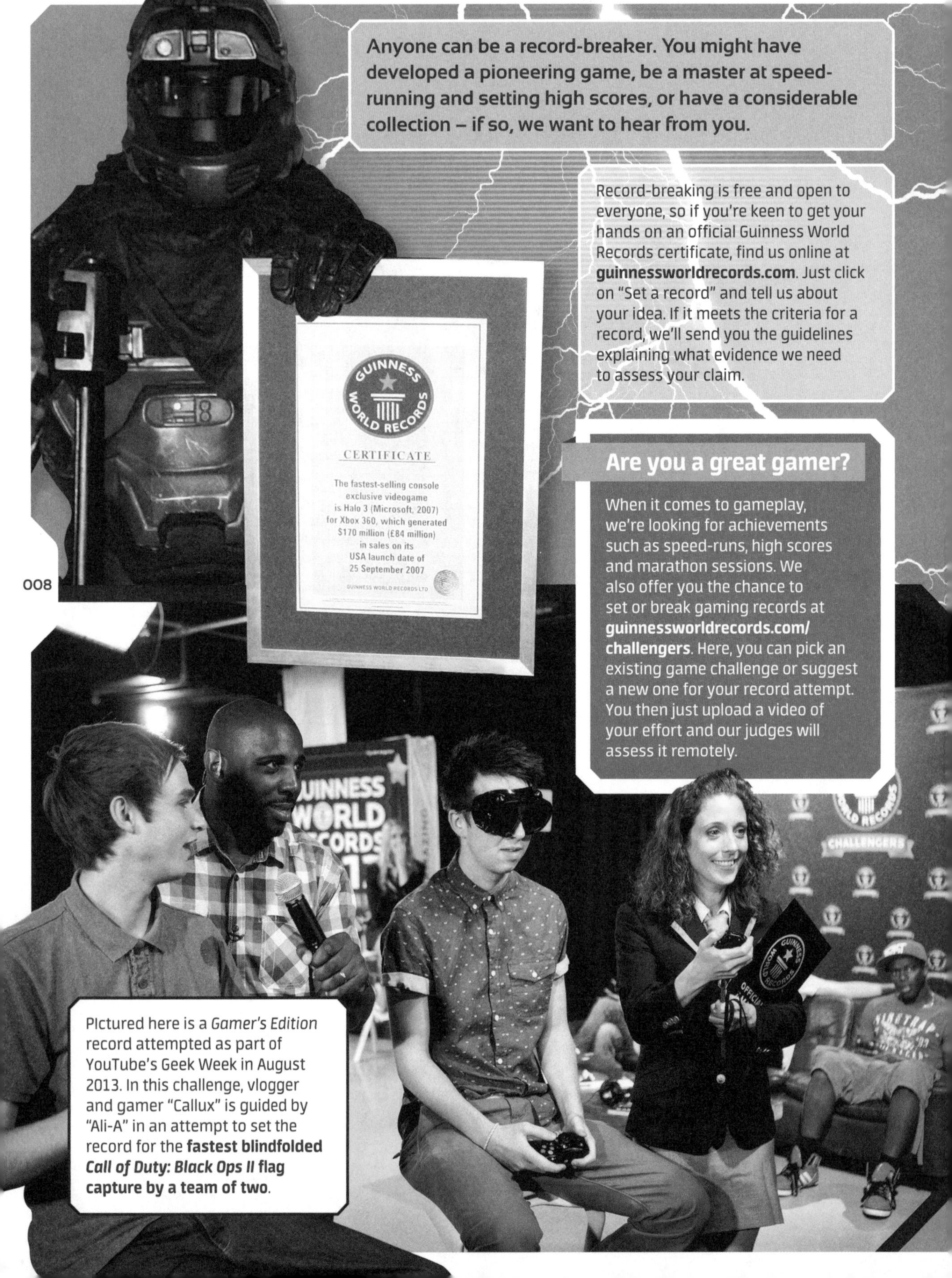

Are you a great gamer?

When it comes to gameplay, we're looking for achievements such as speed-runs, high scores and marathon sessions. We also offer you the chance to set or break gaming records at **guinnessworldrecords.com/challengers**. Here, you can pick an existing game challenge or suggest a new one for your record attempt. You then just upload a video of your effort and our judges will assess it remotely.

GUINNESS WORLD RECORDS

CERTIFICATE

The fastest-selling console exclusive videogame is Halo 3 (Microsoft, 2007) for Xbox 360, which generated $170 million (£84 million) in sales on its USA launch date of 25 September 2007

GUINNESS WORLD RECORDS LTD

Pictured here is a *Gamer's Edition* record attempted as part of YouTube's Geek Week in August 2013. In this challenge, vlogger and gamer "Callux" is guided by "Ali-A" in an attempt to set the record for the **fastest blindfolded *Call of Duty: Black Ops II* flag capture by a team of two**.

Hideo Kojima (Japan) – the writer, designer and godfather of stealth behind the multi-record-holding *Metal Gear* (Konami, 1987–present, *see pp.38–39*) – is just one of many games developers recognized by Guinness World Records.

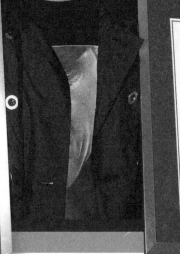

Are you a games developer?

We're not just about *playing* games – we want to hear from the designers, programmers and artists who *develop* the games. Have you created record-breaking graphics or audio? Or maybe you've released a superlative mod or even a game engine? If so, tell us about it. We also want to hear about sales figures from games publishers – such as Microsoft, who issued Bungie's *Halo 3* (2007; *facing page, top*), the **fastest-selling console exclusive game** on the Xbox 360.

Are you a collector?

Being a record-breaker can mean being the first to achieve something, having the most of anything – from in-game aliens to XP – or amassing loads of memorable memorabilia, just like Michael Thomasson (USA, *above*). He has the **largest collection of videogames** – find out how many on pp.204–05 and then get to work beating him! As ever, collect your evidence and drop us a line so we can verify your claim.

The **best-selling videogame** has long been *Wii Sports* (2006) from Nintendo, whose general manager Shigeru Miyamoto is pictured holding their certificate. If you're a producer, composer, publisher or anyone else who works on games and you think you've got what it takes to join the likes of Shigeru, get in touch with us.

ROUND-UP

Roxanne Mackey looks at what's happened in gaming since our previous book went to press.

GAME OF THE YEAR ANNOUNCED

At the Golden Joystick Awards on 26 October 2012, *The Elder Scrolls V: Skyrim* (Bethesda, 2011) was voted the Ultimate Game of the Year, as well as collecting awards for Best RPG and Top Gaming Moment with "Throat of the World". Selling more than 3.5 million copies in its first two days of release, *The Elder Scrolls V* is also the **fastest-selling open-world RPG**.

CALL OF DUTY BREAKS RECORDS

Within 24 hours of its 2012 launch, on 13 November, Treyarch's *Call of Duty: Black Ops II* had grossed $500 million (£315 million). This surpassed *Call of Duty: Modern Warfare 3*'s record as the **highest-grossing videogame in 24 hours**. *Black Ops II* also set the **fastest time for a game to gross $1 billion**, taking just 15 days to reach the landmark. The next instalment, *Call of Duty: Ghosts*, is scheduled for release in November 2013.

PlayStation Mobile

On 3 October 2012, Sony launched PlayStation Mobile, a service for gamers to download third-party and PlayStation games to their handheld console or Android device. Andrew House (*right*), President of Sony Computer Entertainment Europe, announced the service at E3 2012.

BAFTA AWARDS

The 2013 BAFTA Games Awards, held in London, UK, on 5 March, saw *Dishonored* (Arkane Studios, 2012) winning Best Game. But the night belonged to Thatgamecompany's *Journey* (2012), which took five awards including Game Design and Artistic Achievement. An unexpected winner of the Sports/Fitness award was *New Star Soccer* (Simon Read, 2012), beating *FIFA 13* among others. Turn to pp.196–97 for more.

NEW NINTENDO

The first of the eighth-generation consoles, the Wii U was launched on 18 November 2012. The new Nintendo console came with a touchscreen GamePad, a move away from the original Wii Remote, and launch titles included *Nintendo Land* and *New Super Mario Bros. U*. Disappointing sales led Nintendo to announce a price cut ahead of the launches of the Xbox One and PS4. The Wii U doesn't look set to scale the heights of its predecessor, the Wii – the **best-selling Nintendo home console**, with sales of more than 100 million units as of August 2013.

The Wii Mini (*left*), launched in Canada in December 2012, is a bright red, scaled-down version of the Wii, complete with MotionPlus Remote and Nunchuk.

WALKING DEAD HONOURED AT VGAs

The year 2012 saw the 10th anniversary of the Spike Video Game Awards. Held on 7 December, the VGAs saw *The Walking Dead* (Telltale Games, 2012, *left*) win Game of the Year. Indeed, *The Walking Dead* was the night's star, with five wins from six nominations, including Best Adapted Video Game and Best Downloadable Game. *Assassin's Creed III* (Ubisoft, 2012) had the biggest disappointment, receiving no awards despite six nominations.

MoMA VIDEOGAME EXHIBITION

The Museum of Modern Art (MoMA) in New York, USA, chose to explore the connections between art and gaming with an exhibition entitled "Applied Design". Running from 2 March 2013 to 19 January 2014, it includes images from *PAC-Man*, *The Sims*, *Katamari Damacy* and a 1984 still from *Tetris*. Pictured left is Paola Antonelli, the Senior Curator responsible.

FIRST OFFICIAL DIGITAL GAMES CHART

In 2004, the Official Charts Company (UK) began to include digital sales in its weekly music charts. The USA's *Billboard* Hot 100 did the same in 2005. Nine years later, gaming has followed suit. March 2013 saw the Association for UK Interactive Entertainment (UKIE) launch the **first official digital games chart**, combining physical and digital PC sales. The first chart ranked *SimCity* (EA, 2013, *left*) at No.1, with the most combined physical and digital units sold.

2012'S MOST ACCLAIMED

Set in the fictional Japanese town of Inaba, the PS Vita role-playing game *Persona 4: Golden* (Atlus) was the most critically acclaimed game released in 2012. It scored a mammoth rating of 94.16% on GameRankings. *Journey* (Thatgamecompany) for the PS3 came in second place with a score of 92.56%. See page 194 for the full top 10.

2012'S BEST-SELLERS

The best-selling videogame of 2012 – selling almost twice as many copies as *FIFA 13* (EA) in second place – was *Call of Duty: Black Ops II* (Treyarch), which sold 20.6 million copies across the Xbox 360, PS4, PC and Wii U. For the full list of 2012's best-selling games and platforms, as well as a snapshot of 2013 sales, turn to pp.194–95.

2012'S WORST-RATED

Survival-horror flop *AMY* (VectorCell) was the worst-rated game of 2012; the Xbox 360 version had a GameRankings score of 25.81%, while the PS3 release fared little better with 27.24%. Surprisingly, the third worst-rated game was a *Call of Duty* title – *Call of Duty: Black Ops: Declassified* (nStigate Games) for the PS Vita scored just 33.21%.

RAISE YOUR HANDHELDS

Nintendo shocked everyone with their announcement of the 2DS (*right*), a new handheld bundled with the unreleased *Pokémon X and Y* (Game Freak) and priced at $130, or £109.99 in the UK. The 2DS plays all DS and 3DS games (although without the 3D effect) and, while it does contain two screens, it isn't hinged. Nintendo hopes the 2DS' lower price will serve as an "entry-level" system for casual gamers.

Not content with unveiling the PS4 in 2013, Sony also announced the PlayStation Vita TV, a tiny box that hooks up to a TV either wirelessly or via cable. Vita TV will support 1,300 games taken from the PS Vita, PSP and original PlayStation, and offer remote play for PS4 titles. It will also play music, TV and movies.

In what was a very busy year for the Japanese company, Sony developed a redesigned, more affordable, wi-fi-enabled version of the Vita called the PS Vita 2000 (*right*), which is 20% thinner and 15% lighter than the standard Vita.

DEFIANT TIE-IN

Released on 2 April 2013, the *Defiance* TV show and game became the **first videogame and TV show to directly influence one another**. Trion Worlds' MMORPG and the TV series of the same name sees show characters appear in the game, and allows players to influence parts of the show, such as the chance to win their in-game avatar recreated as a character in the second series. Read more on p.144.

SAINTLY SINNER

Australia's "R18+" adult rating for games was introduced on 1 January 2013, and *Saints Row IV* (Volition, Inc.) was the first game to be refused it.

In fact, *Saints Row IV* was twice denied the rating by the Australian Classification Board, who effectively banned it as without certification it could not be put on sale. Publisher Koch Media appealed unsuccessfully before a modified version of the game was resubmitted and granted a delayed release in September 2013.

State of Decay was the second game banned in Australia; developer Undead Labs made cuts to the game in order for it to be granted a rating.

NEWS IN BRIEF

• In May 2013, the first "Game Designer in Residence" was appointed at the Victoria & Albert Museum in London, UK. Sophia George (*above*), aged 22, won a 2014 BAFTA Ones to Watch award, and will use the history of British art and design in galleries from the years 1500 to 1900 to inspire a game that will be released in 2014.

• Hiroshi Yamauchi, president of Nintendo, died aged 85 on 19 September 2013. He took over in 1949 and – with 53 years at the top – made the trading card company into a videogame behemoth.

• NCAA college football player Ryan Hart began legal proceedings against EA Sports for allegedly using his likeness in *NCAA Football* (2004–06) without permission, in a case that rumbles on.

• Namco Bandai announced plans to release a free2play version of its long-running fighting series *SoulCalibur* (1996–present). As reported in Japanese gaming magazine *Famitsu*, *SoulCalibur: Lost Swords* is being developed for the PlayStation 3.

• Microsoft announced that it would support the Xbox 360 until at least 2016 with 100 new games.

• Rockstar's *Grand Theft Auto V* had a huge development and marketing budget of $275 million (£170 million), making it the **largest budget for a game**. The only production to have cost more is 2007 movie *Pirates of the Caribbean: At World's End*, at $300 million (£190 million).

• Apple reported opening weekend sales of new iPhones in September 2013 of 9 million units, breaking its own record of 5 million, to be the **fastest-selling portable gaming system**. Apple's sales were boosted by releasing two models rather than one, and for the first time selling in China on the same day as the USA.

TITANIC TRIUMPH

At E3 in June 2013, the Game Critics Awards Best of Show went to *Titanfall* (Respawn Entertainment, due in 2014). The FPS cleaned up with six gongs. For more on the E3 awards, see p.203. E3 2013 was one of the most exciting ever, notable for Sony's unveiling of the PS4 and Microsoft's Xbox One press conference, at which they announced the console's $499 price tag (£429). Hours later, to raucous cheers, Sony revealed the PS4 would retail at $399 (£349). In addition, several key eighth-generation games were revealed and you can read more about them in *Gamer's 2014*.

GOLDEN APPLES

In July 2013, Apple celebrated five years of the App Store with best-selling lists of iPhone and iPad apps – although they did not release unit sales figures.

Top 5 all-time paid-for iPhone games
1 *Angry Birds* (Rovio, 2009)
2 *Fruit Ninja* (Halfbrick Studios, 2010)
3 *Doodle Jump* (Lima Sky, 2009)
4 *Cut the Rope* (ZeptoLab, 2010)
5 *Angry Birds Seasons* (Rovio, 2010)

Top 5 all-time paid-for iPad games
1 *Angry Birds HD* (Rovio, 2009)
2 *Angry Birds Seasons HD* (Rovio, 2010)
3 *Where's My Water?* (Creature Feep, 2011)
4 *Fruit Ninja HD* (Halfbrick Studios, 2010)
5 *Angry Birds Space HD* (Rovio, 2012)

Source: charts released by Apple, July 2013

BUCKING CONVENTIONS

With 340,000 attendees, Gamescom 2013 in Germany was the **largest videogame convention** ever, and you can read more about it – and other conventions – on pp.70–71. Game premieres included combat MMO *War Thunder* (Gaijin Entertainment) and *Call of Duty: Ghosts* (Infinity Ward), both set for late 2013 release. Bungie's *Destiny* (due in 2014) won the Best of Gamescom award.

CONSOLE GENERATIONS

The first videogame console was released in 1972. With the arrival of Sony's and Microsoft's long-anticipated eighth-generation systems, Andy Davidson opens his console cupboard and looks back at the hits and misses of the past 40 years...

1st GENERATION

1972–1977

BEST-SELLING CONSOLE:
☐ Magnavox Odyssey
△ 330,000 units

Tennis (Magnavox Odyssey, 1968)

The **first videogame console**, the Magnavox Odyssey, was designed by Ralph Baer (USA) in 1968, but it wasn't released until August 1972. Despite an underwhelming start, the Odyssey had shifted a solid 330,000 units by 1975. Basic but fun, it could only produce squares of light on a TV, so gamers were required to attach a translucent, coloured plastic game sheet on to the screen in order to imitate graphics. What's more, the Odyssey had no sound. It came with six removable game chips, carrying 12 games in total, which were ostensibly variations of arcade smash *Pong* (Atari, 1972).

Pong itself landed in the living room in 1975 with Atari's first console, Home Pong, complete with bleepy sounds and on-screen scoring. Nintendo joined the party in 1976 with the Color TV-Game 6, featuring built-in games *Volleyball*, *Tennis* and *Hockey*. Like Home Pong, Nintendo's system only ran built-in titles and did not support game chips.

2nd GENERATION

1976–1984

BEST-SELLING CONSOLE:
☐ Atari 2600
△ 27.64 million units

Pitfall! (Activision, 1982)

The second generation offered gamers far greater choice, with hundreds of games rather than the few that were made for the Odyssey. The **first second-generation console** was the Fairchild Channel F, which came out in 1976. It was also the **first console to use a microprocessor** and the **first console to use ROM cartridges**, which stored the games.

But it was the Atari 2600, released in 1977, that defined this era and led the way with its iconic, stylish wooden panels.

The 2600 made it big with ports of arcade hits such as *Space Invaders* (Taito, 1980) and *Donkey Kong* (Nintendo, 1981). It included an eight-way joystick with one button, making games easier to control.

The 2600 had two main rivals: toy manufacturer Mattel's first foray into gaming, 1979's Intellivision, and the ColecoVision, released in 1982. The latter was part of the second wave of this generation, and boasted superior graphics and sound to the Atari 2600.

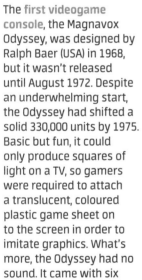

MAGNAVOX ODYSSEY

ATARI 2600

RAY OF LIGHT

Ralph Baer, the man behind the Magnavox, is also the creator of the **first videogame console peripheral**, the light gun that came with the *Shooting Gallery* game for the Odyssey. Some 80,000 units of the innovative gaming rifle were sold. Baer's other famous invention is the electronic game *Simon*.

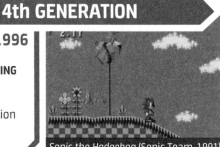

3rd GENERATION

1983–1992

BEST-SELLING CONSOLE:
☐ NES
△ 61.91 million units

Super Mario Bros. (Nintendo, 1985)

Also called the 8-bit era, this generation saw Japan become the centre of the gaming world for the first time with the Nintendo Entertainment System (NES, first released as Famicom in Japan in 1983) and Sega Master System (1985). Both consoles offered far more detailed graphics than their predecessors. The Famicom/NES was the **first 8-bit console**, and it made Mario into a global star. Its iconic controller was the **first console gamepad**, and a template for future versions across different platforms; it contained buttons rather than a stick or wheel, and improved game control markedly.

Rolled out in the USA in 1985, the NES was a global hit and sealed Nintendo's place at the top table of console manufacturers. By comparison, Sega's console sold "just" 13 million. The Master System was, in fact, Sega's second machine of this generation; the SG-1000, released at the start of the era in 1983, was not a big sales success.

4th GENERATION

1987–1996

BEST-SELLING CONSOLE:
☐ SNES
△ 49.1 million units

Sonic the Hedgehog (Sonic Team, 1991)

The **first fourth-generation console** and **first 16-bit console** was the TurboGrafx-16, manufactured by Japanese firm NEC in 1987. A year later, it became the **first videogame console to play CD-ROMs** upon the release of the PC-Engine CD-ROM² add-on.

Despite NEC's enterprise, Nintendo and Sega remained the dominant forces with their 16-bit consoles: the Super Nintendo Entertainment System (SNES, Super Famicom in Japan) and the Mega Drive (Sega Genesis in the USA).

The SNES made use of additional enhancement chips built into game cartridges, such as the Super FX co-processor chip that rendered thousands of polygons. Sega later released its own Mega CD and 32X add-ons, but these extras came out late in the console's life span, by which point most gamers were moving on to the fifth generation. Nevertheless, the Mega Drive/Genesis sold an impressive 40 million.

O15

NES

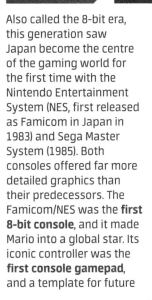

SEGA GENESIS

DREAM CAST-OFF

Despite being the **first sixth-generation console**, the Dreamcast was Sega's fifth and final machine. Poor sales of 10.6 million worldwide led to the company abandoning hardware to focus on developing software.

5th GENERATION

1993–2006

BEST-SELLING CONSOLE:
☐ PlayStation
△ 104.25 million units

Gran Turismo (Sony, 1997)

The fifth generation was notable for the fast rise of 3D games; for the first time, consoles had the power to quickly render high-quality 3D graphics. The N64, which sold 32.93 million, was the **first 64-bit console**, and also the **first console built for four-player use**. *Mario Kart 64* (Nintendo, 1996) allowed up to four players to simultaneously take part in races against each other as well as in-game, unplayable characters.

Competing alongside the Nintendo 64 and Sega Saturn, Sony entered the console market for the first time in 1995 with the PlayStation, and quickly altered the gaming landscape. With killer games such as *Final Fantasy VII* (Square, 1997) and *Gran Turismo* (Sony, 1997), as well as support from all the major publishers, the PlayStation effectively pushed the Saturn out of the market. It became the **first videogame console to ship 100 million units** (including figures for the small version, the PSOne).

6th GENERATION

1998–2013

BEST-SELLING CONSOLE:
☐ PlayStation 2
△ 157.68 million units

Halo: Combat Evolved (Bungie, 2001)

The Sega Dreamcast's 1998 release put it ahead of the sixth-generation pack, but it proved a financial disaster for Sega (*see above*). Nintendo's GameCube shifted 21.74 million units, but was held back by its tiny number of online games – and this era heralded the start of online gaming. The sixth generation opened up new opportunities for gamers keen to compete with others around the world, and Microsoft's Xbox, Sony's PlayStation 2 and the Dreamcast all contained substantial internet gaming services. The Dreamcast and the PS2 required extra hardware to connect to broadband internet, while the Xbox was the **first console to feature built-in ethernet**.

The PS2, released in 2000, also doubled up as a DVD player, thus broadening its appeal. Its phenomenal sales make it the **best-selling console** of all time. Microsoft's first foray into the market, in November 2001, was the final console release of this generation.

N64

PS2

BEST-SELLING GAMES BY GENERATION

1ST-GEN	The 12 games shipped with the Magnavox Odyssey: 330,000
2ND-GEN	**PAC-Man (Atari, 1981): 7.81 million**
3RD-GEN	*Super Mario Bros.* (Nintendo, 1985): 40.24 million
4TH-GEN	**Super Mario World (Nintendo EAD, 1990): 20.60 million**
5TH-GEN	*Super Mario 64* (Nintendo EAD, 1996): 11.89 million
6TH-GEN	**Grand Theft Auto: San Andreas (Rockstar, 2004): 20.81 million**
7TH-GEN	*Wii Sports* (Nintendo EAD, 2006): 81.34 million

7th GENERATION

2004–?

BEST-SELLING CONSOLE:
☐ Wii
△ 100 million units

Wii Sports (Nintendo EAD, 2006)

Coming out a year before the PlayStation 3, Microsoft's Xbox 360 was the **first HD console** when it launched in November 2005. While the 360 supported HD DVD, the PS3 became the **first console to support Blu-ray**, an HD video format that took off with the public. (Sony's format victory in the battle of high-def was complete when Microsoft announced that the eighth-generation Xbox One would support Blu-ray.)

As the PS3 and 360 continued to increase processor power, Nintendo focused on gameplay and accessibility. The result was the Wii, a console that stuck with the graphics of its predecessor, the GameCube, but added innovative motion control via the Wii Remote, offering appeal beyond hardcore gamers. The Wii's rivals released their own motion controllers in 2010: the PS Move and the Xbox 360's Kinect, the **fastest-selling gaming peripheral**, which sold an average of 933,488 units per week in its first 60 days (*see p.20*).

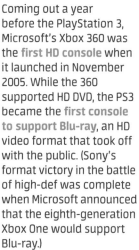

Wii

SYSTEM FAILURES

Some consoles define their generations, while others flop and disappear without a trace…

ATARI JAGUAR 1993–1996

Its advertising slogan was "Do the Math". The "math" added up to sales of around 200,000 and Atari quit the console market for good.

3DO 1993–1996

The 3DO could be manufactured by any number of different companies that licensed it, but the $700 (£465) price tag proved its downfall.

VIRTUAL BOY July–December 1995

Nintendo's first stab at 3D was innovative, but long periods of playing left users feeling dizzy and nauseous. It was pulled after five months.

APPLE BANDAI PIPPIN 1995–1997

Proof that not everything Apple touches turns to gold, slow processor and modem speeds condemned the Pippin to a quick demise after only 42,000 units were shifted.

PLAYSTATION 4

LOWDOWN

In the battle of the next-generation consoles, Sony won the race to reveal theirs before Microsoft got out details of their Xbox One (*see pp.20–21*). On 20 February 2013, Sony showed off the improved Dualshock controller, and when the console itself appeared at E3 in June with a slew of exclusives, the war against Microsoft truly began.

018

NAME THE GAME
Krieg carries an axe and exclaims "I'm here to shank and smile" in which shooter?

INSIDE OUT

Inside that sleek matte box – a parallelogram form seen from the side – lies all-new tech for PlayStation. Similar to a high-performance gaming PC, the PS4 makes the most of an all-new X86-64 AMD Jaguar processor with eight cores, which makes it easier to port over PC code. If you don't speak fluent motherboard, that's a seriously powerful processor for a home console that leaves many gaming PCs eating PlayStation's dust. Add in an AMD Radeon Graphics Processing Unit (GPU) that'll make PS3 titles look like they're on a 1980s ZX Spectrum, and 8 GB of unified memory (one pool of memory rather than the two on PS3) and you have lightning-fast action. The PS4 is an exceptionally powerful piece of technology to slide under your TV.

Despite the gradual shift to digital content, discs are here to stay for the next generation and the PS4 has an improved Blu-ray disc drive with three times the read speed of its predecessor.

Three USB 3.0 ports mean faster charging and speedier data transfer. Plus, unlike PS3, your controllers will charge even when the console isn't awake.

Taking a nod from Vita, the new controller has a touchpad with a light bar, opening up all kinds of new opportunities for game developers.

Sony learnt its lesson from the controversial banana controller – a prototype design for the PS3 pad cruelly nicknamed for its shape and swiftly abandoned – and have gone for a less radical update for the Dualshock 4.

In another first for PlayStation, a speaker on the controller will handle more intimate sound effects such as reloads and will open up a whole new level of fear when it comes to scary sound effects in survival-horror games.

The Wall•E lookalike motion-tracking PlayStation Eye is an optional extra with 3D depth perception from two 1,280 x 800 cameras and the ability to detect even the smallest of movements. It can work with the motion-detecting controller to overlay the real world in games via video capture. New psychological horror game *Daylight* (Zombie Studios), while not using the Eye's full potential, takes photos of your reactions to the game's most terrifying moments.

The Eye features two cameras plus four microphones that can be used for voice control in games.

THE GAMES

Sony's line-up of exclusive titles for launch includes *Knack* (SCE Japan Studio), in which an unlikely hero must harness the power of ancient relics to save mankind; an authentic racer that tests the specifications of the next gen to the full, *Driveclub* (Evolution Studios); and steampunk Victorian actioner *The Order: 1886* (Ready at Dawn Studios). PlayStation classic shooter *Killzone* returns as *Killzone: Shadow Fall* (Guerilla Games), and *inFAMOUS* marches on with *inFAMOUS: Second Son* (Sucker Punch Productions).

Knack

inFAMOUS: Second Son

Killzone: Shadow Fall

019

XBOX ONE

LOWDOWN

Microsoft's 2013 revelations about DRM restrictions went down poorly with commentators and public alike. Similarly, the new 24-hour online check-in got a thumbs down. June's E3 saw a slew of Xbox One exclusives, yet Microsoft was forced into a U-turn (or an Xbox 180...) and took away all online restrictions. This put them on more of an even footing with Sony's upcoming PS4 (see pp.18–19).

NAME THE GAME Ellis – a mechanic turned zombie-hunter – is voiced by Eric Ladin.

INSIDE OUT

A glance inside the Xbox One's black box reveals something similar to a PS4, an X86-64 8-core AMD Jaguar CPU with 8 GB of RAM. The 500-GB hard drive also matches Sony's disk space for content and a high-speed Blu-ray player is included. The shared super-powered specs mean that Xbox One and PS4 are evenly matched for ease of multi-platform development. The Xbox One differs in acting as a hub for TV and as a Skype host for video chat, and has a fully customizable home screen that wakes up to the sound of your voice. With a built-in DVR to match PS4 recording, the Xbox One can also stream straight to website Twitch TV to share your gaming highlights.

The first Kinect sensor launched on 4 November 2010 and, by 3 January 2011, had sold 8 million units, the **fastest-selling peripheral**. Now the Kinect 2 ships with Xbox One with an HD camera that captures video at 30 frames per second. Its field of vision is 60º greater than the previous model. It can track your movements (and how much strength you put into them), render your body as a 3D image and even read your heart rate – useful for fans of fitness games.

An HDMI port at the back of the console connects to a TV set-top box. Microsoft hopes to make the Xbox One your entertainment hub rather than just a games machine.

A first for a Microsoft console, the Xbox One comes with a Blu-ray disc drive as standard for all your high-def movies.

The analog sticks are more subtle and sophisticated than the previous controller. They have been tweaked for more precise control and you need to exert 25% less force than before.

It's not strikingly different but the Xbox One controller has gone through more than 40 tweaks and innovations to reach this sleek form factor.

The plus-shaped directional pad has been updated to a new set-up, with more exact input than ever before, especially when it comes to those finger-contorting fighters.

Minecraft

Ryse: Son of Rome

Forza Motorsport 5

THE GAMES

Exclusive games on the Xbox One include the latest in the **best-selling Xbox sim driving series** with *Forza Motorsport 5* (Turn 10 Studios), *Kinect Sports Rivals* (Rare) and the headlong mix of gore and strategy that is *Ryse: Son of Rome* from Crysis studio Crytek. Also exclusive is mech-FPS *Titanfall* (Respawn Entertainment) – a deal that is considered a serious coup for Microsoft. A new version of the **best-selling Xbox Live Arcade game**, *Minecraft* (Mojang/4J Studios), has bigger worlds and expanded multiplayer features.

O21

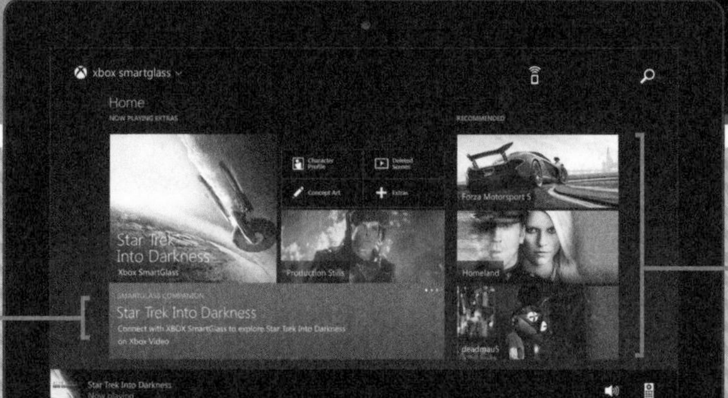

You can navigate the Xbox dashboard and play movies on your TV.

In July 2013, Microsoft announced that the Smartglass app had been downloaded 17 million times since its launch in October 2012.

The Xbox One Smartglass application runs across Windows phones, iOS and Android, and lets you see exclusive game details as well as control your Xbox One. As a second screen, it gives you additional information on movies and TV, as well as extra game content, and helpfully means that you can keep playing with no interruptions.

HANDHELDS & MOBILE

LOWDOWN

The rise of mobile platforms – particularly the Galaxy S4 and the iPhone, updated with iOS 7 – have led to gamers playing for longer sessions. Smartphone gaming experiences are catching up with handheld consoles, such as the Vita, the relatively poor sales of which suggest that the future may indeed belong to tablets and phones.

NAME THE GAME
The Big Boss, aka Willy Mackey, has a machine gun at his disposal.

PLAYSTATION VITA

Sony's handheld features beautiful visuals and a powerful processor but hasn't found its footing in the mobile market. Yet 2013 was a big year for Vita, delivering the **most critically acclaimed PS Vita game**, *Persona 4: Golden* (Atlus, 2013, *right*), with a GameRankings score of 94.16% as of 19 July 2013. The Vita is a must-have addition to the PS4 as the Remote Play feature allows PS4 games to be streamed to the handheld for sneaky bedtime play.

The Vita's 12.7-cm (5-in) OLED touchscreen has been praised for its clarity and is the largest screen on a handheld games console.

Media Molecule followed up *LittleBigPlanet* with an exclusive for Vita. *Tearaway* (Media Molecule, 2013, *below*) takes you on a whimsical adventure with the envelope-headed Iota. On occasion, players' fingers on the back touchpad are made to seem to burst into Iota's world. At another point, the front touchscreen is used to cut up paper to make a crown in a game that uses the Vita's feature set with imagination.

iPHONE & iOS

The **fastest-selling smartphone**, with more than 5 million sold in its initial weekend in September 2012, the iPhone 5 is the travelling gaming companion of choice. The **fastest-selling smartphone game** is *Temple Run 2* (Imangi Studios, *right*). Released on 17 January 2013, in two weeks it was downloaded 50 million times. That's 45 times every second!

The improved Retina display of the iPhone 5 and the 16:9 widescreen format have made gaming with thumbs an easier proposition.

Over 10 million sales of *Minecraft Pocket Edition* (Mojang, 2011) were recorded before May 2013. Available on iOS as well as Android, and with cross-platform, multiplayer support, the world builder is taking over portable devices as well as the PC and Xbox. More *Minecraft* on pp.110–11.

SAMSUNG GALAXY S4

The S4 wields a lofty 13-megapixel camera and the technology to use both front and rear cameras at once to insert the photographer in the image they're taking. More importantly for gamers, the processor has considerable power – more than enough to handle most games without a stutter – although otherwise the phone is more of an evolution than a revolutionary leap.

The Smart Pause technology allows the S4 to register when you are looking away from the screen and to pause your videos accordingly.

The S4 Group Play feature allows up to four players to connect directly and simply without needing to be on a wi-fi network.

Chances are you've already played *Candy Crush Saga* (King, 2012, *right*) and if not, where have you been all this time? As of 10 September 2013, it was the **most popular Facebook game**, with 133.6 million monthly active users (MAU). Making its way to iOS and Android, it promptly became the sweet-swapping, match-three game of choice for all ages. Its increasingly complex levels of puzzling play have seen 1 trillion candies crushed since launch.

3DS

The 3DS, the **first handheld to support glasses-free 3D**, has soared after a shaky start. The introduction of the 3DS XL has increased sales, and exclusive titles mean more Miis StreetPassing everywhere. The console achieved the **best-selling 3DS simulation** with *Animal Crossing: New Leaf* (Nintendo/ Monolith Soft, 2013, *below*), but also has strategy game *Fire Emblem: Awakening* (Intelligent Systems, 2013) – in which the units are characters rather than fodder – and more from Pikachu and co in *Pokémon X* and Y.

NINTENDO **3DS**. XL

Pokémon X and *Pokémon Y* (Game Freak) are the first 3D entries in the franchise and offer new Pokémon types and battle tactics. A new communication system called Player Search System (PSS) allows trainers to connect with friends, battle and trade both locally and globally. Other new features include Sky Battles, as trainers send their monsters for airborne spats.

The StreetPass indication light glows bright green when you meet another 3DS owner. New games in the StreetPass Mii Plaza include *StreetPass Garden* (Grezzo, 2013) for gamers whose fingers are as green as the StreetPass light.

PC, Wii U & NEW SYSTEMS

LOWDOWN

The year of the next-gen console war may have been 2013, but while Sony and Microsoft duelled, the PC market grew ever stronger as gaming PCs raised specs to get one up on the new consoles. Underdogs such as the Ouya and GameStick appeared with their inexpensive and portable Android platforms, and this was also the year that virtual reality, first championed in the 1990s, returned to the scene.

NAME THE GAME
With no rules holding it up, X2011 is the fastest car in the world.

PC

Running on Intel "Haswell" processors that are 10% more powerful than the previous "Ivy Bridge", the new generation of PCs arrived earlier than their console rivals. The 700 series of graphics cards from Nvidia Geforce opened up a bright new world of pixel-perfect graphical prowess; games such as *Crysis 3* (Crytek, 2013) and *Metro: Last Light* (4A Games, 2013) showed gamers just how impressive new titles with updated discrete graphics cards could look.

The Maingear F131 PC (*pictured above right*) is armed with a water-cooled Nvidia GeForce GTX Titan, one of the most powerful single graphics processing units in the world. Utilizing the technology that helps to power the *Titan*, one of the world's fastest supercomputers, it makes for outstanding gaming performance.

Wii U

The Wii U hasn't performed as well as Nintendo would have hoped, with the company CEO blaming disappointing sales ("just" 3.24 million units as of 18 July 2013) on the failure to come up with "one single software [game] with which people can understand, 'OK, this is really different.'" Nintendo will be hoping that 2013 releases *Pikmin 3* (Nintendo, *left*), *Rayman Legends* (Ubisoft) and an HD version of *The Legend of Zelda: The Wind Waker* (Nintendo) will raise fortunes. Nintendo-developed titles planned for 2014 include the Wii U incarnation of *Super Smash Bros.*, *Mario Kart 8* and *Super Mario 3D World* (all Nintendo).

Also arriving for 3DS, *Super Smash Bros.* (Sora Ltd./Namco Bandai Games) mixes classic characters with some new faces such as the Animal Crossing Villager and even Mega Man.

The gamer steps into the treadmill-like ring and dons a belt and shoes, which translates his or her moves into gameplay.

OMNI

This natural-motion interface is primarily a virtual-reality tracking device that lets you walk, run and crouch through games with only a pair of special Omni shoes. This Kickstarter project secured its cash within 3.5 hours. Manufacturer Virtuix claims the device offers an "unprecedented sense of immersion".

STEAM BOX

Valve's long-awaited under-TV box purely for Steam games remains a closely guarded secret. The prototype modular PC shown here, the "Piston", is made by Xi3 and runs the Steam service on Linux. It has numerous features that Valve's final console is expected to include.

While no official Valve product had been revealed as of September 2013, other manufacturers will be free to create micro-machines like this one to make the most of your Steam library and Steam's TV-friendly "Big Picture" mode.

OUYA

This HD Android console set the record for the **most money pledged for a Kickstarter gaming project**; by 2 September 2013, it had total pledges of $8,596,474. In July 2012, it set the record for the **fastest time for a Kickstarter project to reach pledges of $1 million**, in just eight hours. It went on sale in June 2013 with an Nvidia Tegra 3 processor, 1 GB of RAM and 8 GB of storage in a $99 (£65) box.

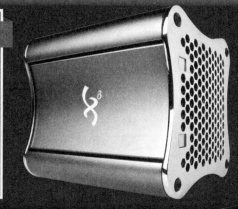

The controller comes with a trackpad because most Android games were originally touch-controlled.

GAMESTICK

PlayJam's GameStick is a micro-console the size of a USB stick. You just plug it into your TV via the HDMI port for full HD Android gaming. It was crowd-funded on Kickstarter and is scheduled for an October 2013 release, priced at $79 (£52).

The bluetooth gamepad removes any need for wires, and the 8 GB of storage can be upgraded via SD Micro memory cards. It even allows for iOS and Android devices to be used as additional controllers.

DEVELOPERS

They are the architects of the record-breaking games featured throughout this book. Andy Davidson presents seven of his favourites from the 25 most critically acclaimed developers.

3 Nintendo®

FOUNDED: 1889
LOCATION: Kyoto, Japan
KEY TITLES: *Mario* (right), *The Legend of Zelda*

One of the world's most famous videogame companies, Nintendo has dominated gaming since the 1980s. Originally a 19th-century gaming cards manufacturer, Nintendo now boasts the **best-selling seventh-generation videogame console**, the Wii, which has sold a staggering 100 million units to date. Its biggest property and most famous star is undoubtedly Mario (*see pp.88–89*).

7 BUNGiE

FOUNDED: 1991
LOCATION: Washington, USA
KEY TITLES: *Halo* (left; below), *Destiny*, *Marathon*

Started by two friends at the University of Chicago, Bungie would be notable for the first *Halo* game alone. *Halo Combat Evolved* (2001) has been credited with saving the Xbox and redefining first-person shooter games, and the *Halo* trilogy has broken a host of records (*see pp.52–53*). Bungie's next big release is eighth-gen FPS *Destiny*, due for release in 2014.

1 VALVE®

FOUNDED: 1996
LOCATION: Washington, USA
KEY TITLES: *Half-Life, Counter-Strike, Portal, Left 4 Dead* (above)

The **most critically acclaimed developer** of all, Valve is as famous for sophisticated games such as the *Half-Life* series as it is for creating the digital platform, Steam. This revolutionary online hub, launched in 2003, allows all developers to sell games directly to a community of more than 40 million gamers, as well as offering multiplayer gaming.

4 ROCKSTAR

FOUNDED: 1998
LOCATION: New York, USA
KEY TITLES: *Grand Theft Auto* (top left; right), *Red Dead Redemption* (bottom left), *L.A. Noire*

Rockstar, which comprises eight studios worldwide, is synonymous with the edgy and innovative *Grand Theft Auto* games, the **best-selling action-adventure videogame series** with sales of over 108 million as of July 2013. Other hits include the Western epic *Red Dead Redemption* (2010).

12 CAPCOM

FOUNDED: 1983
LOCATION: Osaka, Japan
KEY TITLES: *Megaman* (left), *Street Fighter* (right), *Resident Evil*

Capcom started out with arcade games such as *1942* (1984) and *Street Fighter* (1987) before its focus switched to the home-console market. In 1996, Capcom released the first game in the *Resident Evil* series, ushering in a wave of horror-themed titles, and coining the phrase "survival-horror".

24 EA

FOUNDED: 1982
LOCATION: California, USA
KEY TITLES: *FIFA* (below), *NHL*, *Dead Space*, *Need for Speed*

Originally called Amazin' Software, Electronic Arts was founded by former Apple employee Trip Hawkins. It was renamed to highlight the kudos EA would give to developers it worked with. EA is masterful at acquiring licences for sports titles.

11 Bethesda

FOUNDED: 1986
LOCATION: Maryland, USA
KEY TITLES: *The Elder Scrolls* (below), *Fallout*

Bethesda, named after the location of its first offices in Maryland, began by developing games for the Commodore 64 and Atari ST. It hit the big time with the epic open-world *The Elder Scrolls* RPGs. In 2004, Bethesda purchased the *Fallout* series from fellow developers Interplay.

O27

TOP 25 MOST CRITICALLY ACCLAIMED DEVELOPERS

1	**Valve** 94.50%
2	**Naughty Dog** 94.40%
3	**Nintendo** 93.88%
4	**Rockstar** 93.74%
5	**Rocksteady** 93.60%
6	**Irrational Games** 93.55%
7	**Bungie** 93.30%
8	**Infinity Ward** 93.12%
9	**BioWare** 92.95%
10	**Epic Games** 92.84%
11	**Bethesda** 92.78%
12	**Capcom** 92.69%
13	**Atlus** 92.40%
14	**Criterion Games** 92.26%
15	**Kojima Productions** 92.21%
16	**Turn 10 Studios** 91.99%
17	**Harmonix** 91.85%
18	**Blizzard** 91.82%
=	**SCE** 91.82%
20	**Project Soul** 91.75%
21	**Retro Studios** 91.54%
22	**KCET** 91.45%
23	**Ubisoft** 91.33%
24	**EA** 91.18%
25	**Intelligent Systems** 91.16%

Based on games with 90%+ rating, released 2003–13. Data sourced from GameRankings, as of 8 July 2013.

ACTION-ADVENTURE

FASTEST COMPLETION OF *BATMAN: ARKHAM CITY*

Sean "DarthKnight" Grayson (USA) completed *Batman: Arkham City* (Rocksteady Studios, 2011, *shown right*) in 2 hr 3 min 19 sec on 27 May 2012. He also recorded the **fastest completion of Batman: Arkham Asylum** (Rocksteady Studios, 2011), with 1 hr 57 min 8 sec on 16 August 2012. "Some of the fights did not go well," he said, "but I think that's expected. I'm not *actually* Batman."

CONTENTS

GRAND THEFT AUTO

LOWDOWN

PUBLISHER:
Rockstar
DEVELOPER:
Rockstar
DEBUT:
1997

These witty, edgy open-worlders hurl you head-first into the vast and gritty criminal underworld of depraved, fictional cities. Few gaming series have solicited as much controversy and infamy as the *GTA* games; on 20 July 2005, for example, *Grand Theft Auto: San Andreas* (2004), became the **first console game to be rated AO** ("Adults Only").

MOST CRITICALLY ACCLAIMED PS3 GAME

The *GTA* series is as popular with critics as it is with gamers. *Grand Theft Auto IV* (2008) is top of the PlayStation 3 leaderboards, with a GameRankings score of 97.04% as of 29 July 2013. It is also the **most critically acclaimed Xbox 360 game**, with 96.67%. The **most critically acclaimed Nintendo DS game** is *Grand Theft Auto: Chinatown Wars* (2009), which has a 92.71% score.

NAME THE GAME

Miles Prower, aka Tails, is the protagonist's friend in which platform series?

FASTEST GLITCHED COMPLETION OF *GTA: CHINATOWN WARS*

Jordan "Greenalink" Greener (UK) sped through *Grand Theft Auto: Chinatown Wars* in just 2 min 11 sec on 6 November 2011. This speed-run is made possible by a handy glitch that occurs when you save your progress immediately after beginning a new game.

MOST MISSIONS IN AN OPEN-WORLD GAME

Grand Theft Auto IV: The Complete Edition (2010) features a total of 136 main-story missions and dozens of side missions. This edition comprises the original *GTA IV* alongside the two episodes from the *Liberty City* (2009) expansion packs: *The Lost and the Damned* and *The Ballad of Gay Tony*.

FASTEST COMPLETION OF GTA: THE BALLAD OF GAY TONY

With a completion time of 1 hr 43 min 10 sec recorded on 28 May 2010, PC gamer Mihail "SCM" Suraev (Russia) achieved the fastest speed-run for *The Ballad of Gay Tony* expansion pack. By skipping cutscenes and jumping red lights, "SCM" was able to rush his way through the episode's 26 missions.

LARGEST BUDGET FOR AN ACTION-ADVENTURE GAME

With a development and marketing budget of £170 million ($275 million), *Grand Theft Auto V* also has the **largest budget for a videogame** overall. Set for release on 17 September 2013, the game looks likely to smash all-time sales records. (*See Stop Press on pp.214–15 for the very latest figures.*)

(See Stop Press on pp.214–15 for the very latest figures.)

TOP TEN — FASTEST BASE JUMP SEQUENCE IN *GTA: THE BALLAD OF GAY TONY*

MITTTEN1	4 min 6 sec
UNLIMITEDSTREAM WILDESTMIDGET	4 min 21 sec
HUGORL	4 min 25 sec
DOMONLINE	4 min 32 sec
PAREEK5	4 min 34 sec
PAREEK1	4 min 51 sec
SIK MIND 420	5 min 4 sec
MEDEMOTRTAL MEX CRAIGMAC	5 min 5 sec

Source: socialclub.rockstargames.com, as of 29 July 2013

BEST-SELLING ACTION-ADVENTURE SERIES

With worldwide sales of 108.34 million as of 29 July 2013, *Grand Theft Auto* is the best-selling series in its genre. An astonishing 23.61 million of these units belong to *Grand Theft Auto: San Andreas* alone, making it the **best-selling action-adventure game**. Pictured here is the latest title, *GTA V*.

O31

ASSASSIN'S CREED

LOWDOWN

PUBLISHER:
Ubisoft
DEVELOPER:
Ubisoft
DEBUT:
2007

Combining a beautifully realistic open-world environment with the stealth involved in the assassin's trade has proved to be a potent draw. Add in free-running (parkour) and time-flipping fun and the result is a rich, action-packed, historical romp.

032

NAME THE GAME
Wood Jester is one of the larger and more difficult enemies to defeat.

BEST-SELLING SEVENTH-GENERATION FRANCHISE

Assassin's Creed had sold more than 49.56 million units on seventh-generation consoles (PCs excluded) as of August 2013, according to VGChartz. The single-generation hit incorporates the six main games – including *Revelations* (2011, *inset right*) – and four spin-offs.

FASTEST COMPLETION OF *ASSASSIN'S CREED: REVELATIONS*

François "Fed981" Federspie (France) completed *Revelations* in 2 hr 48 min 41 sec on 3 October 2010. Turbo-charged François followed this with the **fastest completion of *Assassin's Creed II*** (2009), taking just 5 hr 42 min 16 sec on 26 March 2011. He later achieved yet another record in the series – for the **fastest completion of *Assassin's Creed: Brotherhood*** (2010), with a time of 2 hr 22 min 41 sec on 3 March 2013.

LARGEST RANGE OF BOMBS IN A STEALTH VIDEOGAME

Assassin's Creed: Revelations allows players to create more than 300 different types of bomb to use on their targets. The hookblade was introduced as a weapon and tool in the game: players can use it to attach themselves to ziplines, navigate the city at speed and send their bombs from above.

HIGHEST AVERAGE KILL COUNT ON ASSASSIN'S CREED: MULTIPLAYER REARMED

The free-to-play iOS exclusive game – based on the "Wanted" multiplayer mode that debuted in *Assassin's Creed: Brotherhood* – was released in 2011. As of 29 July 2013, gamer "Whatsmike" topped the killing charts with an average of 40 assassinations per round.

BOOST

KILLER SCORES

Gamer "Texwiller44" achieved the **highest score on *Assassin's Creed III* "Wolfpack" mode**, with 36,125 points on the PS3 as of 29 July 2013. His associated team score of 369,540 took him to the top of the leaderboards. Playing the PS3 version, "Pinoy47" (USA) set the **highest score on *Assassin's Creed: Brotherhood* multiplayer** across all modes with 109,155,755, as of 30 July 2013. The **highest score on *Assassin's Creed: Revelations* multiplayer**, as of 30 July 2013, is 116,573,255 by "faith_89" (Italy) – more than 17 million points higher than the second-placed leaderboard score.

033

MOST WATCHED E3 GAME TRAILER

The teaser for *Assassin's Creed: Brotherhood* had been viewed 15,876,631 times as of 2 August 2013. The slick presentation of the 2-min 42-sec mini-epic is mirrored in Ubisoft's finely tuned yearly production schedule. They develop in parallel at different studios, so although *Assassin's Creed III* took three years to create, its October 2012 release came 350 days after *Assassin's Creed: Revelations*, the **shortest time between triple-A stealth sequel releases**.

TOP TEN — MOST KILLS BY CLANS IN *ASSASSIN'S CREED III*

Clan	Kills
THE INVINCIBLE CLAN (DIO)	487,912,060
EL GRUPO DE LA MUERTE (DLM)	431,982,950
Legendary A$$a$$in'S (LAS)	414,944,520
Freelance Agents (WAL)	378,634,790
Les Adeptes de l'Animus (ADA)	352,817,030
Capture, Stun, Run (CSR)	286,610,565
ASSASSIN666 (666)	281,735,645
The Polish Champions and Rest of The World (TPC)	277,169,930
Failure To Connect (FTC)	255,128,755
Devils Assassin's TOP!! (TOP)	246,250,155

Source: assassinsnetwork.ubi.com, as of 12 August 2013

RESIDENT EVIL

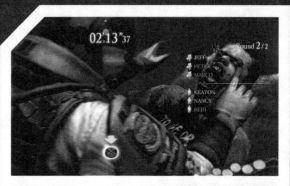

LOWDOWN

PUBLISHER:
Capcom
DEVELOPER:
Capcom
DEBUT:
1996

Puzzles, shooting and zombies – the *Resident Evil* series continues to terrify after 17 years, with the most recent console release, *Resident Evil: Revelations*, arriving in 2013. *Resident Evil 5* (2009) holds the record for the **fastest-selling survival-horror game**, with 1.18 million copies sold in its first two weeks, and the series has the **most novelizations of a gaming franchise** – a total of 18 as of September 2013.

NAME THE GAME
A monkey named Bubbles is trying to rescue his friends from poachers.

FIRST SURVIVAL-HORROR GAME

The term "survival-horror" was coined to describe the original *Resident Evil*. In this scary sub-genre of action-adventure, inspired by horror stories and movies, the gamer must evade attack by solving puzzles and unlocking paths and rooms.

Resident Evil: Outbreak (2003) contained the **first co-op mode in a survival-horror game**, with the introduction of an online multiplayer mode.

MOST KILLS ON...
- ***Resident Evil 6* on PS3** (*top right*)
  1,236,400 kills by "Rocket Launcher"
- ***Resident Evil 6* on Xbox 360**
  1,119,237 kills by "Brutaldactyl"
- ***Resident Evil 6* on PC**
  413,085 kills by "Nesbiandcie"
- ***Resident Evil: Revelations* on Xbox 360**
  312,417 kills by "Prov Drummer"
- ***Resident Evil: Revelations* on PS3** (*above right*)
  236,984 kills by "amatchdrmr"
- ***Resident Evil: Revelations* on Wii U**
  170,535 kills by "doramaru"
  Source: residentevil.net, as of 19 August 2013

BO:OM!

Resident Evil movies are now probably more famous than the games on which they are based (which were themselves inspired by horror movies). As of August 2013, there were a total of five films in the series, with American star Milla Jovovich playing Alice in three of them. There are also three Capcom-produced Japanese CGI movies, separate to the main films.

TOP TEN — HIGHEST-GROSSING MOVIES BASED ON VIDEOGAMES

Prince of Persia: The Sands of Time (USA, 2010)	$335,154,643
Resident Evil: Afterlife (Canada/Germany/USA, 2010)	$296,221,663
Lara Croft: Tomb Raider (USA/UK/Japan/Germany, 2001)	$274,703,340
Resident Evil: Retribution (USA/Canada/Germany, 2012)	$240,159,255
Pokémon: The First Movie (Japan, 1998)	$163,644,662
Lara Croft Tomb Raider: The Cradle of Life (USA/UK/Japan/Germany, 2003)	$156,505,388
Resident Evil: Extinction (UK/Canada, 2007)	$147,717,833
Pokémon: The Movie 2000 (Japan, 1999)	$133,949,270
Resident Evil: Apocalypse (UK/Canada/USA, 2004)	$129,394,835
Mortal Kombat (USA, 1995)	$122,195,920

Source: boxofficemojo.com, as of 19 August 2013

MOST CRITICALLY ACCLAIMED SURVIVAL-HORROR GAME

The GameCube version of *Resident Evil 4* (2005) had an outstanding rating of 95.83% on GameRankings as of 30 July 2013.

The **fastest completion of *Resident Evil 4***, set by Robert Brandl (Germany) on Xbox 360, took 1 hr 37 min 35 sec in Mering, Germany, on 21 November 2011. The **fastest completion of *Resident Evil*** (1996) was quicker still, a mere 1 hr 9 min 17 sec by Brandon "Ekudeht" Armstrong (USA) on 28 May 2005.

GREATEST AGGREGATE TIME PLAYING RESIDENT EVIL 6

Xbox 360 gamer "Brutaldactyl" had played *Resident Evil 6* for a total time of 2,900 hr 46 min 23 sec, the equivalent of more than 120 days, as of 19 August 2013. The **greatest aggregate time playing *Resident Evil: Revelations*** pales in comparison, a "mere" 867 hr 37 min 19 sec by "BobaFett" as of the same date.

BEST-SELLING SURVIVAL-HORROR SERIES

As of July 2013, the *Resident Evil* series had sales of 55 million units worldwide. The series' seventh instalment, *Resident Evil 5* (2009), is the **best-selling *Resident Evil* game** as well as the **best-selling survival-horror game**, with platform-wide sales of 8.2 million by 31 July 2013. The **best-selling single-platform survival-horror game** is *Resident Evil 2* (1998) on PlayStation, with 5.8 million sold as of July 2013. Its PlayStation success saw it ported to PC, N64, Dreamcast and GameCube.

TOMB RAIDER

LOWDOWN

PUBLISHER:
Eidos/Square Enix
DEVELOPER:
Core Design/
Crystal Dynamics
DEBUT:
1996

As gaming icons go, she's up there with Mario and PAC-Man: Lara Croft, the most intrepid archaeologist since Indiana Jones, swung back into action in 2013 with the *Tomb Raider* reboot. The 10 games in the series task players with a global search for various relics, which involves fending off greedy foes. Crystal Dynamics took over development duties in 2006.

NAME THE GAME
Agent Sasha works for the USSR out of a secret bunker in Russia.

BEST-SELLING GAMING HEROINE

With overall sales of 33.26 million following the release of 2013's *Tomb Raider* reboot, the series starring the iconic Lara Croft remains the best-selling game franchise with a female lead, as of 16 August 2013. It's also the **best-selling action-adventure series on the PlayStation**, with five games in as many years generating sales of some 16.5 million on the first Sony console.

MOST UTILIZED *TOMB RAIDER* WEAPON

Lara's twin pistols are almost as iconic as the character herself, yet the new bow weapon introduced in 2013's *Tomb Raider* has proven the most popular with players. In the first 16 weeks of the game's release across the Xbox 360, PlayStation 3 and PC platforms, the bow accounted for 44% of all kills. In contrast, just 4% of kills came via melee combat.

FASTEST-SELLING *TOMB RAIDER* GAME

The 2013 *Tomb Raider* registered the highest first-week sales in the history of the franchise, according to Crystal Dynamics studio head Darrell Gallagher. The game racked up global sales of 3.4 million during its debut month of March 2013, making it the biggest game launch of the year up to that point. Despite this success, Square Enix made the surprising admission that the game had failed to meet its internal sales expectations.

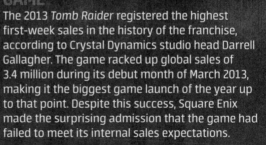

MOST CRITICALLY ACCLAIMED *TOMB RAIDER* GAME

Even if its sales disappointed the publishing executives, the 2013 *Tomb Raider* game proved a success with critics, who scored it an average of 87.41% on GameRankings, as of 13 August 2013. The game's mix of puzzle-solving gameplay and groundbreaking 3D graphics were praised in reviews. *Now Gamer*'s critic said, "each gameplay mechanic is simply top-notch".

BOOST

CROFTWORK

Lara Croft's seminal debut started life on the Sega Saturn in 1996, before being rolled out on the PlayStation and PC. Six developers at Core Designs spent two years creating the original *Tomb Raider*, which went on to sell 6 million copies. The **fastest glitched single-segment speed-run** of *Tomb Raider* is 1 hr 50 min 16 sec, achieved by Ali "AKA" Gordon on 25 May 2007.

TOP TEN

MOST MULTIPLAYER KILLS ON *TOMB RAIDER* (2013)

Player	Kills
wasbeelt (Netherlands)	43,283
Q-BIGBOSS-Q (Saudi Arabia)	39,495
CasPoTe007 (France)	28,549
SilentXSheep (USA)	23,394
Akthar_Cookie (UK)	23,008
NightwishPL (nationality unknown)	22,215
GODHAND73 (Japan)	21,744
Nikopeace93 (France)	21,548
CHIVANDA (Canada)	20,481
IVAN1346 (Hong Kong)	20,479

Source: in-game leaderboards, as of 10 July 2013

FASTEST GLITCHLESS COMPLETION OF *TOMB RAIDER: LEGEND*

Shaun "MMAN" Friend (UK) set the speed-run record for *Tomb Raider: Legend* (2006), with 54 min 19 sec on 22 January 2008. *Legend* is the seventh *Tomb Raider* title, and the first to be developed by US firm Crystal Dynamics. "MMAN" also holds the record for the **fastest glitchless completion of *Tomb Raider 3*** (Core Design, 1998), with 2 hr 4 min 10 sec. This speedy run saw Lara travel a distance of 20.95 km (13 miles).

METAL GEAR

LOWDOWN

PUBLISHER:
Konami
DEVELOPER:
Konami/Kojima
DEBUT:
1987

The *Metal Gear* series spans more than 20 games, the most recent being *Metal Gear Rising: Revengeance* (Platinum Games, 2013). For almost 30 years, these military actioners have been at the forefront of stealth games, a sub-genre of action-adventure in which the main gameplay element is concealment.

⊠
⊠

⊠
⊠

BEST-SELLING STEALTH SERIES

As of 5 August 2013, the *Metal Gear* series, led by Snake (*below left*), had sold some 34 million copies. Creator Hideo Kojima took much inspiration from the movies, commenting, "I always say that, 'Just as humans are 70% made of water, so I'm 70% made of film'." *Metal Gear* influences include World War II classics such as *The Guns of Navarone* (USA, 1961) and *The Great Escape* (USA, 1963).

FASTEST COMPLETION OF *METAL GEAR SOLID 3: SNAKE EATER*

On 11 March 2011, Hidenori "Hikari" Kawamoto completed a segmented run of Konami's 2004 prequel in 1 hr 23 min 37 sec, on the hardest setting. The **fastest completion of *Metal Gear Solid: The Twin Snakes*** (Silicon Knights, 2004) is 1 hr 3 min 7 sec, achieved by Caleb Hart on 30 May 2011 in a single segment, using the "normal" difficulty.

MOST CRITICALLY ACCLAIMED STEALTH GAME

The sixth title in the series, *Metal Gear Solid 2: Sons of Liberty* (Konami, 2001) had a score of 95.04% on GameRankings as of 12 August 2013. Self-described as "tactical espionage action", *Sons of Liberty* was notable for its futuristic look.

C.C.C.P
DIRECT ACTION SUIT

MOST CRITICALLY ACCLAIMED HD COLLECTION ON XBOX 360

Of the many HD updates released for seventh-generation consoles, *Metal Gear Solid HD Collection* (Konami, 2011) is the most acclaimed, with a GameRankings score of 90.14% as of 12 August 2013. It features remastered versions of *Metal Gear Solid 2*, *Metal Gear Solid 3* and *Metal Gear Solid: Peace Walker*. The second-placed HD collection, *Devil May Cry* (Capcom, 2012), scores a distant 77.21%.

LONGEST END SEQUENCE IN A VIDEOGAME

Running for a full 1 hr 8 min, the ending of *Metal Gear Solid 4: Guns of the Patriots* (Kojima, 2008) is the lengthiest in gaming.

The dramatic epilogue includes Solid Snake's suicide attempt, which is interrupted by his genetic father, Big Boss. The tragic fate of clone Solidus Snake is also revealed.

TIP-OFF

There are five hidden Xbox 360 achievements and PS3 trophies in *Metal Gear Rising: Revengeance*. To gain them, you need to defeat the following bosses on "hard" mode (or higher) without sustaining a single hit: Samuel, Monsoon, Mistral, Sen and Sundowner.

TOP TEN
BEST-SELLING STEALTH GAMES

Game	Sales
Metal Gear Solid 2: Sons of Liberty (Konami, 2001)	6.05
Metal Gear Solid (Konami, 1998)	6.03
Metal Gear Solid 4: Guns of the Patriots (Kojima, 2008)	5.79
Tom Clancy's Splinter Cell (Ubisoft, 2002)	5.67
Metal Gear Solid 3: Snake Eater (Konami, 2004)	4.23
Hitman 2: Silent Assassin (IO Interactive, 2002)	3.15
Hitman: Absolution (IO Interactive, 2012)	3.11
Syphon Filter (Eidetic, 1999)	2.88
Dishonored (Arkane Studios, 2012)	2.63
Tom Clancy's Splinter Cell: Conviction (Ubisoft, 2010)	2.15

Source: vgchartz.com, as of 12 August 2013 (figures in millions)

BEST-SELLING HANDHELD STEALTH GAME

With global sales of 1.93 million as of 12 August 2013, *Metal Gear Solid: Peace Walker* (Konami, 2010) for the PSP is the most successful handheld stealth title. *Peace Walker*, which is set in 1974, is also the **fastest-selling handheld stealth game**, with first week sales of 445,138.

THE LEGEND OF ZELDA

LOWDOWN

PUBLISHER:
Nintendo
DEVELOPER:
Nintendo
DEBUT:
1986

For more than a quarter of a century, Princess Zelda has been menaced by the evil Ganon and rescued by bold Link in the pioneering fantasy open-world of Hyrule. There are elements of RPG along the way as Link explores countless dungeons and meets characters he can interact with or battle.

NAME THE GAME
Corruption is in the heart of Cervantes, a ghost pirate in the centre of this fighter.

BEST-SELLING *LEGEND OF ZELDA* GAME (MULTI-PLATFORM)

The Legend of Zelda: Twilight Princess (2006), released for both the GameCube and Wii, had a combined total of 8.40 million copies as of 14 August 2013. Its Wii sales of 6.81 million make it the **best-selling Wii action-adventure game**. A copy of a limited edition Nintendo DS cartridge featuring a promotional video for the game sold on eBay for £200 ($300) on 25 March 2010, the **greatest amount paid for a game trailer**.

FASTEST COMPLETION OF ZELDA: SKYWARD SWORD

A gamer going by the handle "Paraxade" was able to complete *The Legend of Zelda: Skyward Sword* (2011) in 5 hr 39 min using a "save game" glitch. Paraxade recorded the single-segment run on 28 April 2012. Every second counts, and Paraxade used the Japanese version despite being a non-speaker, "because the text scrolls much faster".

FIRST CONSOLE GAME WITH A "SAVE" FEATURE

Published outside of Japan on cartridge for the NES, *The Legend of Zelda* (1986) had a RAM feature for saving progress in the lengthy adventure. This was powered by a battery that had a supposed lifespan of 10 years, and "save" was soon a standard game feature. The **fastest completion of *The Legend of Zelda*** is 31 min 39 sec by "Darkwing Duck" on 25 March 2013.

TOP TEN — BEST-SELLING *LEGEND OF ZELDA* GAMES (SINGLE PLATFORM)

Game	Sales
The Legend of Zelda: Ocarina of Time (1998) on N64	7.60
The Legend of Zelda: Twilight Princess (2006) on Wii	6.81
The Legend of Zelda (1986) on NES	6.51
The Legend of Zelda: Phantom Hourglass (2007) on DS	4.97
The Legend of Zelda: A Link to the Past (1991) on SNES	4.61
The Legend of Zelda: The Wind Waker (2002) on GameCube	4.60
Zelda II: The Adventure of Link (1987) on NES	4.38
The Legend of Zelda: Link's Awakening (1992) on Game Boy	3.83
The Legend of Zelda: Skyward Sword (2011) on Wii	3.68
The Legend of Zelda: Majora's Mask (2000) on N64	3.36

Source: vgchartz.com, as of 16 August 2013 (figures in millions)

BOOST

ZIPPY ZELDA

• Kristian Emanuelsen (Norway) recorded the **fastest completion of Zelda II: The Adventure of Link** (1987) in 57 min 49 sec on 11 January 2011.

• The **fastest completion of The Legend of Zelda: Ocarina of Time** (1998) on the N64 (European edition) is 4 hr 46 min and was achieved by Mauri "Kazooie" Mustonen on 15 November 2006.

• The **fastest completion of The Legend of Zelda: A Link to the Past** (1991, *below*) is 1 hr 24 min 42 sec by "Kryssstal" (USA) on 12 June 2013. Quicker times can be achieved by players using a glitch enabling them to walk through walls.

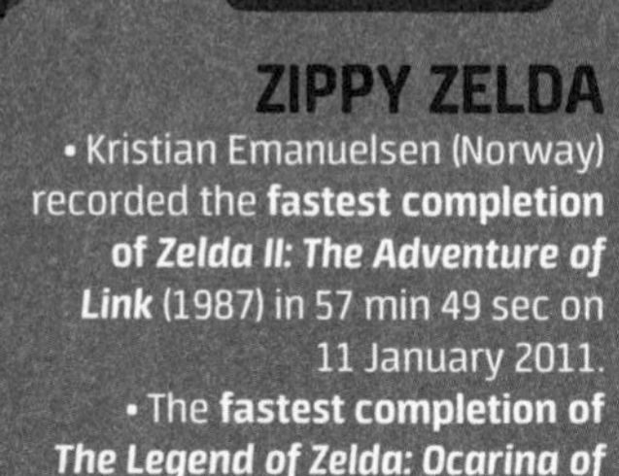

MOST CRITICALLY ACCLAIMED ACTION-ADVENTURE GAME

The Legend of Zelda: Ocarina of Time (1998) on the N64 has a GameRankings rating of 97.54% as of 16 August 2013. Far less well-known is *BS Zelda no Densetsu* (1995), the **rarest Legend of Zelda game**. The "BS" refers to Broadcast Satellite, as the title was developed for the Japanese Satellaview, a satellite modem add-on for the Super Famicom (SNES). In an early example of digital rights management, the games for the quirky device could be played during weekly broadcasts to subscribers. The audience for the satellite service peaked at 116,378 in March 1997.

MOST PROLIFIC ACTION-ADVENTURE GAME CHARACTER

Link stars in 16 official *Legend of Zelda* games and three spin-offs, and makes cameo appearances in *Super Mario RPG: Legend of the Seven Stars* (Square, 1996), *SoulCalibur II* (Namco, 2003) and all three *Super Smash Bros.* titles (HAL Laboratory, 1999–2008). Nintendo's iconic Hyrulean has been collecting hearts and saving princesses across every Nintendo platform since his debut in 1986.

LOWDOWN

The broad scope of titles within the action-adventure genre continues to captivate. E3 2013 was buzzing with announcements of launch titles for the PS4 and Xbox One, from the family-friendly *Knack* (Sony) to the open-world *inFAMOUS: Second Son* (Sucker Punch) via the historical *Ryse: Son of Rome* (Crytek). It was a launch title, actioner *Uncharted: Golden Abyss* (Naughty Dog, 2012), that became the **best-selling PS Vita game**, with sales of 990,000 as of 22 August 2013.

NAME THE GAME
Om Nom is hungry for candy that is often dangling just out of his reach.

BEST-SELLING EPISODIC GAME

The five episodes that make up the first season of *The Walking Dead* (2012) have sold a total of 17 million copies as of August 2013, according to publisher and developer Telltale Games. The series, released on multiple platforms between April and November 2012, also scored huge critical success, picking up more than 90 gaming awards, including two BAFTAs.

FIRST STEALTH GAME

The first game to utilize basic stealth game mechanics was Sega's arcade title *005*, released in 1981. The player is cast as a spy (code-name 005, in a nod to James Bond), who must deliver a briefcase full of secret files to a helicopter while remaining concealed from enemies. There are four tricky environments to negotiate.

MOST SIMULTANEOUS ON-SCREEN ENEMIES IN A GAME

The *Dead Rising* games (Capcom, 2006–present) have always pitted players against vast hordes of hungry zombies. Set for release in 2013, the Xbox One-exclusive *Dead Rising 3* (left) is set to have 21,000 animated corpses onscreen at a single time, according to executive producer Josh Bridge. This is three times the number of undead featured onscreen in *Dead Rising 2* (2010). *Dead Rising 3* will continue the series tradition of wacky combo weapons with the debut appearance of combo vehicles, such as a motorcycle-steamroller hybrid!

TOP TEN

MOST CRITICALLY ACCLAIMED ACTION-ADVENTURE GAMES

Game	Score
The Legend of Zelda: Ocarina of Time (Nintendo, 1998) on N64	97.54%
Grand Theft Auto IV (Rockstar, 2008) on PS3	97.04%
Grand Theft Auto IV (Rockstar, 2008) on Xbox 360	96.67%
Uncharted 2: Among Thieves (Naughty Dog, 2009) on PS3	96.38%
Batman: Arkham City (Rocksteady, 2011) on PS3	96.09%
Resident Evil 4 (Capcom, 2005) on GameCube	95.83%
Resident Evil 4 (Capcom, 2005) on PS2	95.77%
Grand Theft Auto III (DMA Design, 2001) on PS2	95.19%
Grand Theft Auto: San Andreas (Rockstar, 2004) on PS2	95.08%
The Last of Us (Naughty Dog, 2013) on PS3	95.04%

Source: gamerankings.com, as of 22 August 2013

MOST CRITICALLY ACCLAIMED PSP GAME

God of War: Chains of Olympus (SCE Santa Monica, 2008) was the highest-rated game on the PlayStation Portable, with a score of 91.06% on GameRankings as of 22 August 2013. Given that very few new titles are released for the PSP now that the Vita is established as Sony's premier handheld, *Chains of Olympus* is likely to keep hold of that record.

Chains of Olympus is the fourth *God of War* title and serves as a prequel to the original *God of War* (SCE Santa Monica), which was released in 2005.

MOST PROLIFIC ACTION-ADVENTURE SERIES

There are 32 titles in the *Castlevania* series, with the 33rd, *Lords of Shadow 2* (MercurySteam), scheduled for a spring 2014 release. This enduring franchise, which centres on a clan of vampire hunters, began in Japan with *Castlevania* (Konami, 1986) on the Famicom and was ported to the NES in 1987.

The 32-game total excludes those titles that do not feature action elements, such as puzzler *Castlevania Puzzle: Encore of the Night* (Konami, 2010).

BIGGEST POKER CHEAT IN *RED DEAD REDEMPTION*

Of all those caught cheating while playing poker in *Red Dead Redemption* (Rockstar, 2010), the biggest offender is "LordSunQuan" as of 1 July 2013. According to figures published by Rockstar Games Social Club, this wily gamer has been caught cheating a total of 64 times.

Red Dead Redemption is the **best-selling Western-themed game**, with sales of 11.2 million as of August 2013.

THE HEROES

These are the ultimate gaming heroes – the super-men and women achieving the impossible in the name of all things good. **Eddie de Oliveira** checks out some of the games behind the flowing capes.

Most gaming protagonists are heroic in one way or another. After all, Mario has saved Princess Peach countless times and Lara Croft's archaeological adventures make her a heroine of both gaming and academia. But when it comes to superhuman power and sheer indestructible audacity, the comic book legends – the original superheroes – have what it takes, even if some of their videogames don't...

SUPERMAN

First comic: 1938
First game: *Superman* (Atari, 1978)

The Man of Steel has been a mainstay of comics, books, TV series and movies for almost 80 years. But despite his debut being the **first superhero videogame**, Superman hasn't quite managed to transpose his popularity to the games he has starred in. The DC Comics icon fares better when he's sharing the spotlight in ensemble titles such as *Mortal Kombat vs DC Universe* (Midway, 2008) or *Injustice: Gods Among Us* (NetherRealm Studios, 2013, *below*). This fighter sees Superman lead a war between his Regime and an insurgency led by fellow DC hero Batman.

BATMAN

First comic: 1939
First game: *Batman* (Bernie Drummond/Jon Ritman, 1986)

The Caped Crusader is the comic book hero who has most successfully transformed into a gaming hero, particularly in seventh-generation titles. Director Christopher Nolan's *Batman* film trilogy was as well-received as the trio of dark, multi-layered *Arkham* games, the first of which was *Batman: Arkham Asylum* (Rocksteady, 2009).

The **most critically acclaimed superhero videogame** is its sequel, *Batman: Arkham City* (Rocksteady, 2011, *above*), which scored 96.09% on GameRankings as of 16 August 2013.

The latest game starring Bruce Wayne – the third *Arkham* episode – is 2013's *Batman: Arkham Origins* (*above right*), which marks a significant departure. While the first two games were developed by Rocksteady, *Origins* is developed by Warner Bros. Games Montreal. Unlike its predecessors, it includes a multiplayer option.

SPIDER-MAN

First comic: 1962
First game: *Spider-Man* (Atari, 1982)

Peter Parker and his alter-ego have appeared in some 60 videogames, including spin-offs based on the first trilogy of *Spider-Man* movies (*see pp.172–73*). Although prolific, the gaming adventures of the human arachnid have mostly had a lukewarm reception from gamers, notwithstanding 2002's *Spider-Man: The Movie* (Treyarch), based on Sam Raimi's film of the same year. This beat-'em-up is the **best-selling *Spider-Man* videogame**, with sales of 8.4 million across all platforms as of 16 August 2013.

Spidey's most recent gaming enterprise is *LEGO® Marvel Super Heroes* (TT Games, 2013, *right*), which brings together more than 100 playable Marvel Comics heroes.

WHAMM!

Sales of 8.4 million as of 16 August 2013 make *Spider-Man: The Movie* the **best-selling videogame based on a Marvel Comics character**.

CLUNK!

The **first videogame to feature Batman and Superman** is *Justice League Task Force* (Condor Inc., 1995).

045

KAPOW!

The **best-selling superhero videogame** and **best-selling videogame based on a DC Comics character** is *LEGO Batman: The Videogame* (Traveller's Tales, 2008), with sales of 12.15 million as of 16 August 2013.

THOR

First comic: 1962
First game: *Avengers in Galactic Storm* (Data East, 1995)

Even hammer-wielding gods are not immune to savage criticism, and no matter how super their powers, they cannot influence critics' minds. The **worst-rated superhero videogame** is *Thor: God of Thunder* (Liquid Entertainment, 2011), with a GameRankings score of 39.17% as of 16 August 2013. IGN rated it "awful" and ranked it among their top 10 worst games of 2011.

SHOOTERS

BEST-SELLING SCI-FI SHOOTER SERIES

The *Halo* series (Bungie/343 Industries, 2001–present) had sold 53.89 million units as of 30 August 2013. There are nine games in total, the latest being *Halo: Spartan Assault* (343 Industries/Vanguard, 2013, *right*). This Windows 8/Windows Phone 8 exclusive is the first *Halo* game not to launch on an Xbox console, and the first that can be used on touchscreen devices.

CONTENTS

GEARS OF WAR

LOWDOWN

PUBLISHER:
Microsoft Studios
DEVELOPER:
Epic Games
DEBUT:
2006

It's a vicious battle of humans versus the subterranean Locust Horde in this military sci-fi TPS series. The war-hardened veteran holds the record for **best-selling TPS series** with sales of 19.77 million as of 5 July 2013. *Gears of War 2* (2008) represents 6.6 million of those units, making this the **best-selling TPS videogame**.

NAME THE GAME
Judy Nails lives up to her nickname in which rockin' party game?

MOST SUCCESSFUL GAME ENGINE
Now in its fourth iteration, Epic's Unreal Engine, which debuted in 1998, has been the software used to create and power 332 games as of July 2013. The original *Gears of War* (2006) was the **first console game to use the Unreal 3 engine**. All three follow-up titles have utilized the same engine.

TIP-OFF
"OverRun" is a new class-based multiplayer mode for *Gears of War: Judgment* (2013, *below*). Ensure that your team is a balanced squad composed of all the playable classes so that you don't miss out any key skills.

TOP TEN
MOST CRITICALLY ACCLAIMED TPS GAMES

Game	Score
Gears of War (Epic Games, 2006) on Xbox 360	93.97%
Gears of War 2 (Epic Games, 2008) on Xbox 360	93.32%
Gears of War 3 (Epic Games, 2011) on Xbox 360	91.49%
Max Payne (Remedy Entertainment, 2001) on PC	89.26%
Shadow Complex (Chair Entertainment/Epic Games, 2009) on Xbox 360	89.23%
Dead Space 2 (Visceral Games, 2011) on PS3	89.22%
Dead Space 2 (Visceral Games, 2011) on Xbox 360	89.10%
Dead Space (EA Redwood Shores, 2008) on Xbox 360	89.07%
Dead Space (EA Redwood Shores, 2008) on PS3	89.05%
Max Payne 2: The Fall of Max Payne (Remedy, 2003) on PC	88.49%

Source: gamerankings.com, as of 5 July 2013

BOOST

TOP GEARS – OF WAR

The **fastest completion of** *Gears of War* **on "Casual" difficulty** was achieved by Andrew "Brassmaster" Merideth (USA) in 1 hr 30 min 40 sec on 5 November 2012. Compatriot William "Youkai" Welch posted a time of 1 hr 34 min 57 sec on 12 December 2012, the **fastest completion of** *Gears of War* **on "Insane" difficulty**. The two gamers combined on the **fastest co-op completion of** *Gears of War* in 1 hr 34 min 38 sec on 1 September 2011.

FIRST GAME TO FEATURE "DOWN BUT NOT OUT" FUNCTIONALITY

Now a popular feature in many multiplayer co-op shooters, "down but not out" gameplay first appeared in *Gears of War*. The term refers to occasions on which a player has received enough damage to be incapacitated, but not enough to be killed. They must rely on team-mates to revive them before an enemy finishes them off.

MOST MONEY PAID FOR A GAME ENGINE

In March 2012, the US government's Intelligence Advanced Research Projects Activity adopted the Unreal Engine for intelligence training programmes in a deal worth more than $10 million (£6.3 million).

049

FIRST GAME TO FEATURE "HORDE" MODE

"Horde" is a multiplayer mode that made its debut in *Gears of War 2*. It tasks the gamer – and up to four other players – with repulsing 50 successive waves of enemies with ever-increasing resilience and skill. The endurance concept has since been taken up and modified in numerous other games.

FASTEST-SELLING TPS

In September 2011, *Gears of War 3* (2011) sold 3 million copies in its first five days, outselling the first weeks of both previous *GoW* titles combined. The quadrilogy is the first TPS series to gross $1 billion.

LOWDOWN

PUBLISHER:
Activision
DEVELOPER:
Infinity Ward/
Treyarch
DEBUT:
2003

Every year
cynics say this
year will be the
last time *Call of
Duty* captures
war action fans,
whether the
gameplay be
historical, modern
or futuristic – or
zombie. And every
year the series
that gave us
the **best-selling
shooter on the
PS3**, **the Wii**, **the
Xbox 360** and
the Wii U proves
them wrong.

050

NAME THE GAME
Professional thief
Nathan Drake believes
his ancestor to be
explorer Francis Drake.

BEST-SELLING SHOOTER

Call of Duty: Modern Warfare 3
(Infinity Ward, 2011, *left*) had sold
30.11 million units by 22 June 2013.
  Call of Duty is the **best-selling
shooter series** overall, with sales
of more than 162.05 million copies
across all formats as of 1 June 2013,
accounting for a large chunk of
the 187.28 million units that make
Activision Blizzard the **best-selling
shooter publisher**.

FIRST WINNER OF THE *CALL OF DUTY* CHAMPIONSHIP

On 5–7 April 2013, the
might of Microsoft and
Activision combined to
find the best *Call of Duty:
Black Ops II* players at the
Call of Duty Championship
in Los Angeles, USA. The 2013
tournament was won by FARIKO:
team captain Chris "Parasite" Duarte,
Adam "Killa" Sloss, Marcus "MiRx" Carter
(all USA) and Damon "Karma" Barlow
(Canada). They took home $400,000
(£250,000) in the final against EnVyUs (USA),
who won $200,000 (£125,000) as runners-up.
  A prize pool of $1 million (£625,000)
was the **largest prize for a *Call
of Duty* tournament**, matching
that offered at the *Call of
Duty* XP tournament on
3 September 2011 in
Los Angeles, USA.

TIP-OFF

A *Black
Ops II* Easter Egg:
in single-player campaign
"Celerium", after the wing
suit glide, take out the enemy
encampment. Track back to where
you first spotted the enemy, drop
down and follow the water to the cliff
and drop down again. On the right
is a small cave where you can
see Mjölnir, the hammer of
the god Thor.

FASTEST GAME TO GROSS $1 BILLION

Call of Duty: Black Ops II (Treyarch, 2012, *left*) hit $1 billion (£625 million) within 15 days of its 13 November 2012 release and earned $500 million (£315 million) in its first day, overall the **highest revenue generated by an entertainment product in 24 hours**. *CoD: Modern Warfare 3* is the **fastest-selling game** of any genre, with more than 9.3 million units sold in 24 hours on 8 November 2011.

FASTEST CALL OF DUTY: BLACK OPS II FLAG CAPTURE

On 8 August 2013, gamer Roc "Outconsumer" Massaguer Busqueta (Spain, *left*) was blindfolded and Alastair "Ali-A" Aiken (UK, *right*) shouted instructions, as they captured the overflow map flag on *Call of Duty: Black Ops II* in 1 min 00.52 sec. The record was set during YouTube's "Geek Week", live on the GWRomg channel, at Google HQ in London, UK.

BOOST

SHOT IN THE DARK

Since November 2008, gamers have had Xbox Live avatars. The *Call of Duty: Modern Warfare 2* (Infinity Ward, 2009) night-vision goggles are the **best-selling Xbox Live avatar item** and a real pair came in Prestige Editions of the game (*below*). A less successful real-world venture was the 2004 action figure of a Totenkopf Division soldier from the game. Amid complaints about depicting Nazi SS soldiers who were active as mass murderers in concentration camps as dolls, it vanished from stores in weeks.

HIGHEST SCORE ON *CALL OF DUTY: BLACK OPS* "KINO DER TOTEN"

John Lundrigan (USA) stacked up 47,890 points on the zombie-killing level on the Wii. Overall, the **fastest completion of *Call of Duty: Black Ops*** (Treyarch, 2010) is 2 hr 54 min 28 sec on 26 May 2011 by "TheLongshotLegend" aka Oliver Smith (UK).

TOP TEN

MOST NUKETOWN ROUNDS ON *CALL OF DUTY: BLACK OPS II*

Karma Runs You	81
Malicious Devin	74
PsyRoy	70
SiZ mimoun	
aZp DimS	69
scottie 13	
StepUp420 NUKE	68
KING JAQ SUITED	
ItzMe ItzMe 07	67
ZOmbieClutch	66

Source: *Call of Duty: Black Ops II* "Zombie" mode leaderboard, as of 27 July 2013

HALO

LOWDOWN

PUBLISHER:
Microsoft Studios
DEVELOPER:
Bungie, 343 Industries
DEBUT:
2001

These science-fiction shooters are based around an interstellar war between humanity and an alien alliance known as the Covenant. The series hit its stride with *Halo 2* (Bungie, 2004), the **best-selling Xbox game**, with sales of 8.4 million by 15 July 2013. It is also the **fastest-selling Xbox game**, having sold 2.38 million units on its launch day, 9 November 2004.

NAME THE GAME

The leader of the four horsemen, Death is a member of the Nephilim.

BEST-SELLING PLATFORM-EXCLUSIVE SHOOTER SERIES

Halo games are only available on Microsoft consoles, and had sold 53.89 million units by 30 August 2013. Shown here is *Halo 4* (343 Industries, 2012), the latest console release.

Richard Cartwright (UK) set the **fastest completion of *Halo 4* on "Mythic" difficulty** in 2 hr 41 min 20 sec on 23 February 2013.

HIGHEST REVENUE FOR A MICROSOFT GAME FRANCHISE

According to Microsoft Studios head Phil Spencer, *Halo* had generated total revenue of $3 billion (£1.9 billion) as of June 2013. Some $220 million (£137 million) of this came from day-one sales of *Halo 4* alone.

HIGHEST SCORE IN THE *HALO 4* INFINITY CHALLENGE

Michael "Strongside" Cavanaugh (USA, *pictured below*) achieved a score of 522,325 points in the *Halo 4* Infinity Challenges Tournament held between 17 December 2012 and 19 January 2013. "Strongside" won a UNSC-themed Ford F-150 SVT Raptor and a cameo appearance in a future *Halo* game.

The total prize money won by the **highest-earning professional *Halo* team** is an enormous $318,000 (£200,000) secured by Major League Gaming team Final Boss (USA), which comprises Tom "Ogre2" Ryan and his twin brother Dan "Ogre1" Ryan (now retired).

MOST CRITICALLY ACCLAIMED XBOX GAME

Halo: Combat Evolved (Bungie, 2001), the first *Halo* game, tops the critics' list of all Xbox titles, with a GameRankings score of 95.54% as of 23 July 2013.

Source: gamerankings.com, as of 23 July 2013 (excluding compilations and puzzle title *Portal 2*)

BEST-SELLING SCI-FI SHOOTER

With global sales of 11.78 million as of July 2013, *Halo 3* (Bungie, 2007) is the most popular sci-fi shooter. First-day sales of more than 3.1 million on 6 November 2012 make Xbox 360-exclusive *Halo 4* the **fastest-selling single-platform shooter**.

BEST-SELLING SEVENTH-GENERATION RTS GAME

The Xbox 360's *Halo Wars* (Ensemble Studios, 2009) is the first title in the *Halo* series that is not a shooter. It is also the most successful RTS title of any seventh-generation system, with sales of 2.33 million as of July 2013. The game retains the sci-fi setting of the other *Halo* titles, with players controlling human armies in the year 2531.

BATTLEFIELD

054

LOWDOWN

PUBLISHER:
EA
DEVELOPER:
DICE
DEBUT:
2002

Complete your mission, take out the enemy and stay alive – those are the objectives of this prolific military FPS series. The latest instalment, *Battlefield 4*, is set for release in October 2013. Four of its titles are set in World War 2, two during the Vietnam conflict and the remaining 19 are set in the future.

NAME THE GAME Crystal Maiden is an ice queen who uses cool skills to defeat her enemies.

BEST-SELLING TACTICAL SHOOTER

Battlefield 3 (2011, *above*), the 19th title in the series, had global sales of 15.81 million as of 10 July 2013. Games in this shooters sub-genre offer greater realism and require tactical and strategic acumen.

MOST DESTRUCTIBLE ENVIRONMENTS IN A MILITARY FPS

It was owing to the Frostbite 1.5 engine that *Battlefield: Bad Company 2* (2010) had the most destructible environments. Around 90% of the landscape was destroyable and even the ground could be deformed.

Set for late 2013 release, *Battlefield 4* heralds the launch of the company's much-anticipated new game engine, and will be the **first game to use the Frostbite 3 engine**. In development since 2006, the engine features Destruction 4.0, which enhances the in-game annihilation further.

HIGHEST SCORE ON *BATTLEFIELD 3*

UK *Battlefield* fan "ElitestGamer" had amassed 251,186,000 points on the PS3 version of *Battlefield 3* as of 9 July 2013. Fellow PS3 gamer "D3vZ_Kami" (Italy) has the **highest kill-to-death ratio in *Battlefield 3***, with an impressive 218.41 to 1.

MOST MBT KILLS IN *BATTLEFIELD 3*

Romanian gamer FuT-cerealno had achieved a total of 137,396 main battle tank (MBT) kills in *Battlefield 3* on PC as of 9 July 2013.

Acula-3 (Ukraine) fought his way through 201,745 opponents on the multiplayer section of the PC version, achieving the **most melee kills in *Battlefield 3***. The **most kills in *Battlefield 3*** overall is 555,870, achieved by KAIN (Germany), also on the PC version.

QUICK COMPANY

After *Battlefield 3*, the next best-selling title in the series is *Battlefield: Bad Company 2* with sales of 6.71 million. Szymon "-KFC-" Kiendyś (Poland) completed a segmented speed-run of the game in just 1 hr 16 min 3 sec – the **fastest completion of *Battlefield: Bad Company 2*** – on 15 August 2010. Szymon's speed-run advice is simple: "Avoid fighting... run the ways where bots won't see you."

TOP TEN
MOST JET KILLS IN *BATTLEFIELD 3*

-AlphaNerd-Ger- (Germany) on PC	140,787
GrieferKiller (USA) on PC	132,920
Noob_Pwnisher (Puerto Rico, USA) on PC	96,477
Frindly-Fire-4 (Kuwait) on PC	93,324
brxtactics (nationality unknown) on Xbox 360	91,532
souza233 (Brazil) on PC	81,161
Zante666 (Australia) on PC	80,936
CX-Caffeine (USA) on PC	74,459
xSn0wyy (USA) on PS3	73,714
ceasar76 (USA) on PC	73,415

Source: *Battlefield 3* leaderboards, as of 9 July 2013

MOST PROLIFIC FPS SERIES

With its 25 entries (including expansion packs and boosters), the *Battlefield* series is the most prolific FPS franchise. The first six games were PC/Mac exclusives. As of July 2013, the *Call of Duty* series (Infinity Ward/Treyarch, 2003–present) was snapping at *Battlefield*'s heels with 19 titles.

HIGHEST-RANKED TEAM IN *BATTLEFIELD 3*'S "OPERATION EXODUS"

Gamers "NEXTLEVEL_15656" and "Pardaladc" had scored 1,810,710 points apiece in the co-op mission "Operation Exodus" as of 9 July 2013. The pair are ahead of their nearest rivals by more than a million points. "Exodus" is one of six co-operative missions in *Battlefield 3*.

LOWDOWN

The shooters genre continues to be a dominant force in gaming, with the eighth generation heralding a host of slick new games, such as PS4 launch title *Killzone: Shadow Fall* (Guerrilla Games, 2013). The incredible graphics of *Killzone* are a far cry from the **first FPS game**, *Battlezone* (Atari, 1980), a modified version of which was ordered by the US military as a training programme for gunners!

056

NAME THE GAME
Naisha, a Night Elf, is presumed deceased after the Tomb of Sargeras collapses.

MOST CRITICALLY ACCLAIMED TACTICAL SHOOTER

The seventh title in the *Ghost Recon* series, *Tom Clancy's Ghost Recon Advanced Warfighter* (Ubisoft Paris, 2006), had a GameRankings score of 90.47% on the Xbox 360, as of 23 July 2013.

BEST-SELLING SHOOTER FOR Wii

As of 20 July 2013, *Link's Crossbow Training* (Nintendo EAD Group No. 3, 2007) had sold over 4.97 million units, making it the top Wii shooter. Shooters are usually more popular on the Xbox 360 or PS3, but this *Legend of Zelda* spin-off has proved a hit for Nintendo, with its nine stages of tricky crossbow tests.

FASTEST COMPLETION OF *BORDERLANDS 2*

"JoltzDude139" completed a segmented speed-run of FPS *Borderlands 2* (Gearbox Software, 2012) in a speedy 2 hr 5 min 34 sec on 19 April 2013. He claims the trick to running fast is having a depleted shield.

BO:OM!

Hunting games are a crossover sub-genre that traverse both shooters and sports categories. Unsurprisingly, they task the gamer with locating and shooting wild animals such as bears and deer in a number of natural environments, while avoiding the animals' attacks. The most well-known hunter game series is *Cabela's Big Game Hunter* (multiple developers, 1998–present), an FPS that includes a multiplayer mode.

MOST "GAMES CRITICS AWARDS BEST OF E3" WINS

Forthcoming Xbox One and PC title *Titanfall* (Respawn Entertainment) won a total of six "Games Critics Awards Best of E3" titles at E3 in June 2013. The awards are voted for by 30 North American media outlets.

Game	Score
Metroid Prime (Retro Studios/Nintendo, 2002) on GameCube	96.35%
Halo: Combat Evolved (Bungie, 2001) on Xbox	95.54%
Half-Life 2 (Valve Corporation, 2004) on PC	95.48%
BioShock (Irrational Games, 2007) on Xbox 360	95.07%
GoldenEye 007 (Rare, 1997) on N64	94.59%
BioShock (Irrational Games, 2007) on PC	94.58%
Halo 2 (Bungie, 2004) on Xbox	94.57%
Perfect Dark (Rare, 2000) on N64	94.20%
Call of Duty 4: Modern Warfare (Infinity Ward, 2007) on Xbox 360	94.16%
Half-Life (Valve Corporation, 1998) on PC	94.02%

Source: gamerankings.com, as of 23 July 2013 (excluding compilations and puzzle title *Portal 2*)

057

WORST-RATED FPS

Rogue Warrior (Rebellion Derby, 2009) on the Xbox 360, whose protagonist Richard Marcinko is voiced by Hollywood star Mickey Rourke, had a paltry GameRankings score of 29.16% as of 23 July 2013. The **worst-rated TPS** is PS2 game *Army Men: Green Rogue* (3DO, 2001), which scored a feeble 37.77%.

BEST-SELLING PS3 PLATFORM-EXCLUSIVE SHOOTER SERIES

PlayStation 3 series *Resistance* (Insomniac Games, 2006–present) had sold 7.86 million units by 20 July 2013.

The **best-selling platform-exclusive shooter** overall is NES title *Duck Hunt* (Nintendo R&D1, 1984), which sold more than 28.31 million units. This puts it ahead of any *Call of Duty* title on any single platform. *Duck Hunt* utilizes the NES Zapper light gun peripheral.

HOW TO MAKE A
VIDEOGAME

IN 10 EASY STEPS!

The game on your screen began life as an idea in someone's head and made it through coding, design, testing, more testing and another round of testing to your device. Philippa Warr interviews industry figures for insights into the game-creation process.

"I didn't realize people *made* games – I just thought they sort of showed up in a box somewhere." – Ken Levine, on life before writing *BioShock*

1
THINK OF A CONCEPT

You might want to continue a successful series that will sell in the millions or a cult hit that will be remembered for its innovation. Wherever your idea sits, you need to have a strong idea of its unique selling point and the place it will occupy in the crowded market.

2 PREPARE A PITCH

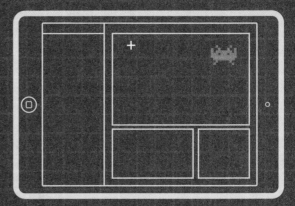

Once you're confident in your concept, you need to pitch it to someone. As Ed Stern, lead writer at Splash Damage points out, "Ideas are free – the problem is trying to find someone with the team and ability to execute that on time and on budget." For a development studio, this means taking the idea to a publisher, a journey that does not always need to be lengthy. "For us, the publisher is next door – we make games for PlayStation and we're owned by PlayStation," says Dave Ranyard, London studio director at Sony. "But you still have to pitch. It's a bit like *Dragons' Den* at times." Tiny indie developers may opt to skip the pitching stage if they don't need mega-budgets and can turn to crowd-funding for cash.

3 START PLANNING

Let's celebrate! Your idea is moving. But don't party too hard. The work has only just begun and the meter is running. "You have production deadlines, marketing deadlines and magazine articles - you have to be focused. If the process is already documented and costed you're more likely to be able to meet those," says Mark Ogilvie, lead developer for *RuneScape* (Jagex Games Studio, 2001–present).

4 GET TO WORK

Often one of the lead developers will sketch out the essentials for the new game, including basic milestones, major design or storyline elements, the intended age certificate and so on. "It's like building a house - you work out the plans and get those approved, then budget for the costs, then you hire the right people to do it," says Dave Ranyard.

5 START BUILDING

Break up big tasks into chunks. Programmers design or rework systems and tools to build the game; scripters and level designers look at plot and missions; artists begin creating the game world and characters. As all the tools, art assets and designs come together, you will begin to see what works as part of the whole. As levels and sections are completed, they are assembled and tweaked.

6 TEST THE GAME

A Quality Assurance (QA) team work as the game nears completion. Once the game is functionally ready, there might be "alpha" testing to make sure nothing is drastically wrong. When the game is all but finished, there may be a "beta" test in which players help iron out kinks and – in the case of online games – stress-test servers. Not every bug gets fixed but there should be nothing capable of ruining the consumer's enjoyment.

7 DON'T WATCH THE CLOCK

A triple-A franchise might take up to three years to complete, while the first in a series can take five years. Major budgets hover around the £30-million ($50-million) mark. "With [an] indie it's difficult to say how much it costs because someone might have done two years' work on it while at college," says Dave Ranyard. If a deal is already secured with a publisher or your studio is owned by one of the big names, you don't need to worry about selling and distribution. Indies may go the digital distribution route to save on producing physical copies. You can try to get on a major service – Valve's Steam, for example, sells games voted in via its Greenlight community.

8 READ (AND IGNORE) THE REVIEWS

Send out review copies, grant interviews to magazines and websites and unleash the marketing and advertising. Publishers keep a close eye on reviews and feedback, although developers are less keen. "You have to take everything with a pinch of salt," says Ranyard. "Don't let your head get too big because of the nice ones and don't get too depressed over the other ones... We look for common issues – you might make something great but everyone got stuck on a certain level so you learn."

9 CREATE A BUZZ

Martin Hollis, director of *GoldenEye 007* (Rare, 1997), says that blockbusters rely more on marketing than reviews: "A good review is important, but if you want your game to sell five or 10 million units you can't reach that level of success through good reviews; you need visibility in the shops and in the news." One game that managed to achieve such visibility was *Call of Duty: Black Ops II* (Treyarch, 2012), which set the record for the **highest revenue generated by a game in 24 hours**, with $500 million (£315 million) on 13 November 2012.

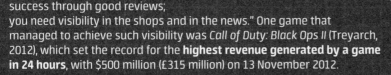

10 SIT BACK AND RELAX (SORT OF)

Games used to be confined to their cartridges, but now developers can tinker with a product long after release. Patches to fix bugs are rolled out, downloadable content is created and, in systems allowing for micro-transactions, new items are made available. When is a finished game really finished? The answer is when players stop playing.

059

SPORTS

LONGEST MARATHON ON AN ICE HOCKEY VIDEOGAME

Canadian gamers James Evans (*right*) and Bruce Ashton (*left*) played *NHL 10* (EA, 2009) for 24 hr 2 min between 30 and 31 July 2011 in Orillia, Ontario, Canada. The record-breaking event was held as part of the Securitas Canada Annual Cure for Cancer Ball Hockey Challenge. For an exclusive chat with the boys, turn to p.185.

For an exclusive chat with the boys, turn to p.185.

CONTENTS

SOCCER

LOWDOWN

The **longest-running soccer videogame series**, EA's *FIFA*, has been scoring with annual innovations since 1993. *FIFA 13* (2012) is the **best-selling soccer videogame**, with 14.5 million copies sold as of June 2013. The many fans of titles such as *Hattrick* (Hattrick Europe, 1997) remind us that there's something for everyone, from simulation to the strategy of management.

062

NAME THE GAME
Eastern European Niko Bellic moved to Liberty City on the advice of his cousin Roman.

FASTEST-SELLING SPORTS VIDEOGAME

No sports videogame has launched more successfully than *FIFA 13*. Released on 25 September 2012, it sold 4.5 million units in less than a week.

MOST SPORTS GAMERS ONLINE SIMULTANEOUSLY

Just days after its release, on 30 September 2012, EA recorded 800,000 gamers playing *FIFA 13*. Few of these have got near the **highest margin of victory against a computer on *FIFA 13*** – 307 goals – achieved by Patrick Hadler (Germany) in Rethem, Germany, on 16 March 2013.

BOOST

MADDENING MOTSON

John Motson (UK, *below*) is the **most prolific soccer videogame commentator**, having voiced nine soccer games, from *FIFA 97* (1996) to *FIFA Soccer 2005* (2004). John Madden is the overall **longest-serving videogame commentator**, with 15 games from 1995 to 2008 in the *Madden NFL* series.

LARGEST ONLINE SOCCER MANAGER GAME

Players manage the fortunes of teams using just a web browser in *Hattrick*, which had 531,130 active users as of 1 July 2013.

Football Manager 2013 (Sports Interactive, 2012) has the **largest soccer database** – with more than 500,000 real-world players and staff.

MOST WIDELY DISTRIBUTED SOCCER SERIES

As of June 2013, *Pro Evolution Soccer* (Konami, 1996–present) has been localized into 19 languages and sold in 62 countries. This compares with 18 languages and 51 countries for the *FIFA* series.

FIRST SOCCER VIDEOGAME FOR KINECT

While *Kinect Sports* (Rare, 2010) features a goalkeeping mini-game, *FIFA 13* is the first soccer-only videogame to support the Kinect.

WORST-RATED SOCCER GAME

Dreamcast game *Virtua Striker 2* (Sega, 2000) has a rating of 51.33% according to GameRankings as of 21 June 2013.

At the opposite end of the scale, *Pro Evolution Soccer 3* (Konami, 2004) is the **most critically acclaimed soccer game**, with a score of 92.97%.

TOP TEN	HIGHEST-RANKED PLAYERS ON *FIFA 13*	
Lionel Messi (Argentina)		94
Cristiano Ronaldo (Portugal)		92
Andrés Iniesta (Spain)		
Xavi (Spain)		90
Franck Ribéry (France)		
Iker Casillas (Spain)		
Nemanja Vidić (Serbia)		89
Wayne Rooney (England)		
David Silva (Spain)		
Robin van Persie (Netherlands)		
Arjen Robben (Netherlands)		88
Radamel Falcao (Colombia)		
Zlatan Ibrahimović (Sweden)		

Source: *FIFA 13* on Xbox 360, as of 15 July 2013

LARGEST GAMING TOURNAMENT

The 2013 FIFA Interactive World Cup took place between 1 October 2012 and 8 May 2013. It attracted 2.5 million participants, with 21 finalists travelling to Madrid, Spain. *Above right*, Bruce Grannec (France) takes the trophy for a second time, having won in 2009, the **most wins of the FIFA Interactive World Cup**, equalling the record held by Alfonso Ramos (Spain) with wins in 2008 and 2012.

LOWDOWN

American football, basketball and baseball are the core sports here. EA's *Madden NFL* series (1988–present) dominates the genre; *Madden NFL 2004* (2003) is the **best-selling American sports game** having sold 7.15 million units by 17 July 2013.

In **baseball**, the **most critically acclaimed game** is PS3's *MLB 10: The Show* (SCEA, 2010), with 90.53% scored on GameRankings, while *World Series Baseball 2K1* (Sega, 2000) on Dreamcast is the **worst-rated** with just 43.79% as of 17 July 2013.

064

NAME THE GAME
"Soap", a canine-hating killer, stars in which series?

FIRST AMERICAN FOOTBALL GAME FOR KINECT

Being able to yell at players is part of the gameplay in *Madden NFL 13*, released on 28 August 2012. The Xbox 360 Kinect peripheral allows a gamer to call out plays and change player formations simply by using their voice. *Kinect Sports* (Rare), released in 2010, was the **first sports game for Kinect**.

LONGEST CAREER AS A BASEBALL VIDEOGAME DEVELOPER

Don Daglow (USA) has been creating and developing baseball games for 42 years, as of July 2013. In 1971, he wrote *Baseball* on a PDP-10 mainframe computer, setting a template for later titles such as *Tony La Russa Baseball* (Beyond Software, 1991, *below*).

BALLS 0
STRIKES 01
OUTS 0
INNING 11

TORONTO
ATLANTA
ALOMAR
GLAVINE 2

BO:OM!

John Madden, the name and voice behind the best-selling *Madden NFL* series, retired from voicing the commentary after *Madden NFL 09* (EA Tiburon, 2008). Although he enjoyed helping devise the games from scratch, Madden says he doesn't miss recording the commentary: "I got bored. The script was literally as thick as a telephone book."

FIRST ROOKIE TEAM TO WIN THE MADDEN BOWL

The Madden Bowl is a gaming contest played on the latest *Madden NFL* title. On 2 February 2013, former Florida State quarterback E J Manuel, former Oregon running-back Kenjon Barner and former Michigan quarterback Denard Robinson (all USA) made up the first rookie team to win the Bowl in its 19-year history, winning 21–7.

065

TOP TEN
MOST CRITICALLY ACCLAIMED AMERICAN SPORTS SERIES

Series	Rating
NFL 2K (Visual Concepts, 1999–2004)	88.89%
World Series Baseball (Visual Concepts, 2002–03)	87.17%
MLB: The Show (SCE San Diego Studio, 2006–13)	87.05%
Madden NFL (EA Tiburon, 1999–2013)	86.46%
NBA Street (EA Canada, 2001–07)	86.37%
NCAA Football (EA, 2001–11)	86.22%
MVP Baseball (EA, 2003–05)	86.12%
NBA 2K (Visual Concepts, 1999–2012)	85.57%
NBA Live (EA, 1999–present)	83.16%
High Heat: Major League Baseball (3DO, 2001–03)	82.84%

Source: gamerankings.com, as of 29 July 2013 (games with 80%+ ratings)

MOST CRITICALLY ACCLAIMED BASKETBALL VIDEOGAME

NBA Street Vol. 2 (EA, 2003, *right*) on the PS2 had a GameRankings rating of 90.16% as of 17 July 2013. The game contains 29 NBA teams and various legends from the history of the sport, such as "Magic" Johnson and Michael Jordan. Xbox title *And 1 Streetball* (Black Ops Entertainment, 2006), on the other hand, had a dismal 49.82% score on GameRankings, making it the **worst-rated basketball game**.

The **worst-rated American football videogame** is *NFL Tour* (EA Tiburon, 2008, *above*) on the PS3, with 48.45%.

FIRST TEAM ON CONSECUTIVE MADDEN NFL COVERS

When Barry Sanders became the cover star of *NFL 25* (2013), he secured a double coup for the Detroit Lions. The team's wide receiver Calvin Johnson Jr had appeared on the cover of *Madden NFL 13* (2012), so Sanders' appearance marked the first time that the same team had featured on consecutive *Madden* covers.

WINTER SPORTS

LOWDOWN

If it's played on snow or ice, it qualifies for our Winter Sports pages. Ice hockey, snowboarding, skiing and Winter Olympic pursuits have long been part of the gaming scene; the **first official Winter Olympics game** was *Winter Olympics: Lillehammer 94* (US Gold, 1993), which included 10 events and was released on various platforms including the SNES and PC.

066

NAME THE GAME Ingward carries a Tin Banishment Catalyst and is dressed in crimson robes in which RPG?

BEST-SELLING SNOWBOARDING GAME SERIES

SSX (EA, 2012) took sales of the long-running alpine sports series to a triumphant 9.69 million units as of 10 July 2013. Predecessor *SSX Tricky* (EA, 2001) for the PS2 is the **most critically acclaimed snowboarding game**, with a GameRankings score of 92.54% as of 19 July 2013.

BEST-SELLING SNOWBOARDING GAME

N64 snowboard racer *1080° Snowboarding* (Nintendo, 1998), which involves performing tricks at high speed, had sold 2.03 million copies as of 19 July 2013.

LONGEST-RUNNING ICE HOCKEY GAME SERIES

EA's *NHL 14*, which won the Best Sports Game in the Game Critics Awards Best of E3 2013, is the 23rd title in a series that began in 1991. The first game, *NHL Hockey*, was a Sega Mega Drive/Genesis exclusive. Its US release included a licence from the NHL to use their players and teams, but in Europe and Japan the game used generic squads. Surprisingly, the **best-selling ice hockey game** is not one of the NHL titles, but an NES game called *Ice Hockey* (Nintendo, 1988), with total sales of 2.42 million.

BEST-SELLING WINTER OLYMPICS VIDEOGAME

Mario & Sonic at the Olympic Winter Games (Sega, 2009), an official title of the 2010 Vancouver Winter Olympics, had sold over 7.72 million copies as of 10 July 2013, making it also the **best-selling winter sports game**. The fourth title in the *Mario & Sonic* Olympics series (*right*) will be the official game of the 2014 Winter Olympics in Sochi, Russia. *Sonic at the Olympic Winter Games* (Venan, 2010) had the **shortest release time for a sports game** – it went on sale on 30 January 2010 and was pulled with no explanation on 3 February 2010.

FIRST FEMALE CHARACTER IN AN ICE HOCKEY VIDEOGAME

A female character option was created in *NHL 12* (EA Sports, 2011), with Lexi Peters (USA) – a 14-year-old at the time – appearing as the default female player. Peters, who lives in Buffalo, New York, USA, plays for the all-girl team Purple Eagles. She was included in the game after writing to EA Sports to complain that women were not represented in the franchise. The NHL then gave its official approval.

067

FIRST THIRD-PARTY Wii BALANCE BOARD GAME

Family Ski (Namco Bandai, 2008, aka *We Ski* in the USA) utilizes the Wii Balance Board to enable players to simulate turning as they ski. In addition, the Wii Remote and Wii Nunchuk simulate the ski poles.

"Third-party" refers to any development company other than a console maker, here Nintendo, who produce the vast majority of titles for their own consoles, including *Wii Fit* (Nintendo EAD, 2007), the **first Wii Balance Board game**.

Family Ski is also the **best-selling skiing game** with sales of 1.63 million copies, by 10 July 2013.

TOP TEN — MOST POINTS ON *NHL 13*

JrPens91 (USA) on PS3	9,641
Shoulder2Chest (Canada) on PS3	9,486
Class_Act_27 (nationality unknown) on PS3	9,324
MiksEi_ (nationality unknown) on PS3	9,304
I3engee xQCx (nationality unknown) on Xbox 360	9,245
AgentSooksta008 (nationality unknown) on Xbox 360	9,226
X Odieeee (nationality unknown) on Xbox 360	9,059
joshfearless13 (nationality unknown) on Xbox 360	8,902
EA_Riivaa (nationality unknown) on PS3	8,791
Akb4r (Thailand) on Xbox 360	8,788

Source: easports.com leaderboards, as of 17 July 2013

BEST OF THE REST

LOWDOWN

Sports gaming has never been so diverse, with a dizzying number of traditional and extreme sports titles vying for gamers' attention. The detail and realism of these sports franchises would have been a pipe dream for physicist William Higinbotham (USA), creator of *Tennis for Two* (1958), the **first tennis videogame**. This basic title simulated a game of tennis on an oscilloscope.

068

NAME THE GAME
In the fourth instalment of which franchise does Leon Kennedy seek to rescue the President's daughter?

MOST PROLIFIC GOLF VIDEOGAME SERIES

EA's *Tiger Woods PGA Tour* series began in 1998. *Tiger Woods PGA Tour 14*, released in March 2013, is the 14th release in the popular series and features all four of golf's majors – the **most tournaments in a golf videogame**.

TOP TEN	BEST-SELLING SPORTS VIDEOGAMES	
Wii Sports (Nintendo, 2006) on Wii		81.445
Wii Sports Resort (Nintendo, 2009) on Wii		31.806
Mario & Sonic at the Olympic Games (Nintendo, 2007) on Wii		7.880
FIFA 12 (EA, 2011) on PS3		6.398
Kinect Sports (Microsoft Game Studios, 2010) on Xbox 360		5.627
Madden NFL 2004 (EA, 2003) on PS2		5.230
Mario & Sonic at the Olympic Games (Nintendo, 2008) on DS		5.023
Tony Hawk's Pro Skater (Activision, 1999) on PlayStation		5.020
FIFA 11 (EA, 2010) on PS3		4.931
Madden NFL 06 (EA, 2005) on PS2		4.910

Source: vgchartz.com, as of 3 August 2013 (figures in millions; includes bundled games, excludes fitness titles)

KICKFLIP
100

MOST CRITICALLY ACCLAIMED SPORTS VIDEOGAME

Tony Hawk's Pro Skater 2 (Neversoft, 2000) on the PlayStation had a GameRankings score of 94.85% as of 30 July 2013. In the list of the top five critically acclaimed sports games, Tony Hawk appears three times. There are 14 *Hawk* titles, the most recent of which is *Tony Hawk's Pro Skater HD* (Robomodo, 2012).

WORST-RATED SPORTS VIDEOGAME

PS2 title *Gravity Games Bike: Street Vert Dirt* (Midway, 2002) is the top of the critical flops, with a rating of just 36.52% as of 30 July 2013. The BMX game met with a chorus of disapproval; IGN writer Chris Roper concluded that it was "easily one of the worst games I've ever played". *Gravity Games Bike* sold 110,000 copies.

FIRST VIDEOGAME TO FEATURE A WOMEN'S TOUR

With a Ladies Professional Golf Association (LPGA) option in *Tiger Woods PGA Tour 14*, in-game females can now compete on the PGA or LPGA Tour as well as in the Kraft Nabisco Championship, even though women are denied the chance to play on many real-world courses. Although tennis series such as 2K Sports' *Top Spin* (2003–11) include females, they don't feature a tour option.

GREATEST INDIVIDUAL PRIZE MONEY IN A GAME COMPETITION

The greatest pay-out to an individual for winning a gaming competition is $1 million (£536,000). There have been two separate contests with such a prize: the inaugural WorldWide Web Games in 2006, won by Kavitha Yalavarthi (USA), and the *MLB 2K* Perfect Game Tournament. The last $1 million winner of the latter was Christopher Gilmore (USA, *below*), who won the tournament final 10–1 on 10 May 2012.

BEST-SELLING VIDEOGAME

Wii Sports, the title bundled with the Wii featuring tennis, bowling, golf, boxing and baseball, had sold 81.44 million copies as of 3 August 2013, making it the all-time best-seller. The **best-selling sports videogame**, excluding bundled titles such as *Wii Sports*, is *Wii Fit*, which has sold 22.75 million.

MOST PROLIFIC TENNIS GAME SERIES

As of 30 July 2013, the biggest pure tennis franchise – that is, one that does not offer side-plots or different games – is *Virtua Tennis* (Sega, 1999–2011). Pictured below is 2011's *Virtua Tennis 4*. There have been seven games in the series, selling a total of 3.8 million copies, making *Virtua Tennis* the **best-selling tennis game series**.

With sales of 5.36 million across all platforms, the **best-selling tennis game** is *Sega Superstars Tennis* (Sumo Digital, 2008), which allows you to play as Sonic, Tails, Gilius Thunderhead, Alex Kidd and various other characters from the Sega universe.

069

GAMING GATHERINGS

They bring together thousands of fans for talks, parties and, of course, some serious gaming. Matthew Edwards **tours the biggest and best gaming conventions in the world.**

With the likes of Xbox Live, PlayStation Network and websites such as IGN, Eurogamer and Kotaku, socializing with other gamers has never been easier. It doesn't matter if you're discussing the latest games on a forum or messaging a player you met in a co-op game, communicating with those who share the same interests is just a click away. But what happens when you break down the online barriers and put a crowd of gamers and developers in a bustling building full of games? In short: a gaming convention.

Back in the 1980s and '90s, one of the few ways to meet fellow gamers was at a local arcade – not only did you get to play the likes of *Street Fighter* (Capcom, 1987) and *Sega Rally Championship* (AM5, 1994) against friends or strangers, but you could also share tips, stories and gossip about the next generation of games and consoles. In this regard, gaming conventions have taken the place of arcade halls, and whether you're a fan of platformers, fighters or Japanese RPGs, there are always games on hand to sample.

While the E3 trade show is undoubtedly the main event in the gaming calendar, with its major premieres and reveals, it isn't a convention in the traditional sense as it is only open to industry pros.

Thankfully, there are several conventions open to gamers, ranging from MineCon, a yearly meet of *Minecraft* (Mojang, 2009) fans that began with around 50 visitors in 2010 and now hosts over 7,000, to Gamescom, the largest of them all.

Gamescom beat its own record in 2013 for the **largest gaming convention**, when more than 340,000 people from 88 countries crammed into the Koelnmesse centre in Cologne, Germany. Highlights included the European debuts of the Xbox One and PS4, and 400 game premieres including *Battlefield 4* (DICE, due in 2013) and Ivory Tower's 2014 title *The Crew*.

MineCon

Gamescom

E3

Conventions have evolved quickly. When gaming enthusiasts attended the first London Eurogamer Expo in 2008, the focus was primarily on the games themselves. Four years later, the convention expanded to include a Games Industry Fair with practical advice on how to pursue a career in videogames. Visitors could also watch presentations and seminars by some of the biggest names in the business. The highlights in 2012 included the iconic British games designer Peter Molyneux (*right*) giving a live demonstration of his "gaming experiment" *Curiosity – What's Inside the Cube?*, and a *Metal Gear* 25th anniversary Q&A with stealth pioneer Hideo Kojima.

As exciting as it may be to play an unreleased game or buy a *Halo* hoodie, conventions also offer fans an unashamed celebration of gaming culture. This is typified by cosplayers – the gamers who dress up as their favourite characters. A simple costume could consist of a red jumper and blue dungarees for the desired Mario effect, while a complex outfit like the Master Chief or Samus Aran's armour will draw the looks and cameras of many an avid gamer. Pictured left are *Star Wars* cosplayers at Gamescom 2012 and, far left, *Assassin's Creed* fan Jerry Yousefian at the Anime Expo 2013. You just need to bear in mind that some costumes are more practical than others...

Anime Expo

Gamescom

Seattle PAX

Gaming and competition have been inextricably linked ever since Midway's *Sea Wolf* (1976) became the **first videogame to log high scores**.

At E3 2012, this competition was channelled into a marathon battle in which 32 gamers attempted the **longest videogame marathon on a tablet**. A range of videogames were played, and 26 of the 32 contestants set a time of 26 hours.

And yet, as much as videogames nurture competition, they're also about working together, whether it's team play in a game or record-setting at a convention. Much like the annual San Diego Comic-Con – the **largest convention of comic book fans**, with more than 130,000 attendees – the multifaceted London MCM Expo covers anime, manga and sci-fi as well as games. In 2009, it hosted the **largest handheld console party** when 586 gamers showed up with a Nintendo DS. And when 536 fans of Kirby were given gum at Seattle PAX Prime in 2012 (*above*), they blew away the record for the **most people blowing a chewing gum bubble simultaneously**.

There's an assumption that conventions are for the hardcore elite only, but in truth they cater for all gamers. Make the pilgrimage to Cologne for Gamescom or take your 3DS to the London MCM Expo for more "Street Passes" than you can use. Gaming is about so much more than your console. Carry on convening.

PUZZLES

MOST DOWNLOADED MOBILE GAME SERIES

With an astonishing download count of 1.7 billion as of March 2013 across all phones and tablets, the *Angry Birds* series (Rovio, 2009–present) is easily the most popular mobile gaming franchise.

The **highest score on Level 1-1 of "Poached Eggs" on *Angry Birds* for Chrome** was achieved by Stephen Kish (UK, *pictured*), who scored a sky-high 37,510 points on 23 August 2011 in East Sussex, UK.

CONTENTS

ANGRY BIRDS

LOWDOWN

PUBLISHER:
Chillingo/Rovio
DEVELOPER:
Rovio
DEBUT:
2009

Eliminate the provoking pigs by launching birds from a slingshot. It couldn't be simpler, which may explain how the game achieved feats such as the **most days as the best-selling iTunes Store app**, with 275 consecutive days at No.1, and **best-selling *Star Wars* app**, with *Angry Birds Star Wars* ranked the 12th most downloaded app on iTunes.

074

NAME THE GAME
Antihero and demi-god Kratos is violent by nature.

HIGHEST SCORE ON *ANGRY BIRDS*

With 42,610,510 points, Swiss gamer "bastieroxxor" is top of the pecking order as of 22 July 2013.

The **highest score on *Angry Birds Rio*** belongs to high-flyer "manu malin", who could lay claim to 30,876,690 points on the same date.

FIRST MOBILE GAME SERIES TO REACH 1 BILLION DOWNLOADS

On 9 May 2012, Rovio announced that *Angry Birds* had racked up a billion downloads, making it the first mobile game franchise to reach this landmark as well as the **most downloaded mobile game series overall**. This total combines figures for *Angry Birds* (December 2009), *Angry Birds Seasons* (October 2010), *Angry Birds Rio* (March 2011) and *Angry Birds Space* (March 2012).

FASTEST #1-RANKING ROVIO GAME

Bad Piggies is Rovio's fastest No.1-ranking app on Apple's App Store. On 27 September 2012, the game took just over three hours to reach the top spot, beating all other Rovio games. *Bad Piggies*' success is owing to a global launch promotion that saw piggy balloons, trucks and electronic displays in cities worldwide.

MOST PEOPLE PLAYING *ANGRY BIRDS*

On 11 June 2011 in Kuala Lumpur, Malaysia, 2,030 people took part in a game of *Angry Birds*. The event was organized by Nokia Malaysia and saw 10 hours of continuous game play, with each gamer playing one level.

Just months before, the **largest game of *Angry Birds*** was held by US talkshow host Conan O'Brien. The human-sized version of the game was built in O'Brien's studio on 3 March 2011, using Ikea furniture, inflatable balls and a catapult taller than the host.

LARGEST IN-APP VIDEO NETWORK

On 17 March 2013, Rovio launched its own cartoon channel "Angry Birds Toons" inside all *Angry Birds* apps, treating the games' audience of 1.7 billion to an animated series starring the flying flockers and their piggy foes. The Mighty Eagle, star of the **most watched *Angry Birds* video** – "Angry Birds & the Mighty Eagle" – had 99,131,980 views on YouTube as of 2 September 2013.

FIRST OFFICIAL THEME PARK BASED ON A PUZZLE GAME

Särkänniemi in Tampere, Finland, is home to Angry Birds Land, which opened on 28 April 2012. The **first official theme park based on a videogame** of any kind, however, was PokéPark, opened on 18 March 2005 in Nagoya, Japan, in honour of Nintendo classic *Pokémon* (Game Freak, 1996–present).

HIGHEST SCORE ON *ANGRY BIRDS SPACE* "EGGSTEROIDS"

German gamer Hendrik "Nintendo S.T.A.R." Bunde racked up a total score of 1,092,235 on 10 May 2013, for all "Eggsteroids" stages combined.

TOP TEN — HIGHEST SCORES ON *ANGRY BIRDS STAR WARS*

wicket182 (USA)	20,059,670
ChiefBumpa (nationality unknown)	19,988,040
bluevertigo (nationality unknown)	19,985,200
alo10w (Ireland)	19,945,410
Yor El (France)	19,912,890
wRm (Germany)	19,900,610
Lancer854 (nationality unknown)	19,801,750
HallieGinSB (USA)	19,704,400
annach (nationality unknown)	19,704,300
Crazy Rider (France)	19,694,730

Source: angrybirdsnest.com, as of 22 July 2013

075

PORTAL

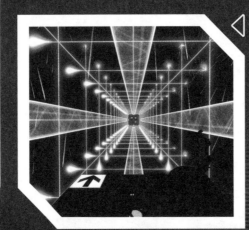

LOWDOWN

PUBLISHER:
Valve
DEVELOPER:
Valve
DEBUT:
2007

This first-person physics-based puzzler began in a 2007 bundle, prior to a full release. Sequel *Portal 2* (2011) for PC is critically acclaimed with a rating of 95.16% on GameRankings. The aim of the game is to solve puzzles set by an artificially intelligent entity named GLaDOS.

076

NAME THE GAME
Kazuya Mishima is also known as the Devil in which fighter?

MOST CRITICALLY ACCLAIMED VIDEOGAME COMPILATION ▷

Portal debuted in Valve's *The Orange Box* compilation (2007) for PS3, Xbox 360 and PC. The five-strong collection introduced *Portal* protagonists Chell and GLaDOS to the gaming world and included the FPS *Half-Life 2: Episode Two* and the online fragfest *Team Fortress 2*. As of 27 June 2013, the collection had a mighty 93.73% average review score on GameRankings.

PC DVD

The Orange Box

FEATURING

Half-Life 2: Episode Two
Team Fortress 2
AND INTRODUCING **Portal**

Also available **Half-Life 2** *and* **Episode One**

◁ ## FIRST CONSOLE GAME TO SUPPORT STEAM

The arrival of *Portal 2* (2011) for PS3 and Xbox 360 marked the first time Valve's Steam platform for PCs and Macs was made available to console players. The digital distribution and multiplayer service allowed *Portal 2* owners across PS3, PC and Mac systems to pair up and tackle co-op courses together, making *Portal 2* the **first cross-platform multiplayer puzzle game**.

BOOST

KEEP ON RUNNING

Sullivan "SullyJHF" Ford braved turrets, lasers and a psychotic AI to finish *Portal* in 13 min 59 sec on 14 June 2013 – the **fastest single-segment speed-run on *Portal***. Alex "Znernicus" Thieke (USA) zipped through *Portal 2* on PC in 1 hr 8 min 17 sec. He recorded the run in a single session on 28 April 2013, making this the **fastest single-segment speed-run on *Portal 2***.

TIP-OFF

Seven secret rooms in *Portal 2* feature artwork by a deranged Aperture Science scientist by the name of Doug Rattmann, aka the Rat Man. They can be found in Chapter 1–Test Chamber 4, 2-3, 2-6, 3-11, 3-12, 3-16 and 3-17.

MOST VIEWED FAN FILM BASED ON A SCI-FI PUZZLE GAME

Portal: No Escape (*below*) is a live-action movie made by Dan Trachtenberg (USA). As of 27 August 2013, it had been viewed 13,054,332 times on YouTube.

The overall **most viewed fan film based on a puzzle game** is "Annoying Orange vs Angry Birds" with 41,619,193 views as of 27 August 2013.

MOST CRITICALLY ACCLAIMED SEVENTH-GENERATION PUZZLE GAME

As of 27 June 2013, *Portal 2* was the highest-rated puzzle game on a seventh-generation platform, earning a 95% aggregate score for PS3 and Xbox 360 on Metacritic in the three years since its release. In its first week on sale, it shifted 926,254 copies, making it also the **fastest-selling puzzle game on a seventh-generation console**.

RAREST ACHIEVEMENT IN *PORTAL 2*

The "Talent Show" PC achievement edged out "Still Alive" in 2013 to become the hardest of its kind on *Portal 2*. The achievement tasks co-op players with completing the sixth chamber of the Mobility Gels co-op course without dropping a single cube. As of June 2013, only 1.5% of *Portal 2* PC gamers had managed to pull it off; 0.2% fewer than "Still Alive".

MOST POPULAR FAN-MADE *PORTAL 2* EXPANSION

Swede Sebastian "CaretCaret" Evefjord's "12 Angry Tests" map pack is the most popular fan-made expansion on Valve's Steam Workshop. As of 18 June 2013, the PC extra had attracted 299,483 unique subscribers. The seven-part download returns players to Aperture Science for more portal-hopping, gel-walking and physics-bending.

TOP TEN	FASTEST SINGLE-SEGMENT SPEED-RUNS ON *PORTAL 2* BY A TEAM
Snernicus	33 min 24 sec
Znernolitic	33 min 33 sec
ZnernoCool	34 min 12 sec
Xebra	34 min 41 sec
Phanger	34 min 48 sec
Phanku	34 min 57 sec
Socnak	35 min 18 sec
Sullsk45	36 min 26 sec
Xelly	37 min 55 sec
Team Britland	37 min 59 sec

Source: cronikeys.com, as of 7 August 2013

FASTEST SEGMENTED SPEED-RUN ON *PORTAL* BY A TEAM

PC speed-running team SourceRuns mastered glitches, skips and tricks to zip through *Portal* in a record time of 8 min 31.93 sec on 16 July 2012. The chambers in the 24-segment run were shared by Nick "Z1mb0bw4y" Roth (USA), Josh "Inexistence" Peaker (UK), Nick "Gocnak" Kerns (USA) and Sebastian "Xebaz" Dressle (Sweden).

PROFESSOR LAYTON

LOWDOWN

PUBLISHER:
Nintendo
DEVELOPER:
Level-5
DEBUT:
2007

For those who want variety with their brain-teasing, the professor's adventures provide an attractive backdrop. The series became the **first puzzle game for the 3DS** on 26 February 2011, with *Professor Layton and the Miracle Mask* (below left), a launch title in Japan.

078

NAME THE GAME
Keith Icahn stops at nothing to destroy zombies in which shooter?

BEST-SELLING 3DS PUZZLE GAME ▷

Professor Layton and the Miracle Mask had sold 1.11 million copies by 27 July 2013. *Mario* still leads the overall field, as *Super Mario 3D Land* (Nintendo 3AD, 2011) is the **best-selling 3DS game**, with more than 8.57 million units sold as of 27 July 2013.

BEST-SELLING PUZZLE GAME ON NINTENDO DS

Professor Layton and the Curious Village (2007) was the elegant gent's first outing and – combining good looks with puzzles – had sold more than 5.08 million copies as of 27 July 2013. As with the 3DS, a *Mario* title takes the overall record – the **best-selling videogame for Nintendo DS** is *New Super Mario Bros.* (Nintendo, 2006), which had sold 29.23 million copies, according to VGChartz, by 27 July 2013.

TIP-OFF

Professor Layton is always one step ahead. Each of his games contains a bonus hidden door that can only be unlocked with an alphanumeric code from the next game in the series – and the password is unique to each DS.

Solved 2 | Entrance

Head for Reinhold Manor!

You found a hint coin!

BOOST

NO LAYABOUT LAYTON

French sleuth Samuel "isu13" Goldstein achieved the **fastest 100% completion of *Professor Layton and Pandora's Box*** (*Professor Layton and the Diabolical Box* in the USA) in 2 hr 33 min on 1 January 2012, after 15 practice attempts. Gamer "mrfredy8" (Colombia) set the **fastest 100% completion of *Professor Layton and the Last Specter*** (*Professor Layton and the Spectre's Call* in Europe) in 4 hr 23 min on 2 December 2011.

FIRST PUZZLE GAME SERIES CROSSOVER

Professor Layton vs. Phoenix Wright: Ace Attorney (Capcom/Level-5, 2012) wittily combines the world of the puzzling prof with the courtroom activities of fictional defence lawyer Phoenix Wright. The game also spawned an officially released soundtrack featuring original music by *Professor Layton* composer Tomohito Nishiura, *Ace Attorney* composer Masakazu Sugimori and Capcom's Yasumasa Kitagawa.

MOST PROLIFIC PUZZLE GAME "MASCOT"

As if six games under his own name weren't enough, the Professor has also appeared in *Ace Attorney* and even has a movie to point to (and indeed in, pointing being a trademark of the character). His son, Alf Layton, has ensured that the family name remains linked with sleuthing and puzzling in the 2012 iOS spin-off *Layton Brothers: Mystery Room* (Matrix Software).

TOP TEN

MOST CRITICALLY ACCLAIMED DS AND 3DS PUZZLE GAMES

Game	Score
Pushmo (Intelligent Systems, 2011) on 3DS	**91.50%**
Meteos (Q Entertainment, 2005) on DS	**87.84%**
Crashmo (Intelligent Systems, 2012) on DS	**87.46%**
Professor Layton and the Unwound Future (Level-5, 2010) on DS	**87.27%**
Tetris DS (Nintendo, 2006) on DS	**87.22%**
Planet Puzzle League (Intelligent Systems, 2007) on DS	**86.81%**
Professor Layton and the Diabolical Box aka *Professor Layton and Pandora's Box* (Level-5, 2009) on DS	**85.41%**
Picross 3D (HAL Labs, 2010) on DS	**84.00%**
Professor Layton and the Last Specter aka *Professor Layton and the Spectre's Call* (Level-5, 2011)	**83.73%**
Professor Layton and the Miracle Mask (Level-5, 2012) on 3DS	**83.09%**

Source: gamerankings.com, as of 8 July 2013

FIRST MOVIE BASED ON A PUZZLE GAME

Pokémon producer Masakazu Kubo worked with series developers at Level-5 on an animated version of the professor that debuted in Japan. *Professor Layton and the Eternal Diva* (Japan) was released in December 2009, treating fans to an original story involving a sailing opera house and the promise of eternal life for those who can solve – of course – puzzles.

MOST PUZZLES IN A GAME SERIES

Professor Layton and the Curious Village was inspired by the *Head Gymnastics* puzzle books by Akira Tago (Japan). *Layton* designer Akihiro Hino had read them as a child and called in Tago to oversee design of the series' 941 in-game riddles from 2007 to 2012. Each title is accompanied by downloadable puzzles. By 2011, 505 bonus daily puzzles had been made available – the **most downloadable content for a puzzle series**.

BEST OF THE REST

LOWDOWN

Puzzle games stretch the mind, entertain and frustrate. Developer King holds the record for the **most popular Facebook puzzle game**, with its *Candy Crush Saga* crushing all opposition with 133.6 million monthly active users as of September 2013. *Tetris* for the Game Boy (Nintendo, 1989) is not only the **best-selling puzzle game**, but also the sixth best-selling game ever, with sales of some 30 million.

080

NAME THE GAME

Big Boss is Solid Snake's main enemy in which action-adventure game?

FIRST APP GAME TO WIN A BAFTA

When *Cut the Rope* (ZeptoLab, 2010) won a BAFTA award on 22 May 2011, it was the first iOS game to do so. According to ZeptoLab, *Cut the Rope* had more than 60 million MAU as of 23 April 2013. The gamer with the **most *Cut the Rope* No.1 spots** on the iPhone leaderboards is "Purple Dream", who in June 2012 held four out of a possible 11 No.1 spots.

BEST-SELLING PUZZLE GAME FRANCHISE

Eternally popular *Tetris* (Alexey Pajitnov, 1985) had shifted more than 170 million units as of June 2010. *Tetris* holds a multitude of records, including the **best-selling Game Boy videogame**, with sales of 32 million, and the **longest-running puzzle game series**, with 28 years of dominance in the genre. The *Tetris* name and gameplay have been utilized by more than 100 games across 65 platforms, making it the **most ported videogame ever**.

FIRST VIDEOGAME IN SPACE

Cosmonaut Aleksandr A Serebrov (Russia, *left*) was the **first person to play a videogame in space** when he packed his Game Boy and copy of *Tetris* (Nintendo, 1989, *right*) for his trip to the *MIR* Space Station. Thus, *Tetris* became the first videogame in space when it travelled on 1 July 1993 in the *Soyuz TM-17* rocket and returned 196 days 17 hr later. Serebrov's copy of *Tetris* sold for $1,220 (£740) at auction on 5 May 2011 – a pittance compared to the version of *Tetris* that is the **most expensive puzzle game**. In April 2008 James Baker (USA) paid $15,000 (£7,500) for a copy – included as part of the ultra-rare 1990 Nintendo World Championships Gold Edition cartridge.

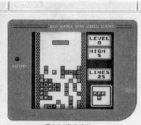

WORST-RATED PUZZLE GAME

Bomberman: Act Zero (Hudson, 2006, *right*) on Xbox 360 had a rating of just 33.97% on GameRankings as of 24 July 2013. On the same date, *Peggle* (PopCap, 2009) was rated 89.33%, making it the **most critically acclaimed Xbox 360 puzzle game**. The **highest-scoring shot in** *Peggle* (PopCap, 2007) is 18,061,920 points achieved by Steve Day (UK) in Portsmouth, UK, in April 2008.

TOP TEN — MOST CRITICALLY ACCLAIMED PUZZLE GAMES

Game	%
World of Goo (2D Boy, 2008) on Wii	94.04%
World of Goo (2D Boy, 2008) on PC	92.27%
Pushmo (Intelligent Systems, 2011) on 3DS	91.50%
Lumines (Q Entertainment, 2005) on PSP	89.80%
Peggle Deluxe (PopCap, 2009) on Xbox 360	89.33%
WarioWare, Inc.: Mega Microgame$! (Nintendo, 2003) on Game Boy Advance	88.99%
Puzzle Quest: Challenge of the Warlords (Infinite Interactive, 2007) on Xbox 360	88.14%
Meteos (Q Entertainment, 2005) on DS	87.84%
WarioWare: Twisted! (Nintendo, 2005) on Game Boy Advance	87.47%
Crashmo (Intelligent Systems, 2012) on 3DS	87.46%

Source: gamerankings.com, as of 24 July 2013

HIGHEST SCORE ON...

- **Bejeweled 2:** 2,147,483,647 points, Mike Leyde, 23 March 2009
- **Bejeweled Blitz:** 938,450 points, Lee Chen Wei, 6 August 2011
- **Dr. Mario:** 2,922,600 points, Will Nichols, 18 February 2011
- **Klax:** 89,090 points, Nathan Page, 11 June 2004
- **Tetris (by a pair):** 23,552 points, Becca Caddy & Gerald Lynch, 18 January 2012
- **Tetris DS:** 67,172 points, Ginger Stowe, 16 September 2006
- **Yoshi's Cookie:** 76,430 points, David Archey, 25 May 2012

TALLEST TOWER BUILT IN *WORLD OF GOO*

As of 24 July 2013, "Peter" had built the tallest tower – with a height of 56.88 m (186 ft).

The **fastest** *World of Goo* **completion** (2D Boy, 2008) took 53 min 41 sec on 7 September 2009 by Nigel Martin (UK).

081

MOST COMIC BOOK CHARACTERS IN A GAME

With more than 2,000 superheroes and villains from the DC universe, *Scribblenauts Unmasked: A DC Comics Adventure* (5th Cell, 2013) has the largest collection of comic book characters in a single videogame. *Super Scribblenauts* has the **most internet memes in a puzzle game**. Of the 30,000-plus entries in the game's vocabulary, 48 are internet memes, such as "ROLFcopter" and "Ninja Shark". *Scribblenauts* also holds records for the **most unique objects in a puzzle game** and **in a videogame**, with more than 10,000 usable items from hot-air balloons to dinosaurs.

THE GREAT GAMING CRASH OF '83

Videogames are such a major part of popular culture today that it's hard to fathom how, in the early 1980s, they almost disappeared. Forever. **Professor James Newman** takes a look back at the crisis that nearly cracked gaming and wonders if it could happen again.

082

IN THE BEGINNING

It was all going so well. In 1983, the games industry was worth $3.2 billion (£2 billion) and enthusiasm for videogames was sky-high. A quarter of US households had at least one console, with market leader Atari having sold some 20 million 2600 systems worldwide. The 2600's popularity was partly due to its conversion of *Space Invaders* (Atari, 1980). The promise of being able to play this popular game at home created a "killer app" – a game so desirable that people would buy a console just to be able to play it. Yet by 1985, the industry was in tatters. Revenues plummeted to $800 million (£480 million) and several companies went bankrupt. Gaming was fast becoming yesterday's fad. What went wrong? Competition from new home computers such as the Commodore 64 played a part, but the industry was ultimately responsible for its own downfall.

TOO MANY GAMES

The 2600 may have been the market leader, but it was far from the only console in the early 1980s. Atari also had its 5200, while the ColecoVision (*bottom*), Intellivision II, Fairchild Channel F System II, Bally Astrocade (*left*), Magnavox Odyssey² and Vectrex (*below*) all vied for gamers' attention. It sounded ideal – plenty of consoles and hundreds of games to play. But by 1983, players were realizing that the games being released for this confusing array of competing systems weren't all of the same high standard. Taking advantage of the lack of restrictions on who could create and publish console games – and seeing opportunities to make easy money – all manner of companies set up gaming divisions in the early 1980s. Before long, the market was awash with below-par games that were hastily developed by often inexperienced teams.

In some cases, as with Purina's *Chase the Chuck Wagon* (1982, *top left*) – the **first videogame about dog food** – games were used purely as marketing tools for companies looking to capitalize on the gaming boom. The glut of what consumers saw as low-quality titles damaged players' interest in gaming so much that retailers began heavily discounting consoles and cartridges. The industry was suddenly in freefall.

SIX FEET UNDER

Having spent more than $20,000 (£12,000) securing the rights to make the videogame of the wildly popular Spielberg movie, Atari rushed the development of *E.T.* (1982, *see p.172*). The resulting game has little in common with the film's plot, with spartan graphics, and sound and gameplay that critics described as "repetitive" and "monotonous". According to Atari's CEO, of the 4 million cartridges produced, 3.5 million were returned to Atari, leaving the company with a huge loss. Consumer confidence crumbled and retailers promptly returned unsellable games and systems. Videogame companies were left with warehouses full of cartridges and consoles that were costing more to store than they would sell for. This led to one of gaming's most infamous incidents: it was reported that Atari loaded thousands of unwanted *E.T.* cartridges and consoles on to a convoy of trucks, took them to the Alamogordo landfill site in New Mexico, USA, then crushed and encased them in concrete. In May 2013, a Canadian documentary team announced plans to dig up the landfill and find the games for a new film.

COULD IT HAPPEN AGAIN?

We can be confident that gaming is here to stay, partly because of lessons learned from the "Great Crash".

There are now more restrictions on who can develop games for consoles. Nintendo, whose NES was key to the recovery of the industry, created its "Official Nintendo Licensed Product Seal" to avoid a repeat of what company president Hiroshi Yamauchi described as a market "swamped with rubbish games".

PLATFORMERS

BEST-SELLING VIDEOGAME SERIES

Starring in 175 games across all platforms and versions over 33 years, Mario had accumulated sales of 511 million units as of August 2013. The diminutive plumber's core platformers, fighting games, kart escapades, dance spin-offs and everything in between make his the most successful series of any gaming genre ever.

The evolution of the *Super Mario* series (Nintendo, 1985–present) is shown right.

1985

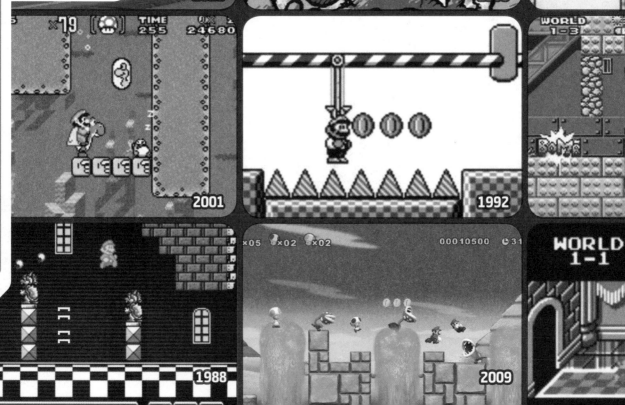

2004

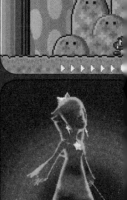

2004

Pick a box.
Its contents
will help you
on your way.

1993

2011

10

1995

x79

TIME
255

UP×
24680

2001

1992

WORLD
1-3

1988

×05 ×02 ×02

00010500

31

2009

WORLD
1-1

2003

1996

2002

MARIO 00 34 TIME 00 5
X15 ★× 158 226980

2010

1990

MARIO×02 WORLD T
4300 ×19 1-1

1989

X05 370

1994

2006

000799000

2012

SCORE
46870

2001

CONTENTS

1988

1999

MARIO WORLD TIME
003000 ×01 5-1 378

2010

2007

TIME: 00:19:66

SONIC

LOWDOWN

PUBLISHER:
Sega
DEVELOPER:
Sonic Team
DEBUT:
1991

You may never have snatched a single gold ring at top speed or seen off the evil Dr Robotnik, but everyone can identify that acrobatic hedgehog. He no longer has quite the profile he did in the 1990s, but in 2013 he could still inspire an arcade running game (complete with treadmills for multiplayers) in *Sonic Athletics*.

NAME THE GAME
Former prince Kaos fled the monarchy with his butler Glumshanks in this RPG.

]]]]

MOST EXPENSIVE *SONIC* GAME ▷

Sonic the Hedgehog (1991) was the last US game for the Sega Master System because the new Sega Genesis was taking over. Instead of creating a localized NTSC version, Sega shipped over stock of the European PAL version. The only difference was a small barcode sticker added for the tills. Few remained intact and it's those copies of the US edition that are collectable. You could pay under £10 ($6) for the regular version, but in December 2011 a rare stickered copy listed on eBay sent collectors into a bidding frenzy with the winner paying $981.33 (£636).

BEST-SELLING VIDEOGAME ON A SEGA PLATFORM

Sonic the Hedgehog was Sega's answer to Nintendo's Mario (*see pp.88–89*), who had ruled gaming in the 1980s. The following decade would be marked as an epic contest between the Blue and Red corners. *Sonic* and sequels sold 13.67 million units across Sega platforms in the early 1990s. Sega itself became a household name in the West and began to rival Nintendo.

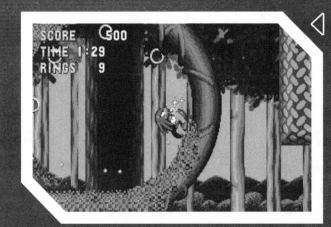

HIGHEST SCORE ON *SONIC & KNUCKLES* ◁

On 22 April 2013, Matthew Felix from Merced in California, USA, racked up 2,120,820 points in just over an hour without losing a life on *Sonic & Knuckles* (1994). On 15 May 2011, Michael Sroka (USA) set the **highest score on *Sonic the Hedgehog***, with 812,140 points. The **fastest completion of *Sonic the Hedgehog*** on the Genesis was set by Charles Griffin on 1 August 2008, with 15 min 5 sec. Mike "mike89" McKenzie recorded the **fastest completion of *Sonic the Hedgehog 2*** (1992) on the Genesis, with 16 min 13 sec on 28 March 2012.

Game	Sales
Sonic the Hedgehog (1991)	6.41
Sonic the Hedgehog 2 (1992)	6.03
Sonic Heroes (2003)	5.46
Sonic's Ultimate Genesis Collection (2009)	3.43
Sonic Rush (2005)	3.06
Sonic Mega Collection Plus (2004)	2.81
Sonic and the Secret Rings (2007)	2.60
Sonic Adventure 2: Battle (2001)	2.56
Sonic Adventure (1998)	2.42
Sonic Advance (2001)	2.24

Source: vgchartz.com, as of 3 September 2013 (figures in millions)

FIRST OFFICIAL FAN CONVENTION FOR A GAME CHARACTER

The first Summer of Sonic convention took place in 2008 in the UK. By 2012, the first 400 tickets for the annual festival moved faster than the blue blur himself, selling out in just three minutes. Over the years guests have included Sonic creator Yuji Naka himself, and among the regular events is the quiz Never Mind the BuzzBombers.

SUMMER OF SONIC 2012

]]]]

SONIC BO:OM!

Imagine Sonic going by the name of Mr Needlemouse and his favourite hobby being break-dancing. It may sound bananas, but it almost happened: one of Sonic's development names was Mr Needlemouse and the debut Sonic game was originally going to have a sound set-up screen with Sonic busting some b-boy moves.

9.766

BEST-SELLING VIDEOGAME FEATURING SONIC

In 2007, Sega and Nintendo, once arch-rivals, joined forces – and made videogaming history. Mario & Sonic at the Olympic Games (Sega) featured eight characters from each franchise competing in Olympic challenges. It had sold 12.91 million copies as of 3 September 2013 on the Wii and DS combined and spawned sequels in which the two icons visited the Winter Olympics (2009) and the London 2012 Olympics. The **highest-ranking player in Mario & Sonic at the Olympic Games** is gamer "becky--jay" (UK) with 1,615 points as of 3 September 2013, according to wii-records.com.

087

LONGEST-RUNNING COMIC BASED ON A GAME

Sonic the Hedgehog is published by Archie Comics (USA) and has been running since 1993. Its 252nd edition was printed in September 2013. Two years before the series started, a comic called Sonic the Hedgehog #1: Promotional Issue was distributed to publicize the first game. Few survived, but a good-quality example of the **rarest Sonic comic** could fetch $1,000 (£640).

SONIC THE HEDGEHOG 200th Issue

MARIO

LOWDOWN

PUBLISHER:
Nintendo
DEVELOPER:
Nintendo
DEBUT:
1983

The **longest-running gaming character**, Mario was originally a carpenter named Jumpman when he made his debut in *Donkey Kong* (Nintendo, 1981), the **first platform game**. He got his big solo break in the arcade game *Mario Bros.* (1983), and has evaded bad guy Bowser ever since.

NAME THE GAME
Wife of Mortimer Goth, the dark-haired Bella's favourite colour is red.

MOST CRITICALLY ACCLAIMED GAME

Super Mario Galaxy (2007) is the most acclaimed game of all time, with a GameRankings score of 97.64% as of 31 July 2013. Sequel *Super Mario Galaxy 2* (2010) is third, on 97.35%, with Nintendo's *The Legend of Zelda: Ocarina of Time* (1998) sandwiched between them on 97.54%. *Super Mario Galaxy's* score makes it the **most critically acclaimed Wii game** and the **most critically acclaimed Mario game**.

TIP-OFF

Before you step through the door in each boss battle of *New Super Mario Bros. U* (2012), hit the hidden "?" block to get a power-up. Stand next to the nearby wall and jump to reveal the block and get a helping hand.

BEST-SELLING PLATFORMER

Super Mario Bros. (1985) sold 40.24 million copies between 1985 and 1995. These phenomenal sales, coming at a relatively early stage in gaming history, helped seal the NES's success as a console and made *Super Mario Bros.* the first blockbuster home-console game. *Super Mario Bros. 2* (1988) had sold 7.46 million units as of August 2013.

FASTEST MARATHON DRESSED AS A VIDEOGAME CHARACTER

Nash Pradhan (*left*) and Dan McCormack (both UK) dressed as Mario and Luigi respectively at the 2012 Virgin London Marathon in the UK on 22 April 2012, completing the race simultaneously in 3 hr 29 min 41 sec. Their run raised funds for the charity Aga Khan Development Network.

FIRST *MARIO* EXPANSION PACK

Compared with rivals Sony and Microsoft, Nintendo has been slow to adopt online multiplayer modes, expansion packs and DLC. However, the release of *New Super Luigi U* (2013), an expansion pack to the Wii U title *New Super Mario Bros. U*, marks the first time an official expansion pack has been available for any *Mario* videogame. Mario himself is not a playable character; brother Luigi takes centre-stage, and there are 82 brand new courses to play.

FASTEST COMPLETION OF *SUPER MARIO GALAXY 2*

On 16 June 2010, gamer "tp3200" (USA) raced through *Super Mario Galaxy 2* to defeat Bowser in a record time of just 5 hr 12 min 46 sec.

On 15 December 2011, Andrew Gardikis (USA) thwarted Bowser in the very first *Super Mario* title in a mere 4 min 58 sec – the **fastest completion of *Super Mario Bros.***

WORST-RATED MARIO GAME

With a GameRankings score of just 56.42% as of 31 July 2013, *Mario Party Advance* (Hudson, 2005) for the Game Boy Advance has the lowest score of any *Mario* title. It sold fewer than a million copies.

MOST PROLIFIC GAME CHARACTER

The character who has appeared in the most games is Mario himself. He'd popped up in 247 titles as of 1 August 2013, including all ports, remakes and re-releases. Mario was created by Nintendo's Shigeru Miyamoto (*see p.192*).

TOP TEN — BEST-SELLING *MARIO* GAMES

Game	Sales
Super Mario Bros. (1985) on NES	40.24
Mario Kart Wii (2008) on Wii	33.85
New Super Mario Bros. (2006) on DS	29.23
New Super Mario Bros. Wii (2009) on Wii	27.02
Mario Kart DS (2005) on DS	22.56
Super Mario World (1990) on SNES	20.61
Super Mario Land (1989) on Game Boy	18.14
Super Mario Bros. 3 (1988) on NES	17.28
Super Mario 64 (1996) on N64	11.89
Super Mario Land 2: 6 Golden Coins (1992) on Game Boy	11.18

Source: vgchartz.com, as of 31 July 2013 (figures in millions)

RATCHET & CLANK

LOWDOWN

PUBLISHER:
Sony
DEVELOPER:
Insomniac Games
DEBUT:
2002

A "Lombax" alien and his robot sidekick team-up to save the universe with an array of exotic weaponry and gadgets in this sci-fi-flavoured series. A combination of humour, action and puzzle-solving helped *Ratchet & Clank* become the **most prolific 3D platform series**, with 14 entries.

NAME THE GAME
London merchant and businessman Reginald Birch can be very persuasive.

HIGHEST SCORE ON *RATCHET & CLANK FUTURE: A CRACK IN TIME* "MY BLASTER RUNS HOT"

"My Blaster Runs Hot" is a mini-game that places players in a top-down shooter in which they blast their way through waves of enemies to defeat a final boss. Hérou "daftpunk" François (France) kept his finger on the trigger to score 15,080 points in the challenge on 15 December 2012.

FIRST ONLINE FOUR-PLAYER MODE IN A 3D PLATFORMER

Ratchet & Clank: All 4 One (2011) allows casual online co-operative play as well as local multiplayer play, with Ratchet and Clank joined by Captain Qwark and Doctor Nefarious as playable characters. A forerunner of the idea was seen on the N64 in 1999, when *Donkey Kong 64* (Rare) allowed multiplay on the **first splitscreen four-player mode in a 3D platformer**.

BO:OM!

Final Fantasy III (Square, 1990) allowed you to turn enemies into toads while *Hexen* (Raven, 1994) allowed you to transform your foes into chickens and pigs. *Ratchet & Clank* continues this fine tradition of animal japes by being the first game series to allow you to turn enemies into a chimpanzee, a boar and even into a baby *T. rex*.

FASTEST COMPLETION OF *RATCHET & CLANK FUTURE: TOOLS OF DESTRUCTION*

Isaac "FlamingMage" McBride (Sweden) completed the 2007 *Tools of Destruction* in 1 hr 58 min 35 sec. McBride took full advantage of the game's time-saving glitches to achieve the record. He said: "The vast majority of the weapons are useless. Besides the Pyro Blaster, which this run uses, the RYNO is the only real option for boss killing."

Daniel "CannibalK9" Burns recorded the **fastest single-segment completion** of *Ratchet & Clank: Up Your Arsenal* (2004) in 2 hr 22 min 38 sec on 9 December 2005.

TOP TEN — MOST CRITICALLY ACCLAIMED *RATCHET & CLANK* GAMES	
Ratchet & Clank: Up Your Arsenal (2004) on PS2	91.54%
Ratchet & Clank: Going Commando (2003) on PS2	90.64%
Ratchet & Clank (2002) on PS2	89.74%
Ratchet & Clank Future: Tools of Destruction (2007) on PS3	88.74%
Ratchet & Clank Future: A Crack in Time (2009) on PS3	87.88%
Ratchet & Clank: Size Matters (High Impact Games, 2007) on PSP	85.33%
Ratchet: Deadlocked (2005) on PS2	82.64%
Ratchet & Clank Future: Quest for Booty (2008) on PS3	77.80%
Secret Agent Clank (High Impact Games, 2011) on PS3	73.48%
Ratchet & Clank: All 4 One (2011) on PS3	70.63%

Source: gamerankings.com, as of 4 September 2013

MOST GUNS IN A PLATFORM SERIES

Excluding Ratchet's wrench, the *Ratchet & Clank* series boasts an impressive 122 standard weapons. If upgrades and variants are included, however, the total is 420.

The **most guns in a game** overall feature in *Borderlands 2* (Gearbox, 2012). The first game in the series had 17,750,000 weapons and a procedural algorithm means that countless more were generated for the second.

FIRST EPISODIC 3D PLATFORM SERIES

Between the *Ratchet & Clank* games *Future: Tools of Destruction* and *Future: A Crack in Time*, Insomniac Games released an episode that took about four hours to complete. Players downloaded spin-off story *Ratchet & Clank Future: Quest for Booty* (2008). *Future: A Crack in Time* then reverted to a standard length and hard-copy retail, leaving *Sam & Max* (Telltale Games) as the **most regular episodic game series**. That other lovable, case-solving duo released three series between 2006 and 2010, the third of which was *Sam & Max: The Devil's Playhouse*.

BEST OF THE REST

LOWDOWN

While the heyday of platformer games was probably in the 1980s and early 1990s, when consoles were becoming a big deal, they have never been more innovative or imaginative than they are now. Action-platformer *Knack* (SCE Japan Studio) is set to be a launch title for the PS4 in November 2013, while many seventh-generation games such as *Rayman Origins* (Ubisoft, 2011) met with great acclaim; IGN described it as "the best-looking platformer this generation".

NAME THE GAME
Teenager Neku Sakuraba teams up with Shiki Misaki in the fight for his life.

MOST PLAYER-CREATED LEVELS IN A GAME

PlayStation platformer *LittleBigPlanet* (Media Molecule, 2008) truly gave power to the people with its user-generated levels. On 6 August 2012, Media Molecule announced that its online servers were jam-packed with 7 million player-created levels. That's more than 5,000 levels generated by gamers every day since the title's launch.

The **most player-created game levels played in 24 hours** is 272 and was achieved by David Dino, Lauren Guiliano and Sean Crowley, who played *LittleBigPlanet 2* (2011) in New York, USA, from 17–19 January 2011.

TOP TEN — MOST CRITICALLY ACCLAIMED PLATFORMERS

Game	Score
Super Mario Galaxy (Nintendo, 2007) on Wii	97.64%
Super Mario Galaxy 2 (Nintendo, 2010) on Wii	97.35%
Super Mario 64 (Nintendo, 1996) on N64	96.41%
LittleBigPlanet (Media Molecule, 2008) on PS3	94.75%
Rayman 2: The Great Escape (Ubisoft Montpellier, 1999) on Dreamcast	92.71%
Journey (Thatgamecompany, 2012) on PS3	92.56%
Super Mario World: Super Mario Advance 2 (Nintendo, 2001) on Game Boy Advance	92.42%
Braid (Number None, Inc., 2008) on Xbox 360	92.25%
LittleBigPlanet 2 (Media Molecule, 2011) on PS3	92.15%
Jet Grind Radio (Smilebit, 2000) on Dreamcast	92.04%

Source: gamerankings.com, as of 26 August 2013

WORST-RATED PLATFORMER

Spyro: Enter the Dragonfly (Equinoxe, 2002) on the GameCube sat at the bottom of GameRankings' platformers chart with a score of just 47.16% as of 25 August 2013. The fourth game in the *Spyro* series (various, 1998–present) was lambasted by, among others, GameSpot UK, whose critic called it "an almost unplayable train wreck of a game that has no direction, no technical merit".

BOOST

DUALITY CHECK

Twin analogue stick controllers such as the PlayStation DualShock have been standard fare for years, and feature on both the PS4 and Xbox One. But the very **first console game to require a dual analogue controller** was a platformer called *Ape Escape* (SCE Japan Studio), released for the PlayStation on 31 May 1999, starring an albino ape.

HIGHEST SCORE ON *KIRBY'S ADVENTURE*

On 7 October 2010, David Archey (USA) achieved the most points on *Kirby's Adventure* (HAL Laboratory, 1993) with a high score of 1,721,370. This NES title was the little pink ball's first home-console appearance after debuting in *Kirby's Dream Land* on the Game Boy in 1992. Like most stars of platformers, Kirby has a neat signature trick: he can inhale enemies and objects.

HIGHEST SCORE ON *DONKEY KONG*

On 9 November 2012, Hank Chien (USA) beat his own world record from May of that year by scoring a total of 1,138,600 points on *Donkey Kong* (Nintendo, 1981). A 2007 documentary called *The King of Kong: A Fistful of Quarters* followed US gamer Steve Wiebe's attempts to beat the high-score record for *Donkey Kong*. He finally achieved it with 1,064,500 points in August 2010, but Hank broke Steve's record in February 2011, before beating his own high score twice.

FASTEST *SUPER METROID* SPEED-RUN

On 10 May 2010, Brandon Moore (USA, *above*) accomplished a *Super Metroid* (Nintendo, 1994) speed-run on a SNES in just 41 minutes. Brandon's effort beat previous record holder Brian Hodge's attempt by a full minute.

Super Metroid, the third game in the *Metroid* series (Nintendo, 1986–2010), puts action-adventure and sci-fi gameplay on to platforms. In *Super Metroid*, series star Samus Aran gets the chance to moonwalk like Michael Jackson.

FASTEST COMPLETION OF *RAYMAN ORIGINS*

On 15 February 2013, seasoned speed-runner Spike Vegeta (USA) uploaded his *Rayman Origins* play-through on to Twitch. He beat the game in 2 hr 10 min, smashing the previous record by almost two minutes. *Rayman Origins'* highly stylized artwork sets it apart from other platformers, and helped scoop it the Best Platformer of 2011 award from GameSpot. Ubisoft released a sequel, *Rayman Legends*, in 2013.

AT THE ARCADES

Rachael Finn looks back on the birth of the coin-op, the golden era of the classic arcade and the influence it exerted on gaming, which is still being felt today.

Arcades encouraged developers to push technology and design while fostering gaming as a social experience. The **first coin-operated arcade machine** was *Galaxy Game* (Bill Pitts and Hugh Tuck, 1971, *far right*). A two-player console unit at Stanford University in California, USA, it was inspired by the mainframe game *Spacewar!* (Steve Russell, 1962). Priced at 10 cents a go, the objective was to destroy rival spaceships, and students queued for an hour or more to play.

Computer Space (Nutting Associates, 1971, *near right*) launched two months later and was 20 times cheaper, costing $1,000 (£400) per unit, the **first commercially available coin-op**. It earned about $3 million (£1.17 million) in sales.

Creators Nolan Bushnell and Ted Dabney founded Atari and produced *Pong* (Atari, 1972, *far right*), the **first commercially successful arcade game**, selling more than 35,000 units.

THE GOLDEN AGE 1978–86

Space Invaders (Taito, 1978) was the first blockbuster, earning over $600 million (then £300 million) from 100,000 units in its first year. Developed by Tomohiro Nishikado, it created the template for shoot-'em-ups. This was the **first game to use the concept of multiple lives**, the first game in which players had to repel hordes of enemies, the **first to have targets that could fire back** and the **first to use a continuous background soundtrack**.

A golden era started with a spate of sci-fi games, including *Asteroids* (Atari, 1979), both the **first arcade game to use real-world physics** and the **first game to allow initials for a top 10 score**, and *Defender* (Williams Electronics, 1980), the **first side-scrolling shooter**.

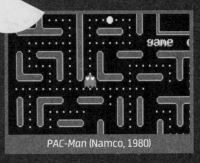

PAC-Man (Namco, 1980)

The **first gaming mascot character**, *PAC-Man* (Namco, 1980) became a 1980s icon, helped establish the maze chase genre and was the **first game with power-ups**. Released in Japan as *Puck-Man*, it was changed in the West amid concerns that the "P" on the case might be vandalized to form a common expletive! By the early 1980s, arcade gaming had become a billion-dollar industry.

SONIC BOOM
MID-1990S

Edged out by home-console gaming (*see pp.14–17*), arcades enjoyed a resurgence as a result of the success of combat fighting games such as *Street Fighter II: The World Warrior* (Capcom, 1991), *Mortal Kombat* (Midway, 1992) and *Virtua Fighter* (Sega, 1993). These classics defined the beat-'em-up genre while attracting a new wave of gamers.

While *Galactic Warriors* (Konami, 1985) was the **first game with multiple playable characters**, *Street Fighter II* was one of the first machines to feature an eight-way joystick and six button controls, offering an array of special moves and "combos". Players chose from eight characters, each with signature moves and distinctive catchphrases. Ryu and Ken's "Hadouken", Guile's "Sonic Boom" and Chun-Li's "Spinning Bird Kick" helped it become the **best-selling coin-operated fighting game**. The franchise continues to this day.

DRIVING FORCE

Released in 1974, Atari's *Gran Trak 10* was the **first racing game**. It was primitive compared to *Turbo* (Sega, 1981), a full-colour game with third-person perspective and a "vanishing point" view.

Pole Position (Namco, 1982) introduced AI opponents on a 3D circuit and set new high standards for the genre.

OutRun (SEGA, 1986) emphasized the driving experience with *Miami Vice* stylings and was the **first game to feature force feedback**.

Although Atari's *Gran Trak 20* (1974) was the **first two-player racer**, multiplaying came into its own with *Final Lap* (Namco, 1987), the **first racing game to support multiple players**. Using linked cabinets, up to eight players could compete on Japan's Suzuka Circuit with the two-screen machines complete with steering wheel, pedals and gear shift.

Turbo (SEGA, 1981)

Street Fighter II: The World Warrior (Capcom, 1991)

Taiko no Tatsujin (Namco, 2001)

INSERT COIN(S)
TO CONTINUE

The advent of fifth-generation consoles (*see p.16*) and online gaming has seen arcades become a rarity, but retro kicks can still be had in places such as Funspot in New Hampshire, USA – the **largest videogame arcade** – which houses 500-plus classics over three floors. These games' legacy is also now seen in gaming-themed bars.

To survive, modern games feature equipment that cannot easily or cheaply be replicated in the home – such as the neon platforms of *Dance Dance Revolution* (Konami, 1998) and the large drums used in *Taiko*

no Tatsujin (*left*), a popular series in Japan. The thriving Japanese arcade culture has bucked the slide and multi-storey geh-sen (gaming centres) are packed with everything from rhythm and fighting games to crane games and horse race sims.

Old titles have been introduced to a new generation with an online purchasing system enabling users to download classics and take on challengers without leaving home. But this misses the point of the arcade – the visceral experience of being in an electronic temple lit by the fluorescent glow of a multitude of games, promising so much fun for a fistful of loose change.

FIGHTING

BEST-SELLING FIGHTING GAME SERIES

With total sales of more than 35.7 million units as of 12 July 2013 (excluding crossover titles), the *Tekken* games (Namco Bandai, 1994–present) have kicked, punched and thrown away all opposition. The series began with an arcade release in 1994 before a hugely successful PlayStation port in 1995. Pictured here is 2012 release *Tekken Tag Tournament 2*.

CONTENTS

STREET FIGHTER

LOWDOWN

PUBLISHER:
Capcom
DEVELOPER:
Capcom
DEBUT:
1987

Each release has tangled up gamers' digits in arcades and at home with the button combinations required for groundbreaking moves. *Street Fighter* set the standard for all fighting games and has gone on to become the **most prolific fighting game series**, with 126 releases across all platforms.

NAME THE GAME
Imps are tiny enemies thrown by weakened Gargantuars.

LONGEST-RUNNING FIGHTING SERIES

Street Fighter began its run of success in 1987 in the arcades, and 27 years later *Ultra Street Fighter IV* is planned for 2014. The series has garnered plenty of praise over the years – *Street Fighter IV* (2009, *below*) had a GameRankings score of 93.23% as of 31 July 2013, the **most critically acclaimed Xbox 360 game**. Overall, the **most critically acclaimed *Street Fighter* game** is the PS3 version of *Street Fighter IV*, with a score of 93.64%.

FIRST FIGHTING GAME TO FEATURE STEREOSCOPIC 3D

Super Street Fighter IV: 3D Edition launched with the Nintendo 3DS in February 2011, creating a sense of depth with its fireball wars and super combos.

HIGHEST EARNINGS IN A FIGHTING GAME TOURNAMENT

Street Fighter player "Infiltration", aka Sun Woo-Lee (South Korea), won the international tournament to celebrate the 25th anniversary of the series in California, USA, on 8 December 2012. Winning both *Super Street Fighter IV Arcade Edition* (2011) and *Street Fighter X Tekken* (2012), he earned $50,000 (£30,000). He also won a Scion FR-S (*above*) for *Street Fighter X Tekken*. The car is priced at $26,000 (£16,000) on the Scion website, making Sun's earnings jump to a dizzying $76,000 (£47,000).

FIRST FIGHTING GAME TO USE COMBOS

A combo is a series of deadly moves triggered by a combination of buttons and controller movements. If well executed, it can be relied upon to drop all but the most skilful (or lucky) opponent and the fighting system has been adopted by many other games since first appearing in 1992's *Street Fighter II*.

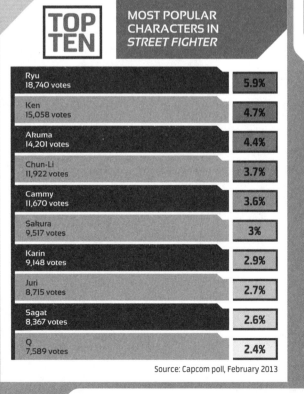

MOST SUCCESSFUL CHARACTER IN *SUPER STREET FIGHTER IV ARCADE EDITION*

In June 2013, the EventHubs site posted character-usage figures ranking characters by the number of top 16 finishes achieved at major fighting tournaments worldwide in the previous year.

The survey of 46 tournaments saw the chubby yet nimble Rufus (*above*) top the table, with 53 top-16 finishes. Ryu and Fei Long came in second and third with 41 and 40 finishes, respectively.

MOST DLC FIGHTING CHARACTERS

The PS Vita release of *Street Fighter X Tekken* featured 12 characters not seen on other platforms. Shortly after release, all 12 were made available as paid-for DLC for the game's home console editions. This expanded the potential cast from 38 characters on the Xbox 360 and 43 characters on the PlayStation 3, to 50 and 55 respectively.

BOOST

CONFLICTS OF INTEREST

X-Men vs. Street Fighter (1996, *below*) pitted teams of heroes from both sides against each other in the **first tag-team fighting game**. *Street Fighter* was also a pioneer in featuring the **first playable female character in a fighting game**, the ex-agent for Interpol Chun-Li. She made her debut in *Street Fighter II* (1991).

TOP TEN
MOST POPULAR CHARACTERS IN *STREET FIGHTER*

Character	Votes	%
Ryu	18,740 votes	5.9%
Ken	15,058 votes	4.7%
Akuma	14,201 votes	4.4%
Chun-Li	11,922 votes	3.7%
Cammy	11,670 votes	3.6%
Sakura	9,517 votes	3%
Karin	9,148 votes	2.9%
Juri	8,715 votes	2.7%
Sagat	8,367 votes	2.6%
Q	7,589 votes	2.4%

Source: Capcom poll, February 2013

TEKKEN

LOWDOWN

PUBLISHER:
Namco Bandai
DEVELOPER:
Namco Bandai
DEBUT:
1995

"Iron Fist", as *Tekken* translates into English, follows the King of Iron Fist Tournament. The innovative 3D fighter gave players control of each limb of their characters. Its 3D environment set the game apart from its genre by allowing players to sidestep.

NAME THE GAME
Master Chief Petty Officer John-117 has nearly 30 years of active duty.

BEST-SELLING FIGHTING GAME SERIES
Tekken titles had sold more than 35.77 million units as of 30 July 2013 (*see p.96*). The 2009 entry in the series, *Tekken 6*, is the **best-selling PS3 fighting game**, with more than 2.54 million copies sold. But *Tekken* has always been popular – its inaugural outing of 1995 was the **first PlayStation game to sell one million units**.

MOST BATTLE POINTS ON TEKKEN TAG TOURNAMENT 2
Using a tag-team combination of Marshall Law and Feng Wei, Xbox Live user "ChopLee" had amassed 299,991 battle points as of 22 June 2013.

The 2012 title has the **most moves in a fighting game**, giving players no shortage of ways to set a high score. Even excluding sample combos and the flashy 10-hit combos, the total is 5,978 moves over its huge roster of 59 characters.

TOP TEN — MOST MOVES BY CHARACTERS IN *TEKKEN*

King	176
Lei Wulong	172
Tiger Jackson	163
Eddy Gordo / Christie Monteiro	162
Hwoarang	161
Yoshimitsu	158
Miharu Hirano	140
Ling Xiaoyu	137
Nina Williams / Steve Fox	129
Anna Williams	127

Source: *Tekken Tag Tournament 2*, as of 2012

FASTEST-SELLING 3D FIGHTING GAME

Shifting 1.17 million units globally in its first week of release, *Tekken 3* (1998) outclasses all of its opponents in terms of speedy sales. The game is also the **best-selling 3D fighting game** overall, with 7.16 million units sold as of 30 July 2013.

LARGEST SCREEN IN A VIDEOGAME TOURNAMENT

Namco Bandai hosted a qualifying tournament for the Tekken European Championships in September 2012 shown on the **largest permanent IMAX cinema screen**, in Sydney's Darling Harbour, Australia. More than 400 fans watched battles on the monolithic screen measuring 35.72 x 29.57 m (117 x 97 ft).

BO:OM!

Tekken was made into a Japanese-only trading card videogame with the release of *Tekken Card Challenge* on the WonderSwan console in 1999. The combatants, taken from *Tekken 3* (1997), used a combat system similar to Konami's *Yu-Gi-Oh!* series of card battlers (1999–2005), itself based on the Japanese manga and anime series of the same name.

MOST SUCCESSFUL *TEKKEN* TEAM

Tekken Turkey had 2,518,078 team points as of 30 July 2013, according to the World Tekken Federation website. The team's 99 players won 92,810 games and lost 56,956 in *Tekken Tag Tournament 2* (2012). Another big hitter is PSN user "Kaz_0519", the **first player to score 30,000 battle points on *Street Fighter X Tekken*** (Dimps/Capcom, 2012), who had amassed 31,017 battle points from 2,824 matches on the PS3 version by June 2012.

LARGEST FAMILY IN A FIGHTING GAME

Street Fighter has the Yun and Yang twins while *Virtua Fighter* has the Bryant siblings, but the Mishima family in *Tekken 6: Bloodline Rebellion* (2008) is the most numerous. Pictured below, as seen in *Tekken 5* (2005), from left, the clan's great grandfather Jinpachi Mishima, grandfather Heihachi Mishima, father Kazuya Mishima and his son Jin Kazama. Jin's mother is Jun Kazama, and Heihachi has an illegitimate son in Lars Alexandersson and an adoptive son in Lee Chaolan. Jun and Jin share a blood relation in Asuka Kazama. That's eight family members in total – and a lot of birthday cards to remember.

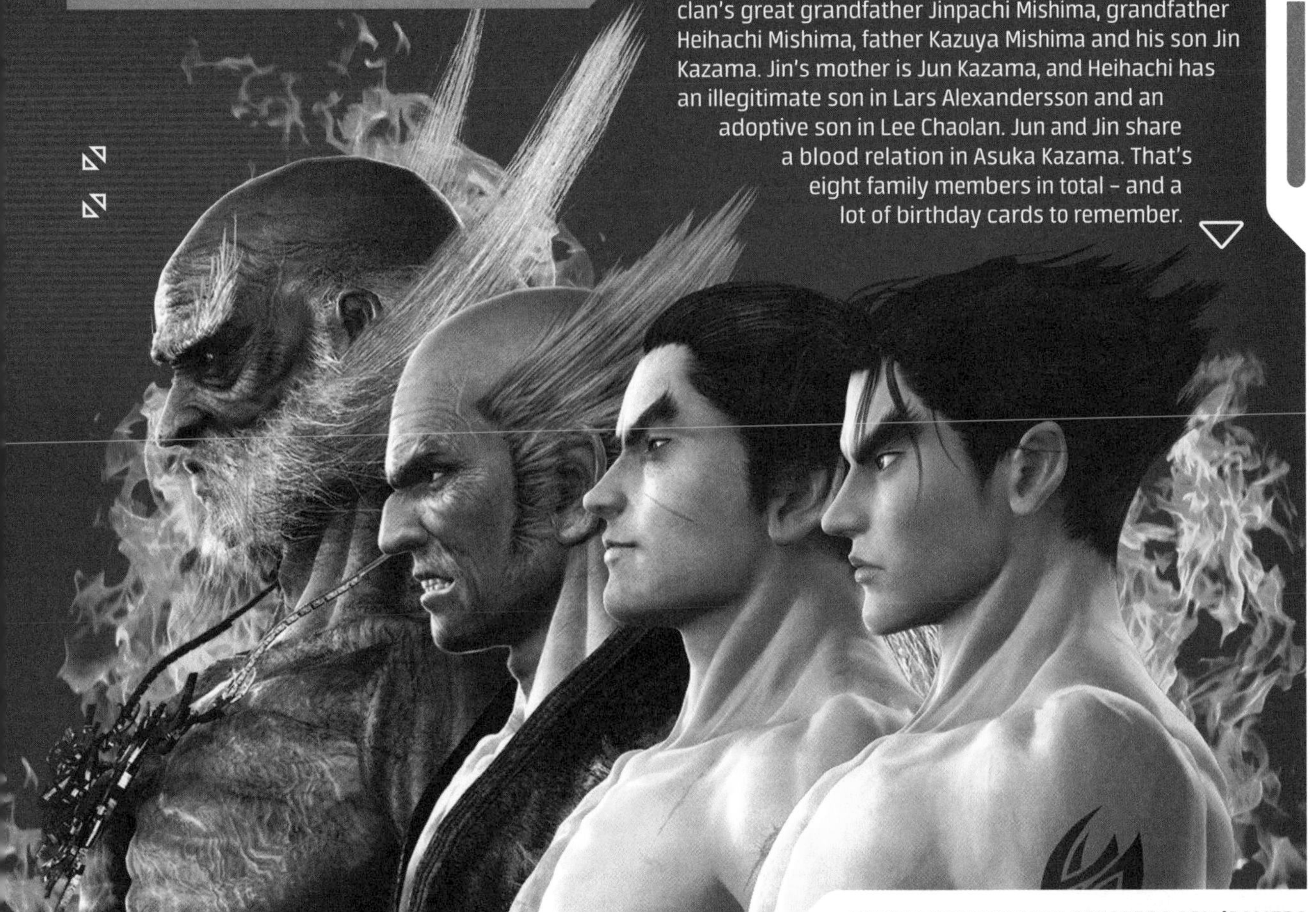

101

SOULCALIBUR

LOWDOWN

PUBLISHER:
Namco
DEVELOPER:
Namco
DEBUT:
1996

The sword called Soul Edge and the 16th-century quest for it is the historical back story for pioneering fighting action. *SoulCalibur* (1998) was the **first 3D fighting game with eight-way movement** – players could run freely in almost any direction. *Soul Edge* (aka *Soul Blade*, 1996) was one of the first fighting games to use weapons and the **first fighting game with multiple weapon choices** in its "Edge Master" story mode.

102

NAME THE GAME
Gamers guide Sackboy and are encouraged to be creative.

FIRST STORY MODE OUTSOURCED TO A THIRD PARTY

Story mode allows players to engage in fights staged as part of an unfolding narrative. When Project Soul commenced work on *SoulCalibur V* (2012), it outsourced the story mode to CyberConnect2, the maestro developers behind both *Asura's Wrath* (2011) and the *.hack* (2002–05) franchise of RPGs. CyberConnect2 handled all storyboarding and motion-capture duties for *SoulCalibur V*.

MOST SUCCESSFUL FEMALE SOULCALIBUR PLAYER

"Kayane", aka Marie-Laure Norindr (France), had 47 *SoulCalibur* top-three tournament placings between 2002 – when she was just 10 years old – and 2012. In 2010, she also became the **first woman to win a pro-*Street Fighter* event**, beating Sola "Burnyourbra" Adesui in the women's *Super Street Fighter IV* (2010) final at the Evolution Championship Series 2010.

The 8WayRun *SoulCalibur* website ranks players by recent tournament wins. Using this measurement, the **highest-ranked *SoulCalibur* player**, as of 14 July 2013, was "LostProvidence" (USA), who scored 4,000 on *SoulCalibur V* in 17 tournament appearances.

MOST CRITICALLY ACCLAIMED FIGHTING GAME

SoulCalibur (1999) on the Dreamcast had a GameRankings rating of 96.94% as of 14 August 2013. An undisputed classic, it is also the **most critically acclaimed Dreamcast game** of any kind.

MOST WEAPONS IN A FIGHTING GAME

SoulCalibur III (2005) featured 284 weapons when it sliced its way on to the PS2. The franchise, well known for its armoury, is also the **best-selling weapons-based fighting game series**, with sales of 12.14 million copies across all platforms as of 6 August 2013.

TOP TEN

BEST-SELLING WEAPON-BASED FIGHTING GAMES

Game	Sales
SoulCalibur II (Project Soul, 2003)	4.56
Mortal Kombat: Deadly Alliance (Midway, 2002)	3.86
SoulCalibur IV (Project Soul, 2008)	2.89
Mortal Kombat: Deception (Midway, 2004)	2.75
Mortal Kombat 4 (Eurocom, 1997)	2.19
Soul Edge/Soul Blade (Project Soul, 1996)	1.59
Battle Arena Toshinden (Tamsoft, 1994)	1.27
Mortal Kombat: Armageddon (Midway/Just Games Interactive, 2006)	1.26
Bushido Blade (Light Weight, 1997)	1.16
SoulCalibur V (Project Soul, 2012)	1.07

Source: vgchartz.com, as of 28 August 2013 (figures in millions)

FIRST FIGHTING GAME WITH A PERFECT *FAMITSU* SCORE

Famitsu magazine is the Japanese gaming bible. It has given only 20 ratings of 40/40 – *SoulCalibur* was the second, in 1998.

103

FIRST PRODUCER AS A NAMED FIGHTING GAME CHARACTER

Tekken producer Katsuhiro Harada (Japan, *below*) appeared in *SoulCalibur V* as NPC Harada TEKKEN. He dressed like Heihachi and used the game's Devil Jin moves.

BEST OF THE REST

LOWDOWN

Fighting games made a name for themselves at the arcades, with *Virtua Fighter* and *Mortal Kombat* joining the likes of *Street Fighter* in the coin-op brawl-off. The **first stereoscopic 3D arcade game** was Sega's 1983 fighting title *Subroc-3D*, which required the player to view the game through a special periscope.

NAME THE GAME

Jennifer Hale portrays Leah, a skilled archer, in which RPG?

MOST PROLIFIC VIDEOGAME NINJA

Iconic ninja Ryu Hayabusa, who has appeared in various gaming franchises, had 27 games to his name as of 1 August 2013. The first title he appeared in was the original *Ninja Gaiden* arcade game (Tecmo, 1988), while his most recent appearance is in *Dead or Alive 5 Plus* (Team Ninja, 2013) on the PS Vita.

MOST LIKED FIGHTING GAME ON FACEBOOK

Mortal Kombat (Midway/NetherRealm Studios, 1992–present) has knocked out the opposition when it comes to popularity among Facebook users, with 4,061,049 "likes" as of 1 August 2013. Rival *Tekken* ranks second with 3,157,659.

The **most fatalities in a *Mortal Kombat* game** is 76, in the PS3 game *Mortal Kombat: Komplete Edition* (NetherRealm Studios, 2012).

TIP-OFF

Risky jumps are crucial in *The King of Fighters XIII* (SNK Playmore, 2010). There are four to master: the short hop, the hyper hop, the standard jump and the super jump. Learning how to use them is a fundamental part of advanced play.

MOST CROWD-FUNDING FOR A FIGHTING GAME

When the team behind *Skullgirls* (Reverge Labs, 2012) needed cash to finish their new DLC character, they turned to crowd-funding site Indiegogo. Some 15,860 backers gave $828,768 (£520,000) from 25 February to 27 March 2012.

Game	Score
SoulCalibur (Namco, 1999) on Dreamcast	96.94%
Tekken 3 (Namco, 1998) on PlayStation	96.30%
Street Fighter IV (Dimps/Capcom, 2009) on PS3	93.64%
Street Fighter IV (Dimps/Capcom, 2009) on Xbox 360	93.23%
Super Smash Bros. Brawl (Game Arts, 2008) on Wii	92.84%
SoulCalibur II (Project Soul, 2003) on GameCube	92.12%
SoulCalibur II (Project Soul, 2003) on Xbox	91.67%
Virtua Fighter 4: Evolution (Sega-AM2, 2003) on PS2	91.59%
SoulCalibur II (Project Soul, 2003) on PS2	91.47%
Super Street Fighter IV (Dimps/Capcom, 2010) on Xbox 360	91.39%

Source: gamerankings.com, as of 1 August 2013

FIRST VIDEOGAME SOUNDTRACK CD

Killer Cuts, which accompanied the SNES port of fighting game *Killer Instinct* (Rare, 1995), was the very first gaming soundtrack album. It came packaged with the game and was not sold separately in shops. The 48-minute-long CD contains 15 tracks plus one hidden bonus.

BEST-SELLING FIGHTING GAME

Super Smash Bros. Brawl (Game Arts, 2008) had achieved sales of 11.74 million as of 1 August 2013, which makes it the best-selling fighter and the eighth best-selling Wii game overall. *Brawl* was the first title in the *Super Smash Bros.* series to feature non-Nintendo characters such as Snake from the *Metal Gear* series (*see pp.38–39*) and Sonic.

105

FIRST FIGHTING VIDEOGAME

Arcade classic *Heavyweight Champ* (Sega, 1976), which came with a boxing-glove controller, was the first game to feature one-on-one brawling. Ten years later, the **first judo videogame** – *Uchi Mata* (Andy Walker/Paul Hodgson, 1986) – appeared on the Commodore 64 and featured British Olympic judoka Brian Jacks (*right*).

WORST-RATED FIGHTING GAME

Fighters Uncaged (Ubisoft, 2010) on the Xbox 360 had a GameRankings score of 35.46% as of 1 August 2013. This martial arts title is the **first motion fighting game for Kinect**. Unfortunately, motion controls did little for its critical reception; GameSpot criticized its "lifeless animation, generic visuals, and a baffling scoring system".

MAKING MONEY PLAYING VIDEOGAMES

Earning a living as a gamer was once a fantasy. Now thousands of professionals compete in eSports for big winnings and sponsorship. **Paul Dean** meets the pros.

Every year, the pro gaming scene grows, as do the prize pools for games such as *DotA 2* (Valve, 2013), *Counter-Strike* (Valve, 2000) and *StarCraft II* (Blizzard, 2010). Is it really that difficult to join the big league? Patrik "cArn" Sättermon is a Swedish pro gamer and part of Fnatic, a multi-disciplinary gaming clan whose members cover eSports from shooters to strategy. He answers the crucial questions about how to make money doing what you love...

How does a player get started as a pro?
My advice is always to find a game that really excites you, then play it with people you like hanging out with. It's important to know that you won't become a star overnight. The gamers you see lifting trophies and prize cheques have all been through years of practice and success does not come easily. In fact, I believe gaming requires more daily practice than a conventional sport simply because you aren't as limited physically.

OCZ PRESENTS

FATAL1TY VS relic

CHALLENGE AT TAIPEI TOL

06.06.2013

COMPUTEX TAIPEI

• FATAL1TY ATTRACTION •

Johnathan Wendel (left), a pro gamer better known as "Fatal1ty", can play for eight hours a day, breaking up his gaming with exercise. It's this level of commitment that has seen Fatal1ty triumph in both the World Cyber Games and the Cyberathlete Professional League – the latter four times.

What should a pro player's daily routine be?
Keeping fit and eating healthy are important factors in eSports. It optimizes your usage of the most important tool to overcome your opponent: your brain.

Should players wait to be recruited by a team?
I would be surprised if the majority of professional players today haven't played for teams created by themselves and their friends.

• Patrik Sättermon (centre) •

How do gamers get spotted?
The great thing with eSports is
that even if you're an amateur or
semi-professional player, there will
be chances to compete with the
best online. There are hundreds of
tournament platforms and qualifiers
that you can participate in. If you
work your way into these leagues
you'll be facing professionals. The
best way of getting on the radar
of eSports organizations is simply
to be active, as well as pushing your
persona on social media and even
live-streaming [games].

• MILLION-DOLLAR GAMERS •
At The International 2012 in Seattle, Washington, USA, Invictus Gaming (above) won
$1 million (£630,000) playing DotA 2. But such prizes are still rare, and outstanding
pro gamers are more likely to earn $20,000–30,000 (£14,000–20,000) a year.

• STARTING YOUNG •
It's never too early to be a pro
gamer. Born on 6 May 1998, "Lil
Poison", aka Victor De Leon III
(USA), entered his first Halo
(Bungie, 2001) tournament aged
four, the **youngest professional
videogamer**. In 2005, Lil Poison
signed an exclusive deal with Major
League Gaming to be the **youngest
signed professional videogamer**.

**How do players know if
they've got what it takes?**
Beating good players online
[shows] that you are of a
reasonable calibre, but the
truth is these players will most
likely outmatch you at a live
event where experience and
confidence comes into the
picture. But don't be afraid
of taking the next step; we've
all been beginners.

**How important are attitude
and temperament?**
I've seen both good
and bad examples
of upcoming players.
What really gets our
attention are players
that are modest about
their success, as well as
professional about their
pro gaming careers.

• CRAFTING A CAREER •
South Korea's Lim Yo-Hwan has made his
living from StarCraft and is widely considered
to be one of the world's best players of the
game. A star with earnings estimated in six
figures, he has his own fan club and has
recently moved into management.

BEST-SELLING PC GAME SERIES

According to VGChartz, as of August 2013, *The Sims* series had sold 46.5 million copies on the PC alone and 72.15 million in all formats. It is now translated into more than 20 languages and sold in at least 60 countries. Publishers Electronic Arts said in January 2013 that the series had shifted 150 million copies across all platforms. Whichever figure is nearer the mark, the franchise remains by far the most popular PC game series. Pictured is expansion pack *The Sims 3: Into the Future*, set for release in late 2013.

CONTENTS

MINECRAFT

LOWDOWN

PUBLISHER:
Mojang
DEVELOPER:
Mojang
DEBUT:
2009

The open-world indie phenomenon keeps building on its own success: the Xbox 360 release made back its entire development costs within an hour of launch and saw sales of 400,000 in its first day. The game's concept is simple: build a shelter and as many items as you like, both for fun and to attack creepy enemies.

NAME THE GAME
An angel-hating New Yorker, Enzo celebrates his birthday at the start of the game.

HIGHEST-GROSSING INDIE GAME
Between October 2010 and December 2011, *Minecraft* made an astounding $80.8 million (£52 million) in gross revenue. During 2012, it took $237.7 million (£154 million). That made its total gross a huge $318.5 million (£206 million) as of 9 September 2013. Mojang said total sales were 33 million as of 3 September 2013, making *Minecraft* the **best-selling indie game**. PC and Mac sales alone were 12,080,037 – that's almost three million more than the population of Mojang's home country, Sweden.

▽

icMcCowan

LONGEST *MINECRAFT* TUNNEL
As of 3 March 2013, gamer Eric McCowan's *Minecraft* tunnel covered a distance of 10,001 blocks, which equates to 10,001 m (3,281 ft). The space is one block wide, two blocks high and is lit by torches placed at 10-block intervals. Undoubtedly impressive, it is some way off Switzerland's Gotthard rail tunnel, the real-world **longest rail tunnel**, at 57 km (35.42 miles) long.

MOST DOWNLOADED *MINECRAFT* PROJECT
Community fansite Project Minecraft is a place for fans of the game to share ideas, texture packs and skins and to talk all things *Minecraft*. With 700,452 downloads, the "Temple of Notch" OCD texture pack produced by "disco_" is the most popular project. *Minecraft* creator Markus "Notch" Persson appears as a giant idol in the pack, which had been viewed 8,053,980 times on YouTube as of 19 September 2013.

TOP TEN
MOST WINS ON *MINECRAFT* SURVIVAL GAMES

Player	Wins
Gravey4rd	2,534
NoahSailer	2,517
Edog786	1,933
Elgoldo	1,879
JustAHotDog	1,814
DevilicCrafter	1,675
reven86	1,652
Brandon6895	1,582
Elisha_Mutang	1,554
PancakeKojo	1,420

Source: minecraftsurvivalgames.com, as of 10 September 2013

In August 2013, the prestigious Victoria and Albert Museum (V&A) in London, UK, ran a special "World of Minecraft" event in collaboration with Mojang. It featured talks, workshops, works of art based on the game and a lifesize Steve. The V&A described *Minecraft* as "more than a game... it is a cultural phenomenon".

LARGEST PLAYABLE AREA

Although *Minecraft*'s map is technically infinite – the farther you go, the more land that is generated; in reality, the game's physics only work effectively on blocks up to 32 million blocks away from the world centre, so the game's maximum playable area is 4,096,000,000 km² (1.5 billion miles²). In theory, with "creative mode" switched on, the game area could stretch to 4,722,366,482,869,645 km² (1.8 quadrillion miles²), the equivalent of 9 million Earths, but players will encounter numerous bugs on their travels.

BIGGEST INDIE GAME CONVENTION

Held at Disneyland Paris, France, MineCon 2012 managed to break Mojang's own record for attendees at an indie convention by hosting more than 7,000 people on 24–25 November 2012. MineCon 2013, scheduled for 2–3 November 2013 in Orlando, Florida, USA, may well break the record again. These conventions reflect the game's quick success; MineCon 2010 was attended by some 50 people, but by 2011 the event was attracting 5,000 enthusiasts. For more about gaming conventions around the world, see our feature on pp.70–71.

MOST POPULAR GAME BETA

With more than 10 million registered users, *Minecraft* is the most successful game beta ever. It was in beta testing from 20 December 2010 to 18 November 2011.

Minecraft's performance on the Xbox 360 has been just as impressive. At a press conference during E3 in June 2013, Microsoft confirmed sales of some 6 million, making *Minecraft* the **best-selling Xbox Live Arcade game**.

111

COMMAND & CONQUER

LOWDOWN

PUBLISHER:
EA
DEVELOPER:
Westwood/
EA Los Angeles
DEBUT:
1995

The first title in this sci-fi strategy franchise is the **most critically acclaimed RTS game**, with a 94% Metacritic score as of 3 September 2013. *C&C* games require players to accumulate resources with which to construct and defend a base, while attacking and conquering opponents' bases.

NAME THE GAME
A homeless petty thief, Faith Connors is voiced by Jules de Jongh.

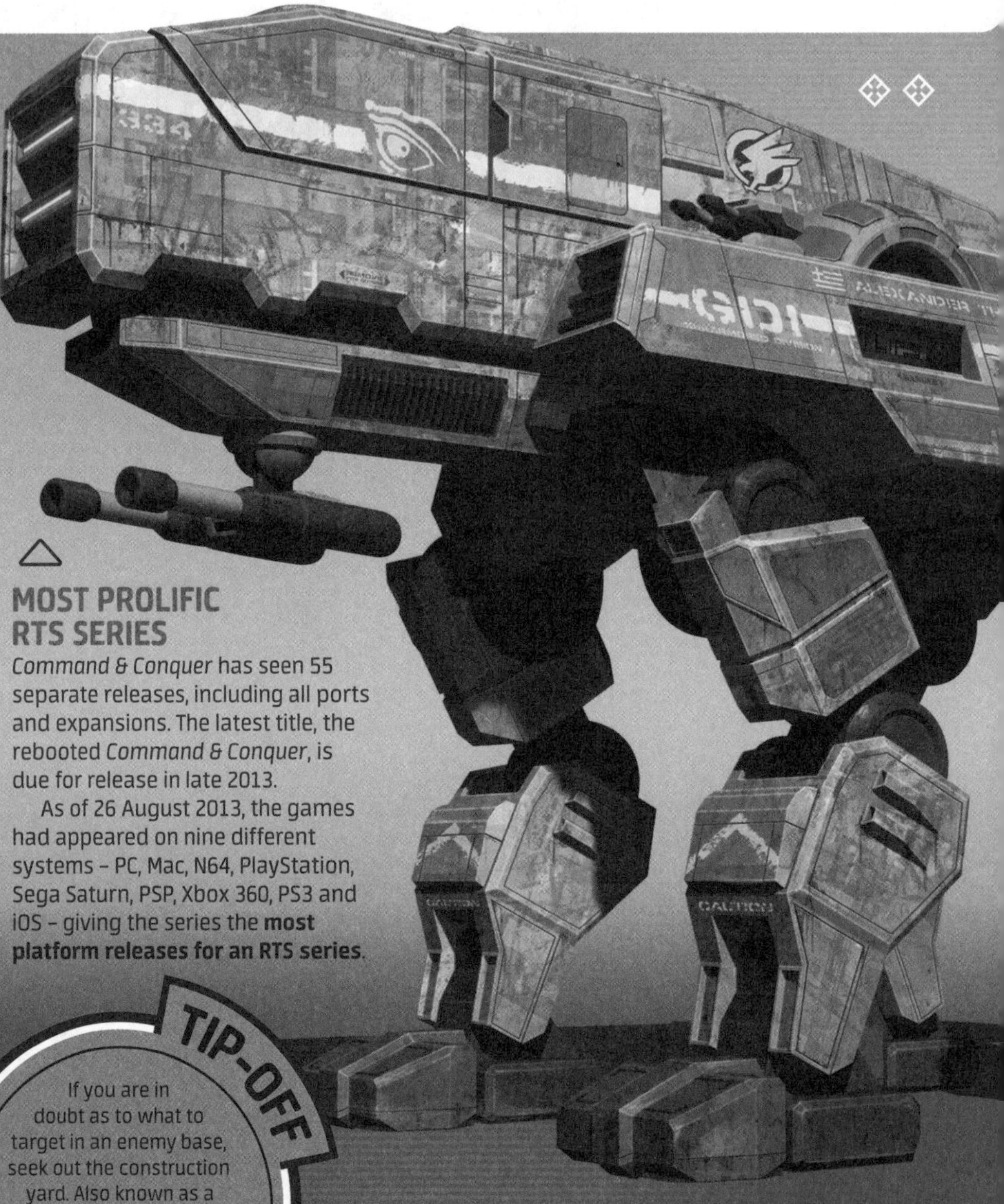

MOST PROLIFIC RTS SERIES

Command & Conquer has seen 55 separate releases, including all ports and expansions. The latest title, the rebooted *Command & Conquer*, is due for release in late 2013.

As of 26 August 2013, the games had appeared on nine different systems – PC, Mac, N64, PlayStation, Sega Saturn, PSP, Xbox 360, PS3 and iOS – giving the series the **most platform releases for an RTS series**.

TIP-OFF

If you are in doubt as to what to target in an enemy base, seek out the construction yard. Also known as a "conyard", this structure produces other buildings and forms the heart of a base, so it makes for a very valuable target.

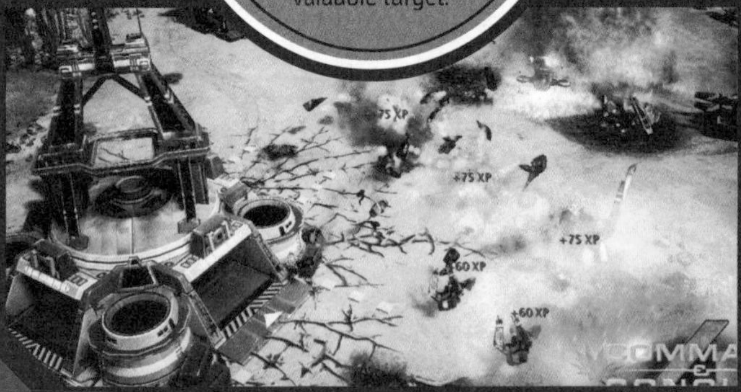

LONGEST TIME IN THE SAME STRATEGY CHARACTER ROLE

Joe Kucan (USA) played the part of Kane, the villainous mastermind of the series, for 15 years from the very first game to *Command & Conquer 4: Tiberian Twilight* (2010; *pictured left*), which marked the end of the six-game Tiberian story. Released to mixed reviews, the game was followed by *Tiberium Alliances* (2012), an online free-to-play, browser-based game.

FIRST INTEGRATED VIDEOGAME COMMENTARY SYSTEM

The earliest in-game commentary system was in *Command & Conquer 3: Tiberium Wars* on PC. Known as Battlecast, the technology allowed gamers to stream matches live or make them available as replays, as well as giving commentators the ability to battlecast matches – offering spectators a running commentary on games. Some 25 episodes of the *Battlecast Primetime* show were broadcast on the *C&C* internet channel between 2007 and its cancellation in 2010, highlighting the latest news, updates and the most exciting multiplayer matches.

FIRST GAME TO USE SAGE

EA Pacific's *Command & Conquer: Generals* (2003) was the first game to utilize the Strategy Action Game Engine (SAGE), which has since been used in *Command & Conquer 3: Tiberium Wars* and *The Lord of the Rings: The Battle for Middle-Earth* (EA, 2004). The engine was created by the Westwood development team in order to introduce full 3D visuals. EA has been using follow-up engine SAGE 2.0 since 2008; the **first game to use SAGE 2.0** was *Command & Conquer: Red Alert 3* (2008).

113

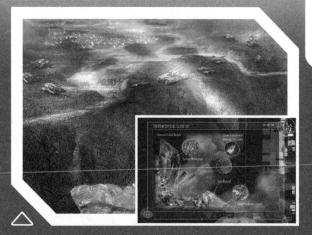

TOP TEN	MOST USER ACCLAIMED *COMMAND & CONQUER* GAMES	
Command & Conquer: Red Alert 2 (Westwood Studios, 2000) on PC		9.2
Command & Conquer: Red Alert 2 – Yuri's Revenge (Westwood Studios, 2001) on PC		9.1
Command & Conquer: Red Alert (Westwood Studios, 1996) on PC		9.0
Command & Conquer: Generals Zero Hour (EA Los Angeles, 2003) on PC		
Command & Conquer (Westwood Studios, 1995) on PC		8.8
Command & Conquer: The First Decade (various developers, 2006) on PC		8.6
Command & Conquer: Generals (EA Pacific, 2003) on PC		8.1
Command & Conquer: Renegade (Westwood Studios, 2002) on PC		7.9
Command & Conquer 3: Kane's Wrath (EA Los Angeles, 2008) on PC		7.8
Command & Conquer 3 : Tiberium Wars (EA Los Angeles, 2007) on PC		

Source: metacritic.com, as of 6 September 2013 (scores out of 10)

FIRST SCIENTIFIC STUDY OF A CHEMICAL COMPOUND IN A GAME

As part of the development of *Command & Conquer 3: Tiberium Wars*, publisher EA commissioned scientists from the Massachusetts Institute of Technology, USA, to come up with a plausible analysis of the game's main resource, Tiberium (*pictured in the field and inset, close up*). In the paper, issued in 2006, the game's executive producer Mike Verdu described Tiberium as a dense "dynamic proton lattice" held together by exotic heavy particles.

DotA

LOWDOWN

PUBLISHER:
Valve
DEVELOPER:
Valve
DEBUT:
2005

The original *Defense of the Ancients*, aka *DotA*, is a multiplayer online battle arena mod for *WarCraft III: Reign of Chaos* (Blizzard, 2002) and its expansion, *The Frozen Throne* (2003). *DotA* is based on the "Aeon of Strife" map for *StarCraft* (Blizzard, 1998). Stand-alone free2play sequel *DotA 2* entered beta in 2011. The game, available on PC, Mac and Linux, is a key part of the eSports scene.

NAME THE GAME
Chun-Li often unleashes a Lightning Kick to defeat her enemies.

MOST CONCURRENT USERS ON STEAM

On 9 July 2013, a posting on the *DotA 2* blog announced that the game's beta period was finally over after two years. On 18 May 2013, while still in beta mode, *DotA 2* set the record for the most simultaneous players on Steam, with a formidable 329,977 gamers in all. This figure also makes *DotA 2* the **most popular game in beta (concurrent users)**. The monthly user base in beta was more than 3 million individual players. As of 3 September 2013, there were 6,545,325 unique monthly players of the officially released *DotA 2*.

TIP-OFF

Struggling with experience and gold? Fire up a bot match. Don't add in other heroes, just practise striking the death blow on creeps. When they're enemy creeps it's called "last hitting", and when they're friendly it's "denying". Last hits give you extra gold, while denies reduce enemy XP gains.

MOST EXPENSIVE ITEM IN *DOTA 2*

DotA 2 offers a formidable selection of digital hats, scarves, swords and capes with which to customize characters. The Fiery Soul of the Slayer, a flaming hair option, costs £22.99 ($35). The **most expensive in-game item in *DotA 2*** that can be bought while playing is the fully upgraded "Dagon". The Dagon is a wand capable of dealing a massive burst of damage to an enemy. The first level costs 2,730 "gold" (the in-game currency), but you can repurchase it up to four times to upgrade, bringing the cost to 26,150 gold.

LARGEST SINGLE eSPORTS PRIZE

The International 3 – Valve's third annual international *DotA 2* championship – used sales of a digital compendium to boost the prize money. As a result, Swedish team "Alliance" walked away from the tournament in Seattle, Washington, USA, not just with the "Aegis of Champions" trophy but with a record-breaking prize of $1,437,204 (£927,000) on 11 August 2013. The International 3's total prize pool of $2,369,892 (£1.53 million) makes it the **largest eSports prize pool for a single tournament**.

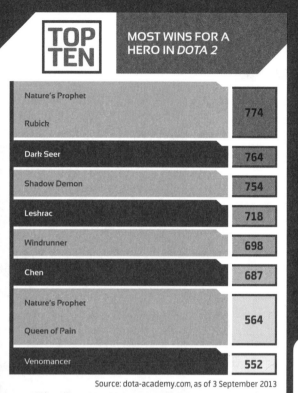

TOP TEN

MOST WINS FOR A HERO IN *DOTA 2*

Hero	Wins
Nature's Prophet / Rubick	774
Dark Seer	764
Shadow Demon	754
Leshrac	718
Windrunner	698
Chen	687
Nature's Prophet / Queen of Pain	564
Venomancer	552

Source: dota-academy.com, as of 3 September 2013

◁ ## MOST CHOSEN HERO IN DOTA 2

Described as "a threat to all creation" in his character bio, Shadow Demon tops the DotA Academy list as the hero chosen most often in tournament matches, notching up 1,665 appearances on the pro scene as of 3 September 2013. Dark Seer lags some way behind on 1,537 appearances, while Rubick breathes down his neck on 1,510. The menacing Shadow Demon was called Eredar in the original *DotA* but was changed in order to avoid legal tangles with Blizzard as the Eredar are a race from the *WarCraft* universe. The **most banned hero in *DotA 2*** is Dark Seer with 2,261 bans.

SMALLEST TERRITORY TO PRODUCE A GAMING CHAMPION

The saying goes, "It's not where you're from, it's where you're going." Although now a Danish citizen, gamer Jacob Toft-Andersen, better known as "Maelk", was born on Norfolk Island, a tiny island in the Pacific Ocean that has a population of 2,302. Maelk has made a name for himself on the *DotA* circuit for leading three teams – BTO, MYM and Ravens – to a total of 32 victories, which is the **most DotA tournament wins** for an individual playing within a team.

HIGHEST WIN PERCENTAGE ON *DOTA 2*

According to *DotA* data aggregator DOTABUFF, as of 4 September 2013 the player with the best win percentage was "aceaceace", who had won 91.63% of matches.

The **most DotA 2 matches played** is 5,694, completed by "bluechipps", although his win rate is 48.96%. The 164 days 15 hr 52 min that "bluechipps" has spent playing the game also gives him the record for the **greatest aggregate time playing DotA 2**. He is almost 20 days ahead of his closest competitor.

StarCraft

LOWDOWN

PUBLISHER:
Blizzard
DEVELOPER:
Blizzard
DEBUT:
1998

Military sci-fi RTS game *StarCraft* is set on a 25th-century Earth, where three species – the Terrans, the Protoss and the Zerg – are battling for control of a sector of the Milky Way. Given the success of the original title, it's surprising that sequel *StarCraft II* took some 12 years to arrive.

NAME THE GAME
Professor Pig may not be the biggest, but he is definitely the wisest.

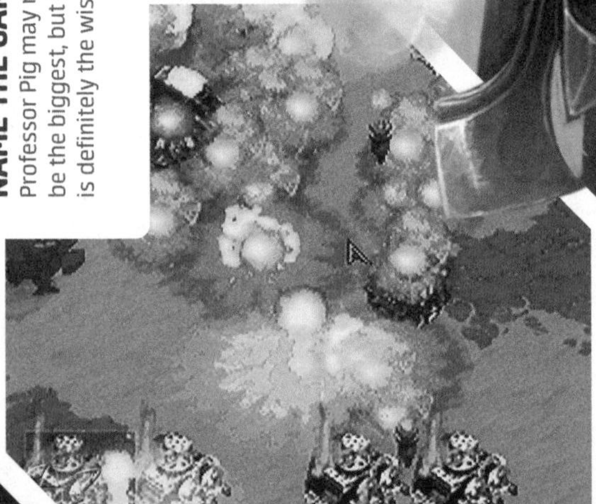

MOST CRITICALLY ACCLAIMED SCI-FI RTS GAME ▷

With an aggregated score of 92.44% on GameRankings as of 14 August 2013, sequel *StarCraft II: Wings of Liberty* (2010) is the most critically acclaimed game in the sci-fi RTS genre, well ahead of the second-placed title, *Homeworld* (Relic, 1999), which scores 88.81%. *StarCraft II* is set four years after events in the *Brood War* (1998) expansion pack.

BOOST

SHOOTING STARS

Gamer "Freezard" held three *StarCraft* speed-run records as of 14 August 2013: the **fastest completion of Protoss mission 1** in 2 min 44 sec on 19 October 2011; the **fastest completion of Terran mission 1** in 2 min 26 sec on 25 September 2011; and the **fastest completion of Zerg mission 1** in 4 min 30 sec on 6 October 2011.

△

BEST-SELLING SCI-FI STRATEGY SERIES

StarCraft has sold 8.99 million copies over all platforms as of September 2013. Blizzard puts the figure at more than 11 million, but either way these figures are impressive, particularly given that the game has only appeared on three platforms – PC, Mac and the N64. The port for the latter, *StarCraft 64* (Blizzard/Mass Media Inc, 2000), included the *Brood War* expansion but didn't offer online multiplayer mode.

FIRST GAME INVOLVED IN MATCH-FIXING

On 13 April 2010, a number of match-fixing revelations surfaced in the *StarCraft: Brood War* league. A total of 16 people were implicated in the scandal, in which pro players accepted bribes worth 6.5 million Korean Won ($5,400; £3,500) in exchange for deliberately losing matches. The 11 pros in question were handed lifetime bans by the Korea e-Sports Association (KeSPA), ending their careers.

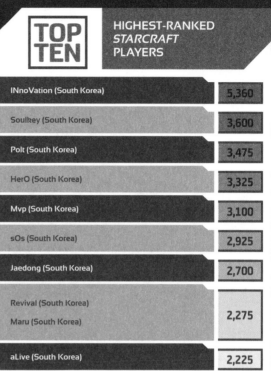

TOP TEN

HIGHEST-RANKED *STARCRAFT* PLAYERS

Player	Rank
INnoVation (South Korea)	5,360
Soulkey (South Korea)	3,600
Polt (South Korea)	3,475
HerO (South Korea)	3,325
Mvp (South Korea)	3,100
sOs (South Korea)	2,925
Jaedong (South Korea)	2,700
Revival (South Korea) / Maru (South Korea)	2,275
aLive (South Korea)	2,225

Source: *StarCraft* World Championship Series standings, as of 14 August 2013

FIRST UNIVERSITY TO OFFER A COMPETITIVE GAMING QUALIFICATION

"Game Theory in StarCraft", a 14-week course covering the theory and practice of high-level gaming in *StarCraft*, began at the University of California, Berkeley, USA, in 2009. The course includes lectures on timing, resource-management and base layout, and requires students to produce detailed analyses of previous games to better understand the strategy of world-class players. It is worth two units of "pass/fail" but not a letter grade.

HIGHEST-EARNING *STARCRAFT II* PLAYER

South Korean Protoss player Jang "MC" Min Chul (*left*) had made $389,802 (£250,700) in prize money as of 14 August 2013. Compatriot Lee Young Ho is the **highest-earning *StarCraft: Brood War* player**, with winnings of $407,228 (£263,000), which also makes him the **highest-earning *StarCraft* player** overall.

LONGEST-RUNNING eSPORTS GAME

As of August 2013, the original *StarCraft* had been played as an eSport for 14 years, with its first pro tournament taking place in 1999.

KeSPA publishes monthly rankings of *StarCraft* players based on wins and recent in-game successes. The **longest time in the KeSPA rankings** is 87 months straight, clocked up by South Korean Terran player Lee Yoon Yeol, aka "NaDa", from March 2002 to May 2009.

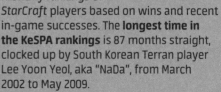

THE SIMS & SIMCITY

LOWDOWN

PUBLISHER:
EA
DEVELOPER:
Maxis
DEBUT:
The Sims, 2000
SimCity, 1989

When *SimCity* creator Will Wright wanted to publish his new game, he started his own development company, Maxis. Acquired by EA in 1997, Maxis now dominates the sim scene with its city-building and life-simulation franchises. The latest games in each series are *SimCity* (2013) and *The Sims 4*, scheduled for a 2014 release.

NAME THE GAME
Genetic Lifeform and Disk Operating System, aka GLaDOS, stars in this puzzle game.

MOST CRITICALLY ACCLAIMED CITY-BUILDING GAME

SimCity 4 (2003) had a score of 85.09% on GameRankings as of 12 August 2013. IGN's critic described the level of detail in the game as "amazing", concluding that *SimCity 4* was "a major evolutionary step in the series", while EuroGamer scored it 9/10.

FIRST CITY-BUILDING GAME

The original *SimCity*, whose early working title was *Micropolis*, was the first fully fledged city-builder. It allowed players to devise and run their own cities – the original gaming urban planner. While Intellivision title *Utopia* (Don Daglow, 1981) allowed players to create cities on the game's two islands, the technology was not advanced enough at the time to actually show the cities.

BEST-SELLING CITY-BUILDING GAME SERIES

According to GameSpot as of August 2013, the *SimCity* series (1989–present) had sold 18 million units. There are six games in the PC series, three console titles, one browser game and five releases for handhelds (including smartphones). The central gameplay has stayed much the same throughout the years: build a city, keep your citizens happy and be ambitious – within budget.

Talking of grand ambitions, the **largest building capacity in *SimCity 4*** is the Hamster Tenement, which has a maximum capacity of 8,146.

FIRST OFFICIAL MUSIC VIDEO IN SIMLISH ▷

Simlish is a fictional language that features in both *The Sims* and *SimCity* series. While many artists appear on the soundtrack of *The Sims 2: Seasons* (2007), British singer Lily Allen's Simlish version of her hit single "Smile" was the first track given an official video, crafted by EA in March 2007.

Lily Allen "Smile"

MOST CONCURRENT PLAYERS ON ORIGIN

The release of 2013's *SimCity* saw EA's Origin service reach a peak of 1.3 million concurrent users on 19 March 2013. Origin, a gaming hub similar to Valve's Steam service, couldn't always handle the high number of gamers, however, so log-in delays, error messages and network outages plagued the launch.

TIP-OFF

Although *SimCity* now allows players to create curving roads, the most efficient city layouts are based around grid patterns. Holding down shift will make rectangular road loops square and keep intersections at right angles.

BEST-SELLING SIMULATION GAME SERIES

With 72.15 million units sold across all platforms as of 12 August 2013, EA's life-sim franchise continues to hold its own. The first game in the series, *The Sims* (2000), is the **best-selling game for PC**, with sales of 11.23 million as of 12 August 2013. *The Sims* is also the **best-selling life sim**, having sold 14.91 million across all platforms. Pictured above is *The Sims 2*, which has sold a total of 7.16 million units.

119

TOP TEN — MOST CRITICALLY ACCLAIMED LIFE SIMS

Game	Score
The Sims 2 (Maxis, 2004) on PC	90.76%
The Sims (Maxis, 2000) on PC	89.74%
Animal Crossing: New Leaf (Nintendo, 2012) on 3DS	87.09%
The Sims 3 (The Sims Studio, 2009) on PC	86.61%
Animal Crossing (Nintendo, 2001) on GameCube	86.36%
Animal Crossing: Wild World (Nintendo, 2005) on DS	86.27%
The Sims (Maxis, 2003) on GameCube	85.80%
The Sims: Hot Date (Maxis, 2001) on PC	85.54%
Viva Piñata (Rare, 2006) on Xbox 360	85.37%
Nintendogs: Lab & Friends (Nintendo 2005) on DS	85.13%

Source: gamerankings.com, as of 13 August 2013

BEST OF THE REST

LOWDOWN

Few activities are too obscure to simulate. Even farming has *Agricultural Simulator 2013* (UIG Entertainment, 2012), boasting more than 100 tractors and extensions. Strategy games, meanwhile, have long put players in charge of armies in a virtual universe, but the real world is also taking notice. In 2013, the US government ruled that professional players of Riot Games' *League of Legends* (2009) were eligible for work visas in the USA.

120

NAME THE GAME
Martial arts competitor Jann Lee was inspired by Bruce Lee.

FIRST DATING SIMULATOR

The first romantically themed simulator was *Sonic the Hedgehog* creator Yuji Naka's debut, *Girl's Garden* (Sega, 1984). The 8-bit title, in which the heroine has to collect flowers for her true love, was released exclusively in Japan for owners of Sega's SG-1000 console.

TIP-OFF

Is Air Traffic Control bugging you in the long haul of *Flight Simulator X* (2006)? Once you're safely at cruising speed and are directed to contact the next controller, ignore the command. Fly in splendid silence until you need to land and then contact them.

LONGEST-RUNNING GAME SERIES

Flight Simulator spans more than 32 years between its first and most recent releases. Originally released by developer subLOGIC in October 1979 for the Apple II, the game was acquired by Microsoft and distributed for PCs as *Flight Simulator 1.00* in 1982. It has 16 main series titles in total.

Further development on expansion packs of the 2012 reboot, the free *Microsoft Flight*, were cancelled later the same year. Eager to take the record is RPG veteran *Ultima* (see p.134).

BEST-SELLING SIMULATION GAME

Nintendogs (Nintendo, 2005) had sold 24.52 million units on the DS as of 22 August 2013. The pet pooches can be trained to score points, although the contests stay firmly in the real world, unlike that other great collection of creatures from Nintendo, *Pokémon* (1996–present; see pp.126–27).

Nintendogs sits up appealingly in the virtual pet category, which has been around for 20 years, and even Japan's *Famitsu* magazine gave it 40/40. Rather less cute is the **first street-cleaning simulator**: *Street Cleaning Simulator* (2011) by Astragon, the people behind *Garbage Truck Simulator* (2008) and *Farming Simulator* (2011).

TOP TEN
BEST-SELLING STRATEGY GAMES

Game	Sales
Pokémon Stadium (Nintendo, 1999) on N64	5.45
Warzone 2100 (Pumpkin Studios, 1999) on PlayStation	5.01
Warcraft II: Tides of Darkness (Blizzard, 1995) on PC	4.21
StarCraft II: Wings of Liberty (Blizzard, 2010) on PC	4.09
RollerCoaster Tycoon (Chris Sawyer Productions, 1999) on PC	3.83
StarCraft (Blizzard, 1998) on PC	3.73
Pokémon Trading Card Game (Nintendo, 1998) on Game Boy	3.70
Command & Conquer: Red Alert (Westwood Studios, 1996) on PC	2.85
Pokémon Stadium 2 (Nintendo, 2000) on N64 / *Age of Empires II: The Age of Kings* (Microsoft, 1999) on PC	2.73

Source: vgchartz.com, as of 22 August 2013 (figures in millions)

FASTEST "BEST ENDING" COMPLETION OF *PIKMIN 2*

Charles Griffin completed Nintendo's real-time strategy game *Pikmin 2* (2004), collecting all 201 treasures on 25 September 2009 in 3 hr 10 min.

Pikmin, the original surreal gardening/strategy combination by *Donkey Kong* developer Shigeru Miyamoto, came out in 2001. The **fastest completion of *Pikmin*** was set by Peter "Dragorn" Branam-Lefkove, who managed it in nine segments in 1 hr 54 min on 16 August 2004.

MOST SPECIES OF TREE IN A STRATEGY GAME

Total War: Shogun 2 (The Creative Assembly, 2011) features 80 species of tree and only 30 different types of combat unit. The series also provided the **first historical game used on TV** – an upgraded version of the engine for *Rome: Total War* (2004). It was used in *Time Commanders* (BBC2, UK, 2003–05).

In May 2011 came another pioneering milestone as *Napoleon: Total War* (2010) became the **first strategy game to win an Ivor Novello award,** for Best Original Videogame Soundtrack. This was composed by Richard Beddow, Richard Birdsall and Ian Livingstone.

121

LONGEST VIDEOGAME DEVELOPMENT PERIOD

Elite (David Braben and Ian Bell) was published in 1984 and had two sequels: *Frontier: Elite II* (GameTek, 1993) and 1995's *Frontier: First Encounters* (Frontier Developments). *Elite: Dangerous* (Frontier Developments, *main picture*) received funding with the help of a Kickstarter campaign in 2012–13.

If the PC version arrives as expected in 2014 it will be 19 years after the previous instalment and 30 after the original, the **first space trading game,** a genre evolved by the likes of MMORPG *EVE Online* (CCP Games, 2003).

WORST-RATED REAL-TIME STRATEGY GAME

Cops 2170: The Power of Law (MiST Land, 2005) had a rating of 41.50%. On the sim front, the record for the **worst-rated simulation game** goes to *Mobile Suit Gundam: Crossfire* (Namco Bandai Games, 2006), rated 35.68% (it did better in Japan, with *Famitsu* magazine awarding it 32/40). The **worst-rated flight sim** is *Over G Fighters* (Taito Corporation, 2006) on the Xbox 360, rated 53.47% (all percentages by GameRankings, as of 22 August 2013).

STAR GAMING

The *Star Trek* phenomenon warped back into cinemas and homes in 2013 with a new movie, videogame and Kickstarter-funded TV pilot. Eddie de Oliveira journeys through a wormhole to look back at a handful of the 70 videogames in Paramount's enduring sci-fi franchise.

TREK: ORIGINS

Star Trek is renowned for its innovation and cultish fan enthusiasm – traits that have reinvented the franchise for new audiences across five decades. Its first re-birth came just two years after *Star Trek* creator Gene Roddenberry's original TV series was cancelled, when an unlicensed *Trek* game arrived on home computers: the **first *Star Trek* videogame** was the text-only *Star Trek* (Mike Mayfield, 1971), in which players were charged with leading the USS *Enterprise* on a mission to destroy a Klingon fleet.

A handful of similarly basic titles followed before *Trek* gaming became juicier in 1983 with Sega's space flight sim and FPS arcade title *Star Trek: Strategic Operations Simulator*. This also centred on leading the *Enterprise* against marauding Klingon vessels, but was most notable for its rather elegant Captain's chair.

BON VOYAGER

With a GameRankings score of 85.65% as of 5 August 2013, FPS *Star Trek: Voyager – Elite Force* (Raven Software, 2000) for the PC is the **most critically acclaimed game based on a sci-fi TV series**. Inspired by the fourth *Trek* TV series, gameplay features the USS *Voyager*, which is stranded 70,000 light years from Earth, with its crew desperate to find a way home under the leadership of the franchise's first female captain, Kathryn Janeway. In single-player mode, players can choose to be a male or female ensign and take part in high-risk away missions to come up against villains, including the Borg and Hirogen.

TREK GOES MASSIVE

Star Trek docked in the sci-fi MMORPG genre for the first time in 2010 with *Star Trek Online* (Cryptic Studios), which went free2play two years later. Set in 2409, the plot revolves around a new war between the United Federation of Planets and the Klingon Empire. Players assume the role of captain on a ship of their choice: Federation, Klingon or Romulan. The first expansion pack, *Legacy of Romulus*, was released in 2013. Original Spock actor Leonard Nimoy can be heard introducing the game.

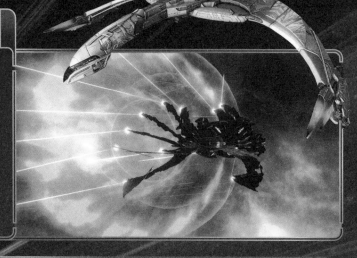

THE NEW, OLD TREK

Brian Miller, Senior Vice-President at Paramount Pictures, talks about the latest *Star Trek* game (Digital Extremes, 2013) and explains just why it captures our imagination...

What was your role on the *Star Trek* videogame project?
My role was to guide the overall creative development of the game – from the story, the casting, game play and sound design. My team and I have worked tirelessly to make sure all parties – our studio, the film-making team, our writers, co-publisher and developer – were working to make the ultimate *Trek* game. The experience of making this game has truly been a dream come true.

How does this *Star Trek* game differ from previous ones?
While we have great affection for many of the *Star Trek* games done in the past, we realized that this was

our opportunity to really bring *Trek* into the triple-A gaming space. Our goal was to create a great game. The fact that it was *Star Trek* was always a bonus for us. We wanted to make the *Star Trek* game that *we* always wanted to play – we wanted to play as Kirk and Spock (which we were surprised had never been done before), we wanted great co-operative game play and we wanted an authentic game based on the rebooted 2009 film. We want you to feel like you *are* Kirk and Spock. I loved the *Star Trek* arcade game where you could sit in a replica of the Captain's chair! You felt like you were part of the crew. That feeling was what we were trying to replicate in the game.

What is it about *Star Trek* – videogames, film and TV series – that makes it such an enduring, popular entertainment franchise that transcends generations?
It's a testament to the vision

of the great Gene Roddenberry. He created iconic characters and stories that still thrive today. It has been very humbling to work on a franchise that was created long before and will survive long past any of us.

Will there be another *Star Trek* TV series?
I want an answer to that question myself!

RPGs

FASTEST-SELLING RPG

Blizzard's *Diablo III* sold in excess of 3.5 million copies within 24 hours of release on 15 May 2012, while a further 1.2 million gamers received the game free with a *World of Warcraft* promotion. The game's release day was also marked by the **first** and **fastest completion of Diablo III**, set by South Korea's "EHG" clan in 5 hr 30 min.

CONTENTS

POKÉMON

LOWDOWN

PUBLISHER:
Nintendo
DEVELOPER:
Game Freak
DEBUT:
1996

The main series puts players in the role of trainers who have to capture the "pocket monsters", or *Pokémon*, and use them to battle other trainers. While their collection of Pokémon may get stronger, trainers have to contend with the threat from evil organizations plotting to take over the *Pokémon* world.

126

NAME THE GAME
Mr Toffee offers advice and level introductions in which sweet game?

FIRST GAME ON THE COVER OF *TIME*

The prestigious *Time* magazine is usually the preserve of presidents, world events and Hollywood stars, but in November 1999 the cover of the magazine was taken over by *Pokémon*, the first time that a single videogame title had been given that honour. "For many kids it's now an addiction," parents of America were warned. "Cards, videogames, toys, a new movie. Is it bad for them?"

TIP-OFF

In *Pokémon Black/ White Version 2* (2010), keep your eyes peeled for hidden grottos, found between two trees in areas of the world where the gap between the trees is dark green. Interact with the tree and you'll enter a secret clearing. Here, you'll find some random items and a Pokémon with hidden abilities.

MOST WINS OF THE POKÉMON WORLD CHAMPIONSHIPS

On 11 August 2012, Ray Rizzo defeated Wolfe Glick (both USA) to win the *Pokémon* World Championships Masters division for the third year in a row. Nintendo added Ray and his characters to *Pokémon Black/White Version 2* via a downloadable update. "Hydreigon is my favourite and, in my opinion, the best Dragon," he revealed. "Rotom-W was the Pokémon I used the least."

LONGEST-RUNNING VIDEOGAME TV SPIN-OFF

The *Pokémon* anime first screened in Japan on 1 April 1997 with the episode "Pikachu, I Choose You!" It charts the adventures of Ash Ketchum – the 10-year-old trainee trainer – Pikachu and friends. The series has been in production ever since, clocking up 795 episodes across 17 seasons as of 1 August 2013.

BO:OM!

The least useful ability in the series is "Splash", introduced in the very first *Pokémon* generation. The signature move of Magikarp, Splash makes the Pokémon bounce, usually causing no damage to opponents and no effect to the user. The exception is *Pokémon Mystery Dungeon* (2005), in which Splash can be used to hop into enemies, causing them to lose five hit points. Other than that, the move has absolutely no practical use in battle at all.

TOP TEN
BEST-SELLING *POKÉMON* GAMES

Game	Sales
Pokémon Red/Green/Blue Version (1996) on Game Boy	31.37
Pokémon Gold/Silver Version (1999) on Game Boy	23.10
Pokémon Diamond/Pearl Version (2006) on DS	18.08
Pokémon Ruby/Sapphire Version (2002) on Game Boy Advance	15.85
Pokémon Black/White Version (2010) on DS	14.74
Pokémon Yellow Version: Special Pikachu Edition (1998) on Game Boy	14.64
Pokémon HeartGold/SoulSilver Version (2009) on DS	11.58
Pokémon FireRed/LeafGreen (2004) on Game Boy Advance	10.49
Pokémon Platinum Version (2008) on DS	7.54
Pokémon Black/White Version 2 (2008) on DS	6.78

Source: vgchartz.com, as of 9 August 2013 (figures in millions)

127

SHORTEST REIGN AS *POKÉMON* CHAMPION

Rubén Puig Lecegui (Spain, *left*) won the UK Master's Division at the *Pokémon* Videogame Championships on 3 March 2012 in Birmingham, UK, but held the title for just three days. He was disqualified following an investigation into an undisclosed "incident" in his hotel on the night of the final. "We found that unacceptable behaviour did take place, and have taken the appropriate steps," said the brand managers. The title was awarded to the runner-up, 19-year-old Ben Kyriakou (UK).

BEST-SELLING RPG SERIES

As of 9 August 2013, *Pokémon* had reached total sales of 218 million units. The game is so popular that when a protein used in the rapid transmission of visual information to the brain was identified in 2008, Japanese biologists named it "pikachurin", after fast-moving Pikachu.

The popularity of the *Pokémon* series is a significant part of Nintendo becoming the **most successful videogame publisher**, with more than 1.64 billion units sold of 1,237 titles across all platforms.

THE ELDER SCROLLS

LOWDOWN

PUBLISHER:
Bethesda
DEVELOPER:
Bethesda
DEBUT:
1994

The epic, fantasy open world of the *Elder Scrolls* series (1994–present) mostly takes place on the empire continent of Tamriel, where the player has a number of spells to cast and quests to fulfil. *The Elder Scrolls Online*, an MMORPG that has been in development for five years, is scheduled for release in spring 2014.

128

NAME THE GAME
Sporting a red bow and a diamond ring, Birdo appears in various editions of which platform series?

LEAST COMPLETED STEAM ACHIEVEMENT IN *THE ELDER SCROLLS V: SKYRIM*

The PC version of *The Elder Scrolls V: Skyrim* (2011) is one of the most popular titles on Steam, but as of 22 July 2013, only 0.8% of its tens of thousands of players have earned the "Dragonrider" achievement awarded for taming and riding five dragons. By contrast, 89.6% of players earned the "Unbound" achievement for completing the game's opening sequence, which is the **most completed Steam achievement in** *The Elder Scrolls V*.

TIP-OFF

Looking for a spooky Skyrim secret? If you're lucky, you may see the ghostly headless horseman who roams Skyrim's roads at night. Follow this sinister but harmless spectre and he'll lead you to Hamvir's Rest, a Nordic ruin containing a master chest full of loot!

MOST POPULAR MOD FOR *THE ELDER SCROLLS V: SKYRIM*

With 8,091,136 views and 6,838,833 total downloads on the Skyrim Nexus site as of 22 July 2013, the Skyrim HD 2K Textures pack – created by 19-year-old user "NebuLa" for the PC version of the game – is by far the most popular user-created modification. The pack enhances the resolution and detail of the graphics by up to eight times as much as the official HD texture DLC created by Bethesda.

SKYRIM HD
BY NEBULA

LARGEST GAME GUIDE

On 4 June 2013, Prima Games released the updated *Legendary Collector's Edition* of its official guidebook for *The Elder Scrolls V: Skyrim*. The revised book now contains an enormous 1,120 pages, 785,000 words and 4,025 screenshots, detailing some 350 quests, 500 monsters and 2,000 items. All told, the guide weighs in at 2.7 kg (5 lb 15 oz).

LARGEST PLAYABLE AREA IN AN RPG

The Elder Scrolls II: Daggerfall, released in 1996, used a randomly generated map that covered a virtual 487,000 km^2 (188,000 miles^2) of terrain – that's twice the size of the UK, considerably bigger than California and the largest fixed-size map of the entire series. It contained 15,000 towns and dungeons, and 750,000 non-player characters.

MOST POWERFUL ENEMY IN *THE ELDER SCROLLS V: SKYRIM*

When the *Dragonborn* downloadable content first expanded the world of *Skyrim* on 4 December 2012, it also introduced a terrifying new foe: the Ebony Warrior, the most powerful enemy in the game. Appearing only when the player has reached Level 81 or higher, the vicious Ebony Warrior can use Dragon Shouts (a form of magic), is 50% resistant to fire, frost and shock, has the ability to paralyze the player for up to 15 seconds, and uses a sword that drains the player's health and refills his own.

FIRST MULTIPLAYER *ELDER SCROLLS* GAME

Originally intended as an expansion pack for *The Elder Scrolls II: Daggerfall*, the 1997 PC game *An Elder Scrolls Legend: Battlespire* was the first in the series to offer both a co-operative story mode and team-based competitive multiplayer modes. The game is set in a tower used to train Battlemages, and pits players against the sinister Mehrunes Dagon, the Daedric Prince of Destruction, Change, Revolution, Energy and Ambition.

TOP TEN — MOST CRITICALLY ACCLAIMED FIRST-PERSON RPGs

Game	Score
The Elder Scrolls V: Skyrim (Bethesda, 2011) on Xbox 360	95.15%
The Elder Scrolls IV: Oblivion (Bethesda, 2006) on Xbox 360	93.85%
The Elder Scrolls IV: Oblivion (Bethesda, 2006) on PC	93.29%
The Elder Scrolls IV: Oblivion (Bethesda, 2006) on PS3	92.98%
Fallout 3 (Bethesda, 2008) on Xbox 360	92.85%
Fallout 3 (Bethesda, 2008) on PC	90.85%
Fallout 3 (Bethesda, 2008) on PS3	90.52%
The Elder Scrolls III: Morrowind – Game of the Year Edition (Bethesda, 2003) on Xbox 360	89.90%
The Elder Scrolls III: Morrowind (Bethesda, 2002) on PC	89.18%
The Elder Scrolls IV: Shivering Isles (Bethesda, 2007) on Xbox 360	87.62%

Source: gamerankings.com, as of 22 July 2013

LOWDOWN

PUBLISHER:
Activision
DEVELOPER:
Toys for Bob
DEBUT:
2011

These innovative games work by placing a *Skylanders* figure on the Portal of Power peripheral, which turns the toys into in-game heroes. Latest title *Skylanders: Swap Force* is scheduled for autumn 2013. *Skylanders* may be a relatively new franchise, but one of its stars, Spyro the Dragon, has featured in games since the 1990s and is one of three characters in the *Skylanders: Spyro's Adventure* starter pack.

130

BEST-SELLING *SKYLANDERS* TOY

Hammer-wielding Crusher from *Skylanders: Giants* (2012) is the most popular *Skylander*, based on UK toy sales rankings and not including starter figures packaged with the games. The most popular character packed with a game is Tree Rex, also from *Skylanders: Giants*. More than 6 million *Skylanders* figures were sold in the UK alone during 2012. As of August 2013, more than 100 million *Skylanders* figures and playsets have been sold around the globe.

Since the launch of *Skylanders: Spyro's Adventure* in 2011, the series has earned more than $1.5 billion (£950 million).

NAME THE GAME
His real name is Bi-Han, but this fighter has also been called Sub-Zero and Noob Saibot.

RAREST *SKYLANDERS* FIGURES

Activision created 600 specially marked *Skylanders* figures to promote the launch of debut title *Skylanders: Spyro's Adventure* at E3 2011. Lucky media recipients were offered a standard Spyro, Gill Grunt or Trigger Happy figure, each of which came in a package that invited the owner to "Bring me to life at the Activision E3 Booth". Packaged versions have sold for $700 (£450) each on eBay.

MOST VIEWED *SKYLANDERS* VIDEO

With 12,030,136 views as of 20 August 2013, the "Tall Tales" television trailer for *Skylanders: Giants* is the most popular *Skylanders* video on YouTube. Uploaded by Activision in October 2012, the 1-min 5-sec CGI spot introduces fans to the *Skylanders: Spyro's Adventure* sequel and its new, super-sized characters. The extended version of the trailer, which runs for 2 min 17 sec, proved less popular, with total views of "just" 5,961,451.

FIRST ONLINE GAME TO USE TOY FIGURES AS PLAYABLE CHARACTERS

Skylanders: Universe, which was originally named *Skylanders: Spyro's Universe*, was an online multiplayer game that launched in October 2011 and was closed down in April 2013 having never left its beta stage. But it did leave its mark on browser gaming: players could plug their Portal of Power into a USB port to unlock new characters in the online world.

TOY MEETS WORLD

As of August 2013, *Skylanders* was the **best-selling videogame toy line**, selling more than 100 million units. A quarter of all videogame accessories sold in the UK in 2012 were *Skylanders* toys. Globally, the figures have outsold toy brands such as *Transformers*. The *Skylanders* toys are priced between £8.99 and £99.99 ($14–$156).

BEST-SELLING GAMES FEATURING SPYRO

Spyro the Dragon (Insomniac Games, 1998)	5.00
Skylanders: Spyro's Adventure (Toys for Bob, 2011)	4.64
Skylanders: Giants (Toys for Bob, 2011)	4.13
Spyro: Year of the Dragon (Insomniac Games, 2000)	3.71
Spyro 2: Ripto's Rage! (Insomniac Games, 1999)	3.52
Spyro: Enter the Dragonfly (Check Six Games, 2002)	2.68
Spyro: Season of Ice (Digital Eclipse, 2001)	2.23
The Legend of Spyro: Dawn of the Dragon (Étranges Libellules, 2008)	2.01
Spyro: A Hero's Tail (Eurocom, 2004)	1.07
The Legend of Spyro: The Eternal Night (Amaze Entertainment, 2007)	0.96

Source: vgchartz.com, as of 17 August 2013 (figures in millions)

LARGEST SKYLANDER

As of 20 August 2013, the largest Skylander is a "life-sized" statue of Tree Rex, which tours the world and appears at exhibitions and trade fairs. Standing 315 cm (10 ft 4 in) tall, the statue was carved from polystyrene by UK-based model company Sculpture Studios and is an exact scale replica of the *Skylanders: Giants* figure, right down to eyes that light up. Fortunately, *this* version of Tree Rex cannot crush his opponents.

FINAL FANTASY

132

LOWDOWN

PUBLISHER:
Square/Square Enix
DEVELOPER:
Square/Square Enix
DEBUT:
1987

The 1987 game that started it all was a turn-based RPG in which the player controlled four characters who each had to quest for crystals to restore balance to the world. But a dark foe was out to stop them... The franchise has evolved over the years and has become a legend among RPG fans.

NAME THE GAME
Dutch van der Linde said: "We all make mistakes, John".

LARGEST REPLICA WEAPON FROM A GAME

In May 2013, Hollywood movie armourer Tony Swatton created a life-sized version of the Buster Sword – a devastatingly accurate weapon belonging to Cloud Strife that was first seen in *Final Fantasy VII*. The real version is appropriately huge: 259 cm (8 ft 6 in) in length, with a blade 29 cm (11.4 in) wide and a weight of 21.6 kg (47 lb).

TIP-OFF

In *Final Fantasy XIII-2* (2011), don't ignore your little Moogle pal, Mog. He is great at detecting hidden items, so if you see the bulb on his head starts to glow or hear him chattering, that means something useful is nearby. Mog will lead you to it.

MOST PROLIFIC RPG SERIES

With 58 individual titles including spin-offs, *Final Fantasy* is easily the most prolific RPG series. From the 2009 entry in the series, *Final Fantasy XIII*, the cold and determined main character Lightning is pictured right. *Final Fantasy VII* (1997) is the **best-selling *Final Fantasy* game**, with sales of 9.72 million as of 3 July 2013. It also has the **best-selling game soundtrack**, with 175,000 copies sold.

TOP TEN

MOST CRITICALLY ACCLAIMED *FINAL FANTASY* GAMES

Game	%
Final Fantasy IX (Square, 2000) on PlayStation	93.32%
Final Fantasy VII (Square, 1997) on PlayStation	92.35%
Final Fantasy X (Square, 2001) on PS2	91.73%
Final Fantasy XII (Square Enix, 2006) on PS2	90.77%
Final Fantasy VI Advance (Tose, 2007) on Game Boy Advance	90.65%
Final Fantasy VIII (Square, 1999) on PlayStation	89.17%
Final Fantasy Tactics: The War of the Lions (Square Enix, 2007) on PSP	88.26%
Final Fantasy Tactics Advance (Square Enix, 2003) on Game Boy Advance	87.64%
Final Fantasy Chronicles (Tose, 2001) on PlayStation	86.70%
Final Fantasy X-2 (Square, 2003) on PS2	86.25%

Source: gamerankings.com, as of 3 July 2013

MOST POWERFUL FINAL FANTASY ATTACK

Anima (*right*), of *Final Fantasy X* (2001), has an oblivion overdrive attack with a 16-hit combo of 1,599,984 HP damage.

The **most powerful *Final Fantasy* monster** is Yiazmat, from *Final Fantasy XII* (2006), with 50 million HP.

In *Final Fantasy VII*, Safer Sephiroth's supernova attack starts a cutscene lasting 2 min 16 sec, the **longest game attack animation**.

The Pandemonium Warden is the **toughest enemy in *Final Fantasy***, from *Final Fantasy XI* (2002). After teams of gamers battled it for hours, Square Enix released an update with reduced abilities.

MOST PROLIFIC RPG PRODUCER

Hironobu Sakaguchi (Japan) was the creator of *Final Fantasy* and had produced and directed 40 RPG titles as of 3 July 2013, including *Final Fantasy XII* (*below*). Each game requires a huge crew, with the **largest development team on a Japanese RPG** being a total of 300 for *Final Fantasy XIII* (2009).

FASTEST COMPLETION OF *FINAL FANTASY IV*

On 24 May 2013, Andrew Melnyk (Canada) set a single-segment time of 3 hr 21 min. The **fastest completion of *Final Fantasy XII*** on PS2 is 6 hr 35 min 17 sec, set on 29 July 2012 by William "Youkai" Welch (USA).

FIRST ALL-FEMALE RPG CAST

PS2 game *Final Fantasy X-2* (2003) revolves around three playable characters: Yuna and Rikku from *Final Fantasy X* and newcomer Paine. The game is set for re-release in HD in 2013. The **first playable female character in a videogame** starred in *Ms. PAC-Man* (Bally/Midway, 1981). Ms. PAC-Man took the same form as the original PAC-Man, with the addition of a hair bow and lipstick.

BOOST

CHOC-O-BLOCK

The chicken-like Chocobo (*below*) is the **most prolific *Final Fantasy* creature**. First seen in *Final Fantasy II* in 1988, it had appeared in 55 games by 12 June 2013. As of October 2012, Bahamut was the **most prolific boss in an RPG**: 27 of his 32 appearances were in *Final Fantasy*.

LOWDOWN

Role-playing games have come a long way since the **first RPG videogame**, *dnd* (Gary Whisenhunt and Ray Wood) – a text-derived game from 1974, based on pencil-and-dice *Dungeons & Dragons*. Today you can roam sumptuous fantasy worlds as anything from a serf to a fully fledged hero. The **longest-running RPG series** is *Ultima* (various developers), which began in 1981 and reached iOS in August 2013. In 1997 it also became an MMORPG with *Ultima Online* (Origin/EA).

134

NAME THE GAME
Barry Bones costs 15,000 coins; win this back by activating his power-up for extra coins.

△

FASTEST-SELLING PC VIDEOGAME

Diablo III (Blizzard, 2012) sold 3.5 million copies in its first 24 hours, and a further 1.2 million players got the game for free as part of a promotion. Just 37 days after the game's launch, the **first completion of *Diablo III* on "Hardcore Inferno" mode** was set by "Kripparrian" (Canada) and "Krippi" (USA), on 19 June 2012.

The **fastest time to reach level 60 in *Diablo III*** was achieved by "Djhunterx" (Sweden), who exploited gameplay to raise his character level in 15 minutes of logged-in playing by 9 October 2012.

FASTEST COMPLETION OF *DARK SOULS*

On 15 April 2013, famously difficult Japanese RPG *Dark Souls* (From Software, 2011) was finished in 26 min 58 sec by gamer "Treynquil", who took a route based on that of previous record holder "Thanatos".

The **fastest time to beat *Dark Souls'* Asylum Demon** is 11 seconds by Steven Craig Epperson (USA) in Florida, USA, on 24 April 2012.

BOOST

DAZZLING DIABLO

The **fastest completion of *Diablo*** (Blizzard, 1996) is a blistering glitched, segmented run by Maciej "Groobo" Maselewski (Poland) of 3 min 12 sec on 16 January 2009. Sören "FraGFroG" Heinrich holds two records on Blizzard's 2001 sequel: the **fastest completion of *Diablo II: Lord of Destruction* as the Assassin** in 58 min 52 sec and even quicker **as the Assassin with deaths** in 58 min 28 sec, both on 11 October 2009. On 12 November 2009, Ricky "LeWoVoc" Mitchell achieved the **fastest completion of *Diablo II: Lord of Destruction* as the Druid** in 1 hr 11 min 43 sec, while it took Alan "Siyko" Burnett longer **as the Sorceress (100% time)** in 4 hr 22 min on 14 November 2008.

MOST STATEMENTS BY CONSUMER BODIES ON A GAME ENDING

The UK's Advertising Standards Authority, the US Better Business Bureau and the US Federal Trade Commission each commented on the conclusion of BioWare's *Mass Effect 3* (2012) after a fan backlash.

It had started so well: the game allowed more than 1,000 decisions to be imported from the first two games in the series, affecting player abilities and how the new game turned out – the **most advanced character import system**. By contrast, it was felt that the trilogy's end scenes were disappointing and contradicted various aspects of the series narrative.

Although fan complaints weren't upheld, BioWare did release a free, extended version of the finale to address them: the **first downloadable alternative videogame ending**.

FASTEST-SELLING MOBILE RPG

Released for iOS on 9 December 2010, *Infinity Blade* (Chair Entertainment/Epic Games) clocked up 271,424 users in four days, each paying $5.99 (£3.87) – a gross of $1.6 million (£1 million). Epic had ported its game engine from PCs to make this the **first mobile game to use the Unreal Engine 3**.

MOST EXPENSIVE RPG

In January 2012, a sealed and certified mint-condition US copy of the 1995 SNES role-playing game *EarthBound* (Ape/HAL Laboratory) sold in an online auction for $4,700 (£2,900).

Nintendo didn't publish the game on other platforms until 20 June 2003, when it was released on Game Boy Advance, and in March 2013 it went on sale on the Wii U virtual console – some five years after it had first been announced.

TOP TEN — MOST CRITICALLY ACCLAIMED RPGs

Mass Effect 2 (BioWare/EA, 2010) on Xbox 360	95.77%
The Elder Scrolls V: Skyrim (Bethesda, 2011) on Xbox 360	95.15%
Mass Effect 2 (BioWare/EA, 2010) on PC	94.52%
Star Wars: Knights of the Old Republic (BioWare/ LucasArts, 2003) on Xbox	94.21%
Persona 4: Golden (Atlus, 2012) on PS Vita	94.16%
Baldur's Gate II: Shadows of Amn (BioWare, 2000) on PC	93.97%
The Elder Scrolls IV: Oblivion (Bethesda, 2006) on Xbox 360	93.85%
Final Fantasy IX (Square, 2000) on PlayStation	93.32%
The Elder Scrolls IV: Oblivion (Bethesda, 2006) on PC	93.29%
Star Wars: Knights of the Old Republic (BioWare/ LucasArts, 2003) on PC	93.19%

Source: gamerankings.com, as of 20 August 2013

FIRST PUBLIC AUTHORITY-FUNDED GAME

The US state of Rhode Island invested a whopping $75 million ($48 million) in developer 38 Studios for the open-world RPG *Kingdoms of Amalur: Reckoning* (2012). The investment was made in a bid to lure Curt Schilling, head of 38 Studios and a former Major League Baseball player, to set up his company in Rhode Island.

WORST-RATED RPG

Metal Dungeon (Panther Software, 2002) on the Xbox had a GameRankings score of 43.63% as of 20 August 2012.

135

GAMING IN SCIENCE

Videogames are not just for fun. Simulators prepare soldiers for battle or replicate life itself while games are developed to research space exploration. David Hawksett finds out how gaming and science influence each other.

SPORT AND HEALTH

Gaming: *Wii Sports* and *Wii Fit* (Nintendo, 2006 and 2007) are the two most popular games that allow players at home to experience a realistic simulation of physical activity.

Science: In recuperation, *Wii Sports* and *Fit* help victims of strokes and brain injuries and patients in intensive care to recover as part of their physical therapy. Focusing on stamina and balance, therapists report that games and mini-games such as *Golf* coax patients into movement that can be tedious when done traditionally. *SnowWorld* (Drs David Patterson and Hunter Hoffman, University of Washington) is designed for patients with extreme pain, such as from burns or war injuries. Players throw snowballs at penguins to a soothing soundtrack in a distraction that can be more effective than morphine.

MILITARY

Gaming: *Operation Flashpoint: Cold War Crisis* (Bohemia Interactive, 2001) is a first-person military sim boasting realistic physics and massive arenas for multiplayer combat.

Science: A reworked edition of the game, *VBS1* (*Virtual Battlespace Systems 1*; Bohemia Interactive Australia, 2001), is used to train real soldiers. Its 2007 sequel counts NATO, the UK Ministry of Defence, the US Secret Service and the armed forces of France, Canada, Finland, Australia and New Zealand among its user base. The trainer supports battles in arenas over 10,000 km^2 (3,861 miles^2) in size and analyzes detail down to the ballistic path of each bullet.

BIOCHEMISTRY

Gaming: Online puzzler *Foldit* (University of Washington, 2008) challenges players to manipulate the structure of proteins by folding them using special tools.

Science: The best *Foldit* results are analyzed by scientists. In 2011 players solved a 15-year-old scientific problem when they helped to decode the Mason-Pfizer virus, which causes AIDS-like immune deficiency in monkeys.

ASTROPHYSICS

Gaming: *Kerbal Space Program* (Squad, alpha version) is an open-world game in which players build rockets and spacecraft to explore the Kerbal solar system, a fictionalized version of our home system. Players perform spacewalks with the little green humanoid Kerbals and can recreate historical endeavours such as the *Apollo* missions.

Science: In August 2013 it was reported that staff at NASA's Jet Propulsion Laboratory had been playing *Kerbal*. Scientist Douglas Ellison said that he had tried to use the method employed by NASA's *Curiosity* rover on Mars to land on the equivalent planet, "and I have killed many Kerbals along the way". He was joined in gaming by Danish aerospace scientists at Copenhagen Suborbitals.

Match This Pattern

Pattern value
-468

0%

BIOTECHNOLOGY

Gaming: Facebook games encourage casual multiplay on a massive scale and scientists are tapping into this base to create "citizen science". *Fraxinus* (Team Cooper/The Sainsbury Laboratory, *right*) on Facebook presents users with patterns of colours representing DNA. They play with data collected by scientists researching ash dieback, a disease affecting ash trees. *EteRNA* (Carnegie Mellon and Stanford Universities, *below right*) is another example of a multiplayer browser game, the goal of which is to create RNA molecules in preset shapes. Shapes are voted on by other players for the chance to be synthesized in a real laboratory.

Science: *Fraxinus* and *EteRNA* may connect players directly with science, but you can't get more cutting edge than a game that has living specimens in it. Stanford physicist Ingmar Riedel-Kruse uses organisms too simple to feel pain or sensation in his work. Player actions influence the behaviour of single cells such as paramecia in primitive games, among them *PAC-Mecium*, *Biotic Pinball* and *Pond Pong*. Riedel-Kruse hopes to get more young people interested in biomedical research through his team's games.

MMORPGS

LARGEST VIDEOGAME SPACE BATTLE

This truly epic space conflict was staged in the star system of 6VDT in *EVE Online* (CCP Games, 2003) on 28 July 2013. At its peak, 4,070 pilots fought in their ships for control of the system. Game time was slowed down by 90% to ensure that the servers could work out who was shooting at who without lag. More than 2,900 ships – bought with in-game currency that can be paid for with real money – were destroyed. This cost players a total of £15,000 ($24,000). Pictured here is the view of the battle as seen by players.

Selected Item
6VDT-H V - 6VDThanie G
Distance: 25 km

Overview (fight)
Default | fight | util | salvage

Distance	Name
70 km	6VDT-H V -
22 km	Waggin
64 km	Khroam
35 km	Shotao
41 km	buryyou
17 km	Sona Dulla
28 km	imayen
78 km	Aefolatt Amo
34 km	Pittsburgh298
71 km	Fenrir Vice
72 km	Rachea
48 km	Gaius Duilius
32 km	Hal Lee
31 km	Aryth
39 km	Atrum Venefi
62 km	xPredat0rz
79 km	Farseer Zeïre
35 km	Mukun
58 km	Hentai-san D
37 km	juggzy
65 km	theo hendrix
503 km	z3phyria
23 km	Enola Naari
19 km	Vald Tegor
84 km	Leeroy Hawke
75 km	Myrddin Calyx
69 km	DrNo8910

Fleet (240 Members) / Wing 2 / Squad 2
My Fleet | History | Fleet Finder
Filters
Broadcast History ▾   Clear History

20:05:58 - Unorthodox Snake: Warp 6VDT-H
20:05:55 - Madz Negro: Warp 6VDT-H V - 6
20:05:26 - Cy Ber: Warp 6VDT-H V - 6VDTh
20:00:35 - Sarah Nahrnid: Align 6VDT-H V -
20:00:30 - RustyNDH: Align 6VDT-H V - 6VD
19:58:56 - Che eHobie: Align 6VDT-H VIII
19:17:05 - Target Internet Explorer 7 (Blackb
19:09:58 - Target Cy Ber (Legion)
18:46:00 - Your fleet has added an advert

Thorax (Proteus) - captain dirka TEST taka (Bambation)

⚡ Unorthodox Snake: Warp 6VDT-H V - 6 ⌃
Watch List [1]
Esildra

ACTIVE
VDThanie Get Out
km

CONTENTS

WORLD OF WARCRAFT

LOWDOWN

PUBLISHER:
Blizzard
DEVELOPER:
Blizzard
DEBUT:
2004

Players take on the role of fantasy characters to explore and interact in an online world of mystery, magic and new quests made available through expansion packs.

NAME THE GAME
Architect Ethan Mars has his life turned upside-down with the death of one son and the kidnapping of the other.

MOST SUCCESSFUL DEVELOPER BY SUBSCRIPTION

Activision Blizzard reported net revenues of $1.23 billion (£760 million) for 2012. Its most popular title is *World of Warcraft*, with gamers not only paying a subscription but buying extra content.

MOST CRITICALLY ACCLAIMED MMORPG

World of Warcraft: Wrath of the Lich King (2008) on the PC had a rating on GameRankings of 92.68% as of 10 July 2013. *Cataclysm*, the third expansion pack, sold more than 3.3 million on its first day, 7 December 2010, the **fastest-selling MMORPG**. It triggered a race among guilds to kill as many bosses for the first time as possible. DREAM Paragon, a guild of players from Finland, was the first to eliminate 14 out of 55, the **most boss kills in *World of Warcraft: Cataclysm***.

TOP TEN — MOST VIEWED VIDEOS ON THE *WORLD OF WARCRAFT* CHANNEL

Video	Views
"World of Warcraft: Cataclysm Cinematic Trailer", 17 October 2010	15,999,787
"World of Warcraft: Mists of Pandaria Cinematic Trailer", 16 August 2012	12,241,239
"World of Warcraft: Mists of Pandaria Preview Trailer", 20 October 2011	5,966,522
"World of Warcraft: Mists of Pandaria 'Best Expansion' TV Commercial", 19 November 2012	4,531,992
"World of Warcraft: Wrath of the Lich King Cinematic Trailer", 22 January 2010	3,498,815
"Fall of the Lich King Ending", 6 May 2011	2,278,186
"World of Warcraft: Mists of Pandaria TV Spot #1", 9 September 2012	2,188,469
"Cataclysm - Patch 4.2: Rage of the Firelands", 14 June 2011	2,049,620
"World of Warcraft: Mists of Pandaria TV Spot #2", 9 September 2012	1,696,073
"World of Warcraft - 8 Year Anniversary", 19 November 2012	1,544,726

Source: youtube.com/worldofwarcraft, as of 12 August 2013

FIRST PLAYER TO REACH LEVEL 90

A Night Elf Druid called Fs (*left*) climbed to the level 90 cap brought in with *Mists of Pandaria* in 4 hours on 25 September 2012. The **first person to complete all the achievements in *World of Warcraft*** was Little Gray (Chinese Taipei), who hit 986 out of 986 on 27 November 2009. He did 7.25 billion points of damage and completed 5,906 quests, averaging 14 quests a day.

DRINKING WITH THE ENEMY

Once a year, the warring factions of the Horde and the Alliance put down their arms and get together for Brewfest, the **largest virtual beer festival** – a virtual homage to Oktoberfest in Bavaria, Germany, with an event-only boss, Coren Direbrew. Like its real-world counterpart, this features the best (virtual) beers. The 2012 event included beer goggles that made all Alliance players look like gnomes and Hordes look like orcs... Hic!

MOST POPULAR SUBSCRIPTION GAME

World of Warcraft had 8.3 million players as of 9 May 2013. This was a drop from its 2010 peak of 12 million, but remains the most for any game at a time when the industry is switching to free-to-play models. Yet even with new content such as 2012's *Mists of Pandaria* (*below*), 1.3 million players left between the end of December 2012 and 31 March 2013 – a drop of 14% and the **greatest subscriber decline for an MMORPG**.

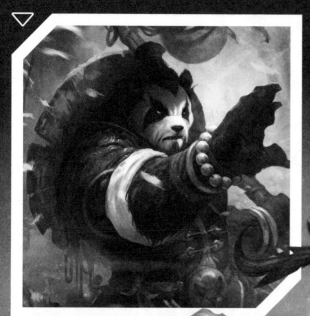

FIRST GAMER ELECTED AS A US STATE SENATOR

When social worker and gamer Colleen Lachowicz (USA) ran for Senator of Maine in November 2012, her political opponents attempted to use her love of *World of Warcraft* against her (*below*). But their campaign backfired and Colleen, who played a level-85 orc rogue named Santiaga, won the election. But not all gamers are so balanced in their playing. In October 2005, gamer Snowly (China) died of fatigue after a three-day, non-stop *World of Warcraft* marathon. Over 100 gamers attended a service in an in-game cathedral, the **most people at a virtual funeral**.

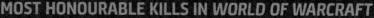

COLLEEN LACHOWICZ SPENDS HUNDREDS OF HOURS PLAYING IN HER ONLINE WORLD AZEROTH, AS AN ORC ASSASSINATION ROGUE NAMED SANTIAGA.

MOST HONOURABLE KILLS IN *WORLD OF WARCRAFT*

An honourable kill is that of a player from an opposing faction who is within 10 levels of your own level. "Fartzwrgoben", a rogue character, amassed 1.81 million such kills as of 10 July 2013. It's a feat that would not impress a gamer called Irenic, who became the **first player to reach level 90 in *World of Warcraft* without a kill** on 12 October 2012. The record took patience and 12 days 4 hr 33 sec of game time to achieve. Irenic explored and carried on professions such as archaeology to build up experience points.

RUNESCAPE

PUBLISHER:
Jagex
DEVELOPER:
Jagex
DEBUT:
2001

Fantasy MMORPG
RuneScape is set
in the medieval
fantasy realm
of Gielinor, a
world filled with
monsters, magic
and mini-games.
Experience points
are gained by
using the 25 in-
game skills, such
as attack, defence
and woodcutting.
In July 2012, *Forbes*
said *RuneScape*
had more than
200 million player
accounts, making
it the **MMORPG
with most user
accounts**.

142

MOST COMPLEX HTML5 CODE IN A GAME

RuneScape comprises 152,472 lines of
HTML5 code and a further 421,196 lines of
client-side-scripting (computer programs
executed by the user's browser). Little
wonder, then, that the working time spent
developing and maintaining *RuneScape*
totals more than 6,700,000 hours. The HTML5
platform is becoming increasingly popular
with developers. HTML5 titles on web
browsers include *Angry Birds* for Chrome
(Rovio, 2011) and *The World's Biggest
PAC-Man* (Soap Creative, 2011).

NAME THE GAME
Quicker than a Jumbo
Jet, the Mighty Eagle
is the top bird.

HIGHEST-RANKED RUNESCAPE CLAN

Based on total "XP" gained, the Maxed clan is at the
top of the *RuneScape* rankings of 118,645 player
clans. Its 478 members had a combined total of
86,194,841,037 XP as of 19 September 2013. XP is
accumulated through successfully completing
training skills, quests, "Distraction and Diversion"
activities such as Penguin Hide and Seek, and
assorted other mini-games. If you fancy joining
Maxed, you'll need 99 in all skills.

GREATEST AGGREGATE TIME PLAYING AN MMORPG

RuneScape players had amassed 443 billion minutes of
game time between them, as of July 2012. That works
out at an average of 36.9 hours of game time on every
registered account – roughly the same number of hours
accumulated in the standard 9-to-5 working week. To put
the 443 billion figure into perspective, if one *RuneScape*
player had played the game for that long, they would
have started in 840,000 BC.

MOST UPDATED MMORPG

RuneScape is the most updated MMORPG ever, with a grand total of 912 content updates as of 19 June 2013, according to Jagex. An average 200 new skills, quests, activities and gameplay features are added to *RuneScape* every year.

Jagex has also researched the **most used term in *RuneScape*** and found it to be "lol". This is said an average of 6,048,000 times every week. The *RuneScape* community posts an average of 27,000 posts every 24 hours on the game's forums – the **most game-related forum posts per day**.

MOST FISH IN A GAME

More than 8 billion fish were caught by *RuneScape* players in 2012. Jagex claims that, laid head to tail, this number of fish would fit around the Earth's circumference 20 times. Species include salmon, trout and herring. Most of the fish in the game can be caught using various methods with the Fishing skill, before being turned into a tasty dinner with the Cooking skill.

TIP-OFF

Are you considering selling an item? It's always a good idea to check the item's price history to see whether or not it has the potential to make you more gold at a later date or if now is the right time to try to shift it.

	CLANS	FACTION	SEA

OVERALL ▼   Categories ▼

View: **All** | Friends | Your Rank

Page 1/22362   Next ▶

RANK	CHARACTER NAME	LEVEL	XP
1	SUOMI	2,496	5,000,000,000
2	Jake	2,496	4,513,985,349
3	Jdelacroix	2,496	4,270,441,837

FIRST *RUNESCAPE* PLAYER TO "MAX OUT" XP

Gamer "S U O M I" was the first player to reach the maximum attainable XP in *RuneScape* – 5 billion – on 18 March 2013. He averaged a gain of 4 million XP every day. Due to a glitch with the way numbers were stored, "S U O M I" dropped from 1st to 1,955th position on 26 May 2012 but the situation was quickly rectified by Jagex. Suomi means Finland in Finnish, and as of 19 August 2013 his "total level" was 2,496.

TOP TEN — HIGHEST XP ON *RUNESCAPE*

Character	XP
SUOMI	5,000,000,000
Jake	4,517,657,355
Jdelacroix	4,275,340,138
Drumgun	4,269,411,135
Elvis	3,828,644,622
Dragonseance	3,729,013,066
Elias	3,724,695,109
AlmostLost	3,566,450,265
Paperbag	3,562,714,045
Geel	3,430,741,896

Source: *RuneScape* rankings, as of 19 August 2013

LOWDOWN

Long considered the province of PC gamers, MMOs of all genres – not just RPGs – are increasing their share of console players, with the eighth generation promising plenty of MMOpportunity. At Gamescom 2013, Sony announced *War Thunder* (Gaijin Entertainment), a free-to-play combat flight sim MMO that joins *Planetside 2* and *DC Universe Online* (both Sony) as planned launch titles for the PS4 in November 2013.

144

NAME THE GAME Vampire-hunter Simon Belmont is a deadly threat to archenemy Dracula.

MOST CONCURRENT PLAYERS ON AN MMO BEAT-'EM-UP

On 12 June 2013, the Chinese server of monster-brawler *Dungeon Fighter Online* (NeoPle, 2005) witnessed a total of 3 million concurrent players. Bizarrely, the very next day, publisher Nexon closed the US version of the game after announcing their decision in April of the same year. In a move that shocked players, Nexon said that the game "was not able to grow beyond its very special and proud core following".

FIRST GAME TO FEATURE A LICENSED BANK

Swedish MMORPG *Entropia Universe* (MindArk, 2003) became the first game with its own built-in bank in March 2009, when its application for a banking licence was approved by the Swedish Financial Supervisory Authority. As a result, the game's currency, Project Entropia Dollars (PED), has a real-world value on the stock exchange fixed to the US dollar at a rate of 10 PED per $1, as of August 2013.

FIRST MMO-BASED TV SHOW

Sci-fi shooter *Defiance* (Trion Worlds, 2013) was the first MMO to tie in to a TV show. Sharing the same characters, locations and weapons as the game, *Defiance* the TV show launched on 2 April 2013, around a week after the game. The show is broadcast by TV channel Syfy (formerly Sci-Fi Channel), who renewed it for a second season to be broadcast in 2014. Both the game and TV show are set on Earth in the year 2046. The science-fiction trail was blazed by **first sci-fi MMORPG** and **first console MMORPG** *Phantasy Star Online* (Sonic Team), released for the SEGA Dreamcast on 21 December 2000.

BO:OM!

Despite shaky initial reviews, sci-fi space sim *EVE Online* (CCP Games, 2003) garnered praise for its gigantic, meticulously detailed galaxy. Hilmar Pétursson CEO of CCP, attributes the game's success to its element of danger. In February 2013, CCP announced the game had more than 500,000 subscribers.

LONGEST-RUNNING MMORPG

Before *World of Warcraft* (Blizzard, 2004), *EVE Online* (CCP Games, 2003) and *EverQuest* (Sony, 1999), there was *Ultima Online* (Origin Systems, *below*). The fantasy MMORPG began life on 24 September 1997 and is still going strong 16 years later, as of 28 August 2013. *Ultima Online* was also the **first MMORPG with 100,000 players**, an achievement that it set in December 1998.

TOP TEN — MOST CRITICALLY ACCLAIMED MMORPGs

Game	Rating
World of Warcraft (Blizzard, 2004) on PC	91.89%
Guild Wars 2 (ArenaNet, 2012) on PC	90.20%
Dark Age of Camelot (Mythic Entertainment, 2001) on PC	88.08%
EverQuest (Sony, 1999) on PC	87.68%
The Lord of the Rings Online: Shadows of Angmar (Turbine, Inc., 2007) on PC	86.73%
City of Heroes (Cryptic Studios, 2004) on PC	85.66%
Rift (Trion Worlds, 2011) on PC	85.20%
Final Fantasy XI (Square, 2002) on PS2	85.13%
Warhammer Online: Age of Reckoning (Mythic Entertainment, 2008) on PC	84.81%
Star Wars: The Old Republic (BioWare, 2011) on PC	83.87%

Source: gamerankings.com, as of 28 August 2013 (list excludes expansions)

FIRST IN-GAME PIZZA DELIVERY SYSTEM

In February 2005, the developers of *EverQuest II* (Sony, 2004) added a pizza delivery system to the game. When players typed in "/pizza", they were linked directly to the Pizza Hut ordering website. This tasty function made *EverQuest II* the **first MMORPG to accept orders for real-world items**. While useful for long gaming sessions, the pizza played no part in the game, which is set in the fictional world of Norrath.

145

Hunger pains interrupting *your game?* Order *pizza while playing!* EVERQUEST II

WORST-RATED MMORPG

Final Fantasy XIV Online (Square Enix, 2010) on the PC had a GameRankings rating of 50.27% as of 25 June 2013. The GameSpot review lamented the "valleys of aimlessness and unfriendliness", stating that the game "isn't fun, it's work". Perhaps because of its critical panning, the game was relaunched as *Final Fantasy XIV: A Realm Reborn* in August 2013. Due to phenomenal demand, digital downloads were suspended after just one day in order to expand server capacity.

ACTING UP

Lights, camera, action? Try shaders, coders, motion-capture. As games become increasingly cinematic, actors are taking centre-stage. Matt Bradford goes behind the scenes...

Ares from *God of War: Ascension*

Wolverine from *Lego Marvel Super Heroes*

Videogame actors have become household names among gamers. Perhaps the most well-known star is Steve Blum (USA), pictured here, who is the **most prolific videogame voice actor** of all, with 333 credits as of 2 August 2013. As well as acting in *God of War: Ascension* (SCE Santa Monica Studio, 2013) and *Lego Marvel Super Heroes* (TT Games, 2013), Blum has lent his voice to an eclectic mix of games, including *Call of Duty: Black Ops II* (Treyarch, 2012), *Uncharted: Drake's Fortune* (SCE Santa Monica Studio, 2013), *Star Wars: The Old Republic* (BioWare, 2011) and *Crash Nitro Kart* (Vicarious Visions, 2003).

Blum's nuanced work is a far cry from videogame acting's rather rudimentary beginnings in the 1980s, with synthesized voice samples in arcade classics such as *Stratovox* (Sun Electronics, 1980), *Berzerk* (Stern Electronics, 1980) and *Sinistar* (Williams Electronics, 1982). The latter taunted players with the sinister, computer-generated phrases, "I am Sinistar!" and "Run, coward!". Later

🔊 MOVIE STARS GO GAMING

SAMUEL L JACKSON
On screen: *Snakes on a Plane, Pulp Fiction, The Avengers*
In game: *Grand Theft Auto* (Officer Frank Tenpenny, *left*), *Afro Samurai* (Afro Samurai)

RON PERLMAN
On screen: *Hellboy & Hellboy II: The Golden Army, Drive*
In game: *Marvel Super Hero Squad Online* (Abomination, *left*), *Fallout 3 & Fallout: New Vegas* (as narrator)

adventures such as *Gauntlet* (Atari Games, 1985) and even home-console title *Altered Beast* (Sega, 1988) further popularized the use of recorded phrases in videogames. As a result, snippets of real human voices began popping up in videogames across all platforms.

The 1990s saw game acting move on from single words and phrases into full in-game scripts. The survival-horror classic *Resident Evil* (Capcom, 1996) was one of the first major releases to thrust voice acting into the spotlight with its memorable, oddball one-liners. From that point forward, videogame actors became far more central to the games' style and direction.

Notable 1990s performances included David Hayter as Solid Snake in *Metal Gear Solid* (Konami, 1998), Shelley Blond as Lara Croft in *Tomb Raider* (Core Design, 1996) and Charles Martinet as the voice of Mario in *Mario's FUNdamentals* (Presage Software, 1995) and *Super Mario 64* (Nintendo EAD, 1996).

What's more, actors' roles during the development of the games

began to evolve beyond voicing with the advancement of motion-capture technology, which made it possible to detect and track physical movements and facial expressions via computers and cameras and reproduce them in games (*below*). Although the **first motion-capture animation in a videogame** was used to depict realistic human movement in *Prince of Persia* (Brøderbund, 1989), the practice of hiring an actor and filming their movements for videogame roles didn't truly gain traction until the mid-90s. *Soul Edge* (Project Soul, 1996) was the **first game to use passive optical system markers**, an early motion-capture technique, and *Actua Soccer* (Gremlin Interactive, 1995) was one of the first sports titles to use real-life soccer stars as motion-capture models.

As the technology improved throughout the 2000s, motion-capture became standard practice in AAA releases, and today – with games now multi-billion-dollar entertainment franchises – videogame acting by big-name Hollywood stars is the norm.

Aaron Staton being motion-captured for his role as Detective Cole Phelps in *L.A. Noire* (Team Bondi, 2011).

GLaDOS SPEAKS!
An interview with the voice of *Portal*

From opera singer to the voice behind *Half-Life*'s Overwatch, *Left 4 Dead*'s witch and *Portal*'s GLaDOS, Ellen McLain (USA) has breathed life into some of the most memorable characters in gaming.

■ **How did you get your start in voice acting?**
When we moved out to Seattle, John [Patrick Lowrie], who is also a videogame voice actor, got a voice demo. He eventually convinced me to get one too. Soon, I was getting auditions for Valve games like *Half-Life 2*, *Team Fortress 2* and then *Portal*. Overall, it was a natural step in my career. I knew how to create a character from my previous acting experience, and my ear was more attuned to creating different voices thanks to my singing.

■ **Can you describe a typical videogame acting session?**
Physically, you're in a recording room, but emotionally and intellectually there's a lot of things happening. You're putting yourself into the character, and letting that character get inside of you. When I was voicing GLaDOS, I would actually imagine that I was hanging from the facility's ceiling, or lying in a heap on the floor when I said things like, "Oh, it's you."

■ **What was your favourite acting scene in *Portal 2*?**
The end of the story where GLaDOS realizes that working with Chell has taught her a lot. I think when she says goodbye to Chell, there's some sadness there, and I think GLaDOS has really learned something about her own humanity. That was a wonderful turning point for her character.

■ **And you got a chance to sing...**
Singing Mike Morasky's "Cara Mia Addio" was so satisfying, because I actually got to sing some opera.

ELIZA DUSHKU
On screen: *Dollhouse*, *True Lies*, *Buffy the Vampire Slayer*, *Angel*, *Jay and Silent Bob Strike Back*
In game: *Wet* (Rubi Malone, left), *Saints Row 2* & *Saints Row: The Third* (Shaundi), *Fight Night Champion* (Megan McQueen), *Yakuza* (Yumi)

RACING

MOST EXPENSIVE VIDEOGAME

GRID 2: Mono Edition (Codemasters, 2013) is a special-edition game package. It includes one copy of the game itself, a driveable BAC (Briggs Automotive Company) Mono Supercar, a PS3, a branded race suit and a visit to the BAC factory. The game costs £125,000 ($189,555) and has just one unit on sale.

CONTENTS

LOWDOWN

While the term "racing games" covers all titles on four or two wheels, we categorize "driving games" as both hyper-realistic games (such as *Forza Motorsport* and *Gran Turismo*) and more serious pro racers. Kart racers may not have real-world cars, but they are competitive and a whole heap of fun. One name rules the karting genre: *Mario Kart* (Nintendo, 1992–present), whose 9 million sales as of July 2013 make it the **best-selling racing game series**.

NAME THE GAME
Born in Serkonos, Corvo Attano is a bodyguard turned assassin.

◁ **BEST-SELLING RACING GAME**

As of July 2013, *Mario Kart Wii* (Nintendo EAD, 2008) had sold over 33 million copies, extending its lead over the game in second place, *Mario Kart DS* (Nintendo EAD, 2005), by a gigantic 11 million copies. Its sales figure also makes it the **best-selling kart racing game**. *Mario Kart 7* (Nintendo EAD/Retro Studios, 2012) on the 3DS was the best-selling racing game of 2012, shifting 3,413,189 units. A staggering 8.14 million copies of the game have been sold since its release in December 2011.

BO:OM!

If imitation is the sincerest form of flattery, Mario Kart 64's (Nintendo, 1996) track designers must be delighted by the most-played track in *LittleBigPlanet Karting* (Sony, 2012). The level named "MooMoo Farm – MKART 64", created by gamer MooJook, is a recreation of the Moo Moo Farm farmyard track from the N64 game. It has been played 184,620 times and received 22,904 "hearts".

MOST CRITICALLY ACCLAIMED KART RACING GAME

Crash Team Racing (Naughty Dog, 1999) for the PlayStation, which features characters from the *Crash Bandicoot* series (multiple developers, 1996–2010), has the highest rating of any karting title, with a score of 91.78% on GameRankings as of 16 July 2013. It is just 0.35% ahead of second-placed *Mario Kart: Super Circuit* (Intelligent Systems, 2001).

FIRST KART RACING GAME LICENSED BY FORMULA ONE

When it was released in North America on 13 November 2012, *F1 Race Stars* (Codemasters, 2012) became the first karting title to carry an official F1 endorsement. The game caricatures all 24 drivers from the 12 teams in the 2012 F1 season.

TOP TEN	FASTEST TIMES ON *SONIC & SEGA ALL-STARS RACING*	
e123omega (UK) on PS3		19 min 50.10 sec
E-103Delta (UK) on PS3		19 min 57.82 sec
AmyOfAmz!Emz! (UK) on Wii		20 min 0.13 sec
NickstahhH (Netherlands) on PS3		20 min 12.85 sec
PK Fiyah (Australia) on Xbox 360		20 min 31.44 sec
Cytryz (USA) on PS3		20 min 34.90 sec
SuperAiAi (Netherlands) on PS3		20 min 35.81 sec
Lyca (Germany) on Wii		20 min 36.86 sec
7Alvin (Switzerland) on Wii		20 min 37.28 sec
The MH (Germany) on Wii		20 min 40.26 sec

Source: SSASR World Ranking, as of 22 July 2013 (times are combined from all tracks)

FASTEST SPEED-RUN OF LAVA LAIR IN *SONIC & SEGA ALL-STARS RACING*

On 19 January 2013, racer "GrimmJowX" (UK) achieved a lightning-quick time of 53.89 seconds around the tricky Lava Lair track in *Sonic & Sega All-Stars Racing* (Sega, 2010), the fastest speed-run of the circuit as of 16 July 2013 and a full 5.5 seconds faster than any other gamer.

FIRST KART RACING GAME

The first game in the karting genre was *Super Mario Kart* (Nintendo), released on the SNES in 1992. It sold an impressive 8.76 million copies worldwide, making it the **best-selling racing game on the SNES**. What's more, it kickstarted the *Mario Kart* series, which is the **longest-running kart racing game series** of them all.

WORST-RATED KART RACING GAME

Wii game *Donkey Kong: Barrel Blast* (Paon, 2007), originally developed for the GameCube, is at the back of the grid when it comes to critical acclaim. It had a score of just 43.94% on GameRankings as of 16 July 2013. The *Nintendo Life* review claims the game is "literally a waste of money" with "very little depth... and repetitive music".

GRAN TURISMO

LOWDOWN

PUBLISHER:
Sony
DEVELOPER:
Polyphony Digital
DEBUT:
1997

Sony's PlayStation-exclusive racing series is back after three years with the much-anticipated *Gran Turismo 6* scheduled for an autumn 2013 release. The 1997 original is the **best-selling PlayStation game**, with sales of 10.95 million by August 2013. The *GT* phenomenon extends beyond the console; in 2009, the Gran Turismo Café opened at the Twin Ring Motegi circuit in Japan.

NAME THE GAME
Little is known about Kane – one of the most commanding villains ever.

BEST-SELLING DRIVING SERIES

Gran Turismo boasted total series sales of an extraordinary 67.77 million across the three PlayStation consoles and the PSP, as of 6 August 2013. By contrast, the rival *Forza Motorsport* series (Turn 10 Studios, 2005–present) had sold 15.91 million. Although the *Mario Kart* games (*see pp. 150–151*) have sold considerably more, they do not simulate real-life driving experiences.

TOP TEN

MOST CAR MODELS FEATURED IN *GRAN TURISMO 5*

Nissan (Japan)	144
Honda (Japan)	101
Mazda (Japan)	100
Toyota (Japan)	90
Mitsubishi (Japan)	73
Subaru (Japan)	38
Chevrolet (USA)	37
Ford (USA)	29
Audi (Germany)	26
Volkswagen (Germany)	23

Source: *Gran Turismo 5*, as of July 2013

LONGEST CHART RUN FOR A RACING GAME

With an incredible worldwide chart run of 141 weeks as of 6 August 2013, *Gran Turismo 5*, which is still charting, was clearly worth the wait for racing fans. Originally announced at E3 2000, it spent five years in development before its release on 24 November 2010 – the **longest development period for a racing game**.

MOST CRITICALLY ACCLAIMED RACING GAME

As of 6 August 2013, *Gran Turismo 3: A-Spec* (2001) had a GameRankings score of 94.47%, which also makes it the **most critically acclaimed driving game**. Among its many accolades was a perfect 10 from Eurogamer.

The third game in the *GT* series is also the **best-selling driving game**, with sales of 14.98 million by August 2013, and is therefore also the biggest overall seller in the franchise. Its sales are all the more impressive given that *GT3* was a PS2 exclusive.

MOST REAL-WORLD CARS IN A GAME

Choosing from a garage of hundreds of real vehicles has been a big draw in *Gran Turismo* games since the series' PlayStation debut, but no game takes that automotive smörgåsbord farther than the latest title, *Gran Turismo 6*. With 1,200 cars featured in total, *GT6* stretches its vehicle count even higher than its immediate predecessor, which previously held this record with 1,083 cars.

GRAN FINALE

Gran Turismo 5's online time-trial events offer a chance for players from across the globe to compete for the fastest overall time in certain tracks and particular categories of vehicle. With 11 fastest times across 142 events, Belgian time-trial expert "Amo_Racing87" holds the record for the **most *Gran Turismo 5* time-trial victories**.

FASTEST CAR IN A RACING GAME

The Red Bull X2011 has a 1,635-horsepower engine capable of 500 km/h (311 mi/h). The car, from *Gran Turismo 5*, is a collaboration between Polyphony Digital president Kazunori Yamauchi and Red Bull Racing's chief technical officer Adrian Newey. Although not a real-world car, the original X2010 prototype and a 2011 model are available as DLC and might only be beaten in speed by the likes of *Wipeout* spacecraft.

FASTEST LAP OF "LAGUNA SECA" BY A TEAM OF TWO

Sharing one controller between them on *Gran Turismo 5*, Callum "Callux" McGinley (*right*) and Olajide "KSIOlajidebt" Olatunji (both UK) recorded a single lap time of 1 min 38.20 sec at the Guinness World Records OMG! YouTube channel live stream. The event, part of YouTube's "Geek Week", was held at Google HQ in London, UK, on 8 August 2013. The *Gran Turismo* circuit is an exact replica of the real-world Laguna Seca track in Monterey, California, USA.

PRO RACING

LOWDOWN

Enthusiasts of pro racing have long searched for authenticity in their driving games. The blend of realistic controls and high-speed competition has attracted fans since videogames first became popular.

Formula One is the **motorsport with the most associated games**, with some 147 titles dating from 1976 to July 2013. NASCAR comes in second place, with 47 games, and the *World Rally Championship* series (Evolution Studios/Milestone 2005–10) takes third place with 21 virtual outings.

154

NAME THE GAME
Gomez collects cubes in this puzzle-platform videogame.

FIRST 3D POLYGON-BASED RACING GAME

Indianapolis 500: The Simulation (Electronic Arts, 1989) recreated 200-lap, 33-car races with unparalleled visual realism for its time. Designer David Kaemmer was born within one hour's drive of the racetrack in Indiana, USA.

MOST CRITICALLY ACCLAIMED F1 GAME

As of 8 August 2013, the Xbox 360 version of *F1 2011* (Codemasters, 2011) had a GameRankings rating of 84.37%, putting it ahead of *F1 2012* by .07%. Back in 1996, the **first game licensed by Formula One**, in the shape of governing body the Fédération Internationale de l'Automobile (FIA), was *Geoff Crammond's Grand Prix 2* (MicroProse, 1996). It depicted the 1994 season, except that drivers Ayrton Senna and Roland Ratzenberger – who both died in racing accidents that year – were left out as a mark of respect.

BO:OM!

You could get your motor running as long ago as 1969, when Sega released *Grand Prix*, which was an electro-mechanical game rather than a videogame. The road was projected on to a screen and cutout cars were the player's competition. The controls comprised a steering wheel and accelerator pedal, and it even had crash sound effects. The trade adverts promised a cabinet "in easy to clean 'Formica' type finish".

TOP TEN
FASTEST LAP TIMES ON THE MONACO CIRCUIT IN *F1 2012*

Randytheracer (Switzerland)	1 min 2.03 sec
Nazar (Germany)	1 min 6.75 sec
Racingking90 (Germany)	1 min 7.63 sec
Croxon (UK)	1 min 7.88 sec
Skillzzz (Italy)	1 min 7.91 sec
Stig90 (Poland)	1 min 7.95 sec
Lturuani (nationality unknown)	1 min 8.05 sec
Kevin080498 (Finland)	1 min 8.19 sec
Agostonp28 (nationality unknown)	1 min 8.42 sec
Merimax87 (Finland)	1 min 8.62 sec

Source: in-game leaderboard, as of 23 June 2013

The *Monaco GP* (Sega) series began in arcades in 1979 and lasted for 13 years across four releases. Its high point was the 1989 Mega Drive/Genesis port of *Super Monaco GP*, the success of which led to a 1992 sequel endorsed by F1 champion Ayrton Senna.

BEST-SELLING NASCAR GAME

The right-turn-averse racing spectacular recorded its highest gaming sales with *NASCAR 2000* (EA Sports, 1999) selling more than 2.11 million units as of 8 August 2013. *NASCAR*'s distinctive brand of close-quarters endurance racing usually makes the most impact on North American sales charts, although more than 700,000 of these sales were outside the USA.

FIRST RACING SERIES

Pole Position II (Namco/Atari) was released in 1983, a year after the pioneering original, which gave gamers their first taste of realistic racing. The 1982 release offered the **first real-world racing track in a game** – the Fuji Speedway, Japan. In another innovation within the same game, players first took part in a qualifying session before a championship race.

BEST-SELLING RALLY GAME SERIES

The *Colin McRae Rally/DiRT* franchise by Codemasters (1998–2012) had achieved sales of 10.75 million units by 7 August 2013. The first game, *Colin McRae Rally*, was released in 1998. McRae himself advised on the series until his death in a helicopter crash in 2007.

Colin McRae Rally 2005 on the N-Gage won the **first BAFTA for a rally game** at the awards of 2005 for the Best Handheld Game. Pictured below is the last game in the series to feature the driver's name, *Colin McRae: DiRT 2* (2011).

▽

155

NEED FOR SPEED

PUBLISHER:
EA
DEVELOPER:
Various
DEBUT:
1994

Thriving on its rich range of developers over the years as much as it has done on its shifting line-up of motors, the series has evolved through many incarnations. It has the sports cars that dreams are made of, and the grittiest of urban settings. When EA formed real-life driving squad Team Need for Speed in 2010 they boasted the **most drivers sponsored by a game publisher**.

156

MOST PROLIFIC RACING SERIES

EA has been as quick in producing games as the series title suggests. Since 1994, there have been 24 titles (including three *V-Rally* games given the *NFS* stamp for US release). *NFS* has spanned platforms as diverse as the 3DO and iOS and has even delved into the MMO genre, with *Motor City Online* (2001) and the free2play *Need for Speed World* (2010). *Need for Speed: Rivals* (*main picture*) is set to take the score to a quarter-century in November 2013.

NAME THE GAME
Gordon Freeman appears in this FPS battling Combine collaborators and aliens.

TIP-OFF

An easy way to get ahead of your competitive friends on the *Need for Speed: Most Wanted* leaderboard – if your pace isn't up to the task – is to complete some collection and exploration-based challenges such as smashing all the billboards in the city.

FASTEST CIRCUIT TIMES ON

- **Beachfront:**
  "SKYCODE", 2 min 5.398 sec
- **Burrows:**
  "BITPOR", 11.22 seconds
- **Campus Interchange:**
  "PERFECT1ON", 3 min 45.777 sec
- **Eagle Drive:**
  "DANIELCXC2", 1 min 24.843 sec
- **Kempton Docks:**
  "SKYCODE", 2 min 27.626 sec
- **Lyons & Hwy 201:**
  "DutchSkill5", 1 min 22.848 sec
- **Welcome to Palmont:**
  "DutchSkill5", 59.625 seconds

Source: nfs-s.com leaderboard, as of 10 September 2013

MOST POPULAR CAR IN *NEED FOR SPEED: MOST WANTED*

According to EA's own internal statistics, 9,521,487 events had been started using the Lamborghini Aventador LP700-4 on both Xbox 360 and PS3 versions of *Need for Speed: Most Wanted* (2011) online, as of 30 June 2013, making it the choice for testing skills against others.

The Porsche 911 Carrera S 2012 (*left*) is the **most popular car in *Need for Speed: Most Wanted* (offline mode)**, with 7,690,800 racing events started on Xbox 360 and 11,785,704 on PS3 as of 30 June 2013.

MOST STUDIOS TO WORK ON ONE RACING GAME SERIES

As of September 2013, an amazing 24 different development studios had worked on all iterations of *NFS*, from original creators Pioneer Productions and EA Canada to Ghost Games and Criterion Games, who are currently collaborating on the latest in the series, *Need for Speed: Rivals* (2013).

TOP TEN — MOST CRITICALLY ACCLAIMED *NEED FOR SPEED* GAMES

Game	Score
Need for Speed: Hot Pursuit (Criterion Games, 2010) on PS2	88.86%
Need for Speed: Hot Pursuit 2 (Black Box, 2002) on PS2	88.01%
Need for Speed: Hot Pursuit (2010) on Xbox 360	86.89%
Need for Speed: Most Wanted U (Criterion Games, 2013) on Wii U	86.46%
Need for Speed: Most Wanted (2012) on PS3	85.09%
Need for Speed: Underground 2 (EA, 2004) on PC	84.52%
Need for Speed: Porsche Unleashed (EA, 2000) on PC	84.36%
Need for Speed: Underground (Black Box, 2003) on PS2	84.29%
Need for Speed: Underground (EA, 2003) on GC	83.73%
Need for Speed: Shift (Slightly Mad Studios, 2009) on PS3	83.48%

Source: gamerankings.com, as of 10 September 2013

BEST-SELLING *NEED FOR SPEED* GAME

Battling for pole position in this close-fought record are *Need for Speed: Underground* (2003), with 7.20 million units sold as of 10 September 2013, and its sequel from the following year. *Underground 2* (*right*) is just behind in sales with 6.90 million copies shifted. *Need for Speed* is the overall **best-selling driving series**, with 87.96 million copies sold as of September 2013, according to VGChartz. EA themselves insist the series clocked 100 million back in 2009.

MOST AUTOLOG RACING EVENTS

The hook in *Need for Speed: Most Wanted* is racing in a constantly connected world that gives you bragging rights via the *NFS* social network, EA's Autolog. EA reported a total of 12,174,323 Autolog recommendations having been sent on PS3 and Xbox 360 versions of the game, from one racer challenging another to beat their time, as of 30 June 2013. Those invitations spawned at least 357 million events.

BEST OF THE REST

LOWDOWN

In a plentiful year for racing games, new titles were released in many major franchises – including Turn 10's *Forza Motorsport* (2005–present). The importance of the series to Microsoft was made clear when *Forza 5* was announced as a launch title for the Xbox One. And eye-catching new racers were announced at E3: Evolution Studios' *Driveclub* and Ubisoft's *The Crew*, both for the PS4.

158

NAME THE GAME Commander Shepard can be played as a man or a woman in this RPG.

MOST CRITICALLY ACCLAIMED RACING SERIES

As of 15 August 2013, the Xbox-exclusive *Forza Motorsport* series had a GameRankings score aggregate of 90.42% across its five releases, which means it is also the overall **most critically acclaimed driving series**. By comparison, the Sony-exclusive *Gran Turismo* games (Polyphony Digital, 1997–present) scored an average of 85.82%.

Forza Motorsport 5, pictured below, is scheduled for November 2013 release and will be an Xbox One exclusive.

LARGEST PLAYABLE AREA IN A RACING VIDEOGAME

Open-world racing games provide huge playable areas to explore without constraints, and the one in off-road racer *FUEL* (Codemasters, 2009) offers a breathtaking 14,400 km² (5,560 miles²) of driveable terrain – approximately the size of Connecticut, USA. It even has its own weather system, containing spontaneous sandstorms and tornadoes.

BOOST

DRIVING RHYTHMS

It's as hard to imagine a racing game without adrenaline-pumping music, as it is a road trip without a car radio. But gamers didn't always have sonic accompaniment: the **first racing game with background music** was *Rally-X* (Namco, 1980), while the **first racing game soundtrack CD** was the *Wipeout* (Psygnosis, 1995) score.

TOP TEN

BEST-SELLING NON-KART RACERS

Game	Sales
Gran Turismo 3: A-Spec (Polyphony Digital, 2001) on PS2	14.98
Gran Turismo 4 (Polyphony Digital, 2004) on PS2	11.66
Gran Turismo (Sony, 1997) on PlayStation	10.95
Gran Turismo 5 (Polyphony Digital, 2010) on PS3	10.51
Gran Turismo 2 (Polyphony Digital, 1999) on PlayStation	9.49
Need for Speed: Underground (EA Black Box, 2003) on PS2	7.20
Need for Speed: Underground 2 (EA Canada, 2004) on PS2	6.90
Forza Motorsport 3 (Turn 10 Studios, 2009) on Xbox 360	5.38
Need for Speed: Most Wanted (EA Black Box, 2005) on PS2	4.37
Excitebike (Nintendo, 1984) on NES	4.16

Source: vgchartz.com, as of 15 August 2013 (figures in millions)

FIRST "CAR-PG"

Final Lap Twin (Namco, 1989), released for the fourth-generation TurboGrafx-16 console, is the first game to combine racing and role-playing game elements, hence the term "car-PG". Its "Quest" mode features random battles and map-based adventuring. *Final Lap Twin* is a spin-off from arcade game *Final Lap* (Namco, 1987), which was a pure racer.

WORST-RATED RACING GAME

Smashing Drive (Point of View, 2002) on the GameCube never really got out of first gear, with a GameRankings score of just 42.76% as of 14 August 2013. This arcade port puts the gamer in the driving seat of a New York City cab, with plenty of power-ups and passengers to pick up around the city. IGN's verdict was damning: "offensive graphics... revolting soundtrack".

LONGEST-RUNNING FUTURISTIC RACING SERIES

The *Wipeout* series has been running for 16 years, with its first release in September 1995 and its most recent, *Wipeout 2048* (Studio Liverpool), arriving on the PS Vita in January 2012. *Wipeout* games offer gravity-defying, speedy racing thrills to a backdrop of equally speedy electronic music.

LONGEST-RUNNING RACING SERIES

Spanning 25 years, the 19 titles in the *Test Drive* series (various developers, 1987–present) cover the longest time span of any racing franchise, as of 14 August 2013. *Test Drive* (Accolade, 1987) began the series' marathon journey on the Amiga, Amstrad CPC, Apple II, Atari ST, Commodore 64 and DOS platforms, while the most recent release, *Test Drive: Ferrari Racing Legends* (Evolved Games, 2012), appears on the PC, Xbox 360 and PS3. Pictured here is *Test Drive Unlimited 2* (Eden Games, 2011), an open-worlder in which the player takes on the role of a valet on the Spanish island of Ibiza.

GLOBAL GAMING

When we think of game-development centres, the USA, Japan, UK and Canada immediately spring to mind. But which other countries are home to respected gaming hubs? Martyn Carroll takes a global perspective...

ICELAND

CCP Games, developers of the sci-fi MMORPG *EVE Online*, was founded in Reykjavík in 1997. *EVE*'s subscriber numbers have steadily increased year-on-year – as of July 2013, the figure stood in excess of 500,000. CCP was crowned Best Independent Studio at the 2012 Develop Industry Excellence Awards.

SWEDEN

Stockholm is the stomping ground of Digital Illusions Creative Entertainment (DICE), developers of the smash-hit *Battlefield* series (2002–present), which has racked up sales in excess of 50 million. The company was established in 1992 and acquired by US behemoth EA in 2006. Groundbreaking visuals are a foundation of the series and *Battlefield 3* (2011, *below*) was voted No.1 in the "Top 50 Videogame Graphics" readers' poll in *Gamer's Edition 2013*.

Stockholm is also the base of Mojang, makers of sandbox sensation *Minecraft* (2009).

URUGUAY

Montevideo-based indie gaming studio Ironhide was founded in 2010 by three friends who say they had always dreamed of working in the industry. The dream became reality with the success of tower-defence browser game *Kingdom Rush* (2012), which was later ported to iOS and Android platforms. A sequel was released in 2013.

CZECH REPUBLIC

2K Czech was founded in 1997 as Illusion Softworks and renamed in 2008 following its acquisition by Take-Two Interactive. Their 2011 sports title *Top Spin 4* (*below*) is the **first tennis game in stereoscopic 3D**. Another of 2K Czech's acclaimed titles is actioner *Mafia II* (2010).

NETHERLANDS

Killzone developer Guerrilla Games, formerly Lost Boys Games, is based in Amsterdam. Formed in 2000 and acquired by Sony in 2005, the firm employs around 160 staff. It's just as well Sony is in charge, as *Killzone 2* (2009) has the **largest budget for a PS3 shooter** at a whopping €41 million (£35 million; $52 million).

FINLAND

Those famous *Angry Birds* were hatched in Finland's second largest city, Espoo, the home of developer Rovio Entertainment. Formed in 2003 under the name Relude, the company produced a string of mobile phone games before landing the mother lode with the release of *Angry Birds* in 2009. With total downloads in excess of 1.7 billion, *Angry Birds* is the **most downloaded mobile game series** (*see p.74*).

GERMANY

In Frankfurt you'll find Crytek, best known for creating the original *Far Cry* (2004) and the *Crysis* series (2007–13). The free version of its game platform CryEngine 3 (*pictured below*) is the **fastest-downloaded free software development kit**, with 108,462 downloads in its first six days.

UKRAINE

The Ukrainian capital Kiev is home to 4A Games, developer of shooters *Metro 2033* (2010) and *Metro: Last Light* (2013, *below*). The publishing rights were auctioned off in January 2013 following the collapse of original publisher THQ; German videogame label Deep Silver snapped up the rights with a bid of €4.5 million (£3.8 million, $5.8 million).

BULGARIA

Although it didn't create the original *Tropico* game, Haemimont Games has become synonymous with the quirky sim series, having developed *Tropico 3* (2009, *below*) and *Tropico 4* (2011). Founded in 1997, the firm is based in Sofia and currently employs around 50 staff, making it Bulgaria's largest videogame company.

AUSTRALIA

Operating out of Brisbane is Halfbrick Studios, creators of the multi-platform *Fruit Ninja* (2010). During its first two years of release, the game was downloaded more than 300 million times, with the number of fruit sliced standing at a mouth-watering 1.5 trillion! Halfbrick say the game has been installed on a third of all iPhones in the USA.

PARTY TIME

LONGEST MARATHON ON A DANCE GAME

Carrie Swidecki (USA) didn't stop dancing to *Just Dance 4* (Ubisoft, 2012) for 49 hr 3 min 22 sec on 15–17 June 2013 at "Otto's Video Games and More!" store in Bakersfield, California, USA. In doing so, she also set the record for the **longest marathon on a motion-sensing dance game**.

Carrie, a school teacher of 2nd-grade pupils, says that "exergaming" has helped her lose 34 kg (75 lb). Read more of Carrie's story on p.184.

CONTENTS

DANCE

LOWDOWN

Dancing, keep fit, music and gaming all rolled into one – what's not to love about dance games? But boogie gaming isn't just popular with gamers: in January 2006, the education authority in West Virginia, USA, announced plans to make Konami's *Dance Dance Revolution* games (1998–present) part of gym class in all of the state's 765 schools, the **most widely used videogame in schools**, in an effort to tackle child obesity.

NAME THE GAME
Appearing when her song is sung, Epona proves a faithful companion.

WORST-RATED DANCE GAME

Breakdancing game *B-Boy* (FreeStyleGames/Evolved Games, 2006) on the PS2 had a score of 56.12% on GameRankings as of 5 August 2013. The aim of the game is to master up to 800 motion-captured moves, build up a crew and battle in-game versions of real-life b-boys.

BEST-SELLING CASUAL GAME

Casual games are targeted at a mass audience – they are accessible and can be played in a spare moment. As of 5 August 2013, *Just Dance 3* (Ubisoft Paris, 2011, *left*) had sold 12.25 million copies across the Wii, PS3 and Xbox 360. This makes it the **best-selling dance videogame**. Its Wii sales of 9.86 million mean it is the **best-selling third-party Wii game**, and the *Just Dance* series is the **best-selling third-party Wii series**, with sales of 41.08 million. The fifth game in the series is *Just Dance 2014* (2013, *below*).

FIRST FULL-BODY MOTION DANCING GAME

The first dancing game to track players' movements in both the upper and lower body was *Dance Dance Revolution Hottest Party* (Konami, 2007), which utilized the Wii Remote and dance pad for full motion detection.

TOP TEN

HIGHEST SCORES ON *JUST DANCE 4* ON Wii

Song	Score
"Hit 'Em Up Style (Oops!)" by Blu Cantrell lokthrow (Spain)	12,896
"Hit the Lights" by Selena Gomez & The Scene manii (Mexico)	12,823
"Oops!...I Did It Again" by Britney Spears emily-anne7 (USA)	12,684
"So What" by Plnk regis7390 (Brazil)	12,643
"Hot For Me" by A.K.A lokthrow (Spain)	12,612
"Never Gonna Give You Up" by Rick Astley atbaum (Germany)	12,579
"Livin' La Vida Loca" by Ricky Martin chris_pizza (Mexico) "Time Warp" by Cast of *Rocky Horror Picture Show* regis7390 (Brazil)	12,530
"Asereje (The Ketchup Song)" by Las Ketchup westgarrett (USA)	12,508
"What Makes You Beautiful" by One Direction westgarrett (USA)	12,505

Source: wii-records.com, as of 5 August 2013

FIRST DANCE MAT GAME

Part of the Japanese *Family Trainer* series, *Aerobics Studio* (Human Entertainment) made its debut in that territory on the Famicom in 1987. The game was subsequently released for the NES and the Power Pad pressure-pad mat (*right*) in 1989 under the name *Dance Aerobics*.

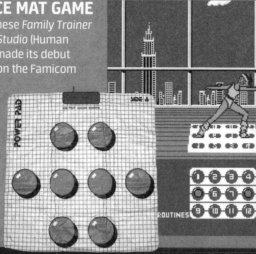

MOST CRITICALLY ACCLAIMED DANCING GAME

Dance Central 3 (Harmonix Music Systems, 2012) for the Xbox 360 had a GameRankings score of 86.88% as of 5 August 2013. *Dance Central 2* (Harmonix Music Systems, 2011) is in second place on 86.55%. New DLC for *Dance Central 3* ended in March 2013, with Harmonix shifting development staff to different projects. The game comes with 46 tracks, including hits by LMFAO, Gloria Gaynor and 50 Cent.

GOOD FEELING

As of 5 August 2013, "I Gotta Feeling" by The Black Eyed Peas was the **most downloaded Dance Central 3 track on Xbox Live** – exact figures were not supplied by Microsoft. The song was released as DLC on 23 November 2010.

GREATEST PRIZE MONEY IN A DANCE GAME TOURNAMENT

The 2007 World Pump Festival, a tournament centred on the *Pump It Up* series (Andamiro, 1999), offered a total prize pot of $148,000 (£74,000) across three categories: Speed (Female), Speed (Male) and Freestyle. Cash prizes were awarded to those placed in the top eight of each category. The '07 festival was held in Mexico.

165

BAND

LOWDOWN

This is where we showcase the games that encourage you to be a musician, or, at least, to do a very good impersonation of one. Rhythm games include any title that relies for its gameplay on copying a rhythm – including instrument and singing-based games and dancing games.

Neversoft's *Guitar Hero III: Legends of Rock* (2007) is the **best-selling rhythm game**, with sales in excess of 16 million as of 7 August 2013.

NAME THE GAME
Jim Raynor is a rebel in this real-time strategy game.

Dropout
Main Menu

● Beginn
▤ Easy
▥ Medium
✦ Hard
✖ Expert

BEST-SELLING RHYTHM VIDEOGAME SERIES

As of 7 August 2013, the *Guitar Hero* franchise (various developers, 2005–10) had total sales of some 57 million. Publisher Activision announced in 2011 that it would no longer release new titles, citing "declines in the music genre". But *Hero* significantly out-sells its rivals, with *Guitar Hero III* selling 16.09 million copies over all platforms. *Guitar Hero II* (Harmonix, 2006) had sold 5.12 million copies on the PS2 – the **best-selling instrument game on a single platform**.

FIRST DJ SIMULATION GAME

Beatmania (Konami, 1998) was the first game to allow wannabe DJs to have a go on the ones and twos, and it even utilized a stylish turntable controller. Originally an arcade title released in December 1997, several home editions were available on the PlayStation in Japan before a European version was published in 2000, with a PS2 release following in North America and Europe in 2006.

BO:OM!

When Guns N' Roses guitarist Slash featured as a playable character in *Guitar Hero III: Legends of Rock*, the band's singer, Axl Rose, tried to sue Activision over Slash's appearance. Rose claimed he allowed the use of their hit "Welcome to the Jungle" only if no images of the band were used. The lawsuit was dismissed.

MOST CRITICALLY ACCLAIMED RHYTHM GAME

Rock Band 3 (Harmonix, 2010) on the Xbox 360 scored 92.44% on GameRankings as of 7 August 2013. It is also the **most critically acclaimed instrument game**. The third *Rock Band* game is the first in the main series to support a keyboard and include three-part vocal harmonies. It comes with 83 songs, plus thousands of DLC tracks from the *Rock Band* Network.

TOP TEN — BEST-SELLING INSTRUMENT GAMES

Game	Sales
Guitar Hero III: Legends of Rock (Neversoft, 2007)	16.09
Guitar Hero: World Tour (Neversoft, 2008)	9.77
Guitar Hero II (Harmonix, 2006)	7.22
Rock Band (Harmonix, 2007)	7.13
Rock Band 2 (Harmonix, 2008)	6.17
Guitar Hero 5 (BudCat Creations/Neversoft, 2009)	4.70
Guitar Hero: Aerosmith (Neversoft, 2008)	4.09
The Beatles: Rock Band (Harmonix, 2009)	3.98
Guitar Hero: On Tour (Vicarious Visions, 2008)	3.44
Band Hero (Vicarious Visions/Neversoft, 2009)	3.09

Source: vgchartz.com, as of 29 August 2013 (figures in millions)

HIGHEST *ROCK BAND 3* SCORE – ALL SONGS, SINGLE INSTRUMENT

As of 7 August 2013, the highest cumulative score logged across all *Rock Band 3* songs achieved by one player on a single instrument was 536,969,531, set by "VladTepz" using a keyboard on the Xbox 360. The **highest Rock Band 3 score – all songs, vocals** is 608,545,773, notched up by "ZDAAVEEDZDIVAS9999", who has a total of 781,544,704 in-game fans.

FIRST LICENSED GAME TO INCLUDE A ROCK BAND

The first game with licensed names and likenesses of a real rock band was *Journey Escape* (Data Age, 1982), which starred US band Journey. The game tasked the player with guiding Journey to their "Escape" vehicle – named after the band's 1981 album – while avoiding groupies, photographers and promoters. Journey gained new relevance when "Don't Stop Believin'", from *Escape*, was covered by the cast of *Glee* in 2009.

ARE YOU HOT ENOUGH TO PLAY WITH JOURNEY?

FIRST GAME TO WORK WITH ANY AMPLIFIED GUITAR

In contrast with rival real instrument games, *Rocksmith* (Ubisoft, 2011) allows players to plug *any* guitar – as long as it has an output jack – into their console with the game's "Real Tone Cable". It sold more than one million copies by 7 August 2013. The **first game to work with a real guitar** is *Power Gig: Rise of the SixString* (Seven45 Studios, 2010), whose controller is a real six-string guitar.

LOWDOWN

If you've watched TV talent shows and fancied having a go in a more private, less embarrassing arena, karaoke games are for you. From the comfort of your home, all you need is the game, a microphone peripheral and a basic sense of rhythm. Although *Karaoke Revolution* (Harmonix, 2003–11) spearheaded the modern karaoke game genre, *SingStar* (London Studio, 2004–present) is very much the dominant force.

BEST-SELLING KARAOKE GAME SERIES

The PlayStation-exclusive *SingStar* series (*below*) is the undisputed king of karaoke, with more than 22 million units sold and over 15 million tracks downloaded from the SingStore, as of 23 August 2013. More than 1.5 million players have uploaded nearly 300,000 videos of their performances to the "My SingStar" online service.

As of 5 August 2013, the **best-selling song in the SingStore** was "Call Me Maybe" by Carly Rae Jepsen.

You're tox - **ic**
I'm slip - pin' un - der

BEST-SELLING BAND-SPECIFIC KARAOKE GAME

A number of band- or singer-specific titles have been released in the karaoke genre. And it's *SingStar ABBA* (London Studio, 2008) that has shifted the most copies – a total of 2.2 million as of 23 August 2013.

NAME THE GAME
Samus Aran uses a variety of weapons including a power suit, missiles and bombs.

MOST CRITICALLY ACCLAIMED KARAOKE GAME

Karaoke Revolution Volume 3 (Konami, 2004) on the PS2 has a GameRankings score of 84.69% as of 28 August 2013. The third game in the series was the first to include a duet option, and it featured tracks by, among others, The Beatles, Usher, Britney Spears and Evanescence.

TOP TEN

MOST PROLIFIC ARTISTS IN THE SINGSTORE

Artist	Songs
Queen (UK)	31
Take That (UK)	20
Coldplay (UK)	18
Blur (UK)	16
Depeche Mode (UK)	15
Pink (USA)	13
Kylie Minogue (Australia)	12
Robbie Williams (UK)	12
Crowded House (Australia/New Zealand/USA)	11
Roxette (Sweden)	11
Snow Patrol (UK)	11

Source: data from singstar.com, as of 29 August 2013 (figures represent number of songs available in the SingStore)

FIRST FREE KARAOKE APP

In October 2012, *SingStar* launched as the first free karaoke app on the PS3. Tracks can be played from the game discs or purchased via the SingStore's catalogue of more than 3,000 songs. This instant access is a far cry from Bandai's *Karaoke Studio* (1987), a cartridge subsystem for the Famicom (NES), which was the **first karaoke videogame**.

BEST-SELLING KARAOKE GAME

High School Musical: Sing It! (Artificial Mind and Movement, 2007) had sold 3.63 million copies worldwide as of 23 August 2013. Available for the Wii and PS2, it is based on the 2006 TV movie *High School Musical* and its sequel *High School Musical 2* (2007). *Sing It!* features animated versions of all the characters from those films, including Troy, Gabriella and Sharpay. They – and the player – sing classic tracks from the movies, such as "Breaking Free".

FIRST CUSTOMIZABLE SOUNDTRACK IN A KARAOKE GAME

SingStar (2007) for the PS3 was the first karaoke game that allowed players to devise their own track listing. The game disc featured 30 songs, but extra tracks can be chosen and downloaded from the SingStore.

LONGEST-RUNNING KARAOKE GAME SERIES

The first game in the *Karaoke Revolution* series was released on 5 November 2003, while the most recent, *Karaoke Revolution Glee: Volume 3* (2011), featured 35 songs from the hit TV series.

The **most prolific karaoke game series** is *SingStar*, with 71 releases between 2004 and 2012, including country-specific titles such as Spain's *SingStar Operación Triunfo* (2008) and Germany's *SingStar Fussballhits* (2010).

BEST OF THE REST

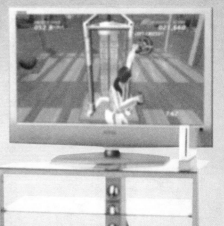

LOWDOWN

Fitness and party games feature here – the former aim to burn calories, the latter usually involve teaming up on a number of mini-games within a game. The **first rhythm game** – Bandai's *Family Trainer: Aerobics Studio* – was released in 1987, but it was the Wii that saw fitness games surge in popularity. The **best-selling fitness game** is *Wii Fit* (Nintendo, 2007), with sales of over 22.75 million as of 8 August 2013.

170

MOST CRITICALLY ACCLAIMED FITNESS GAME

EA Sports Active: Personal Trainer (EA, 2009) on the Wii has garnered the most positive reviews in the fitness genre, scoring 83.25% on GameRankings as of 8 August 2013. The game includes a resistance band and pouch to hold the Nunchuck controller. A virtual personal trainer observes the in-game workout.

TOP TEN	BEST-SELLING PARTY GAMES	
Wii Play (Nintendo, 2006) on Wii		28.74
Mario Party DS (Hudson Soft, 2007) on DS		8.74
Wii Party (Nintendo, 2010) on Wii		8.15
Mario Party 8 (Hudson Soft, 2007) on Wii		7.92
EyeToy: Play (SCE London Studio, 2003) on PS2		4.20
Carnival Games (Cat Daddy Games, 2007) on Wii		3.93
Crash Bash (Eurocom, 2008) on PlayStation		3.39
Mario Party (Hudson Soft, 1998) on N64		2.70
Mario Party 9 (Nintendo, 2012) on Wii		2.56
Mario Party 2 (Hudson Soft, 1999) on N64		2.50

Source: vgchartz.com, as of 8 August 2013 (figures in millions)

FASTEST COMPLETION OF "TEAMWORK TEMPLE" ON *Wii* PARTY

The Geren brothers – Tristen (*far left*), aged 15, and Taylor, aged 10 (both USA) – completed "Teamwork Temple" in just 57 seconds on 16 February 2013 in Fredericksburg, Texas, USA. The mini-game requires players to pair up in a quest for treasure hidden deep inside a temple.

MOST PROLIFIC PARTY GAME SERIES

Mario Party (Hudson Soft/Nd Cube, 1998–2012) has nine main series titles and a further three spin-offs, as of August 2013. The gameplay revolves around a number of mini-games starring characters from the *Mario* universe, including the plumber himself, his brother Luigi and Bowser.

BOOST

FUNKY MONKEY

Super Monkey Ball (Amusement Vision, 2001) on the GameCube scored 88.89% on GameRankings as of 7 August 2013, making it the **most critically acclaimed party game**. Originally an arcade title, this platformer contains three party games named "Monkey Race", "Monkey Target" and "Monkey Fight". *Super Monkey Ball* was a launch title for the GameCube.

FIRST Wii-BASED UNIVERSITY COURSE

The University of Houston in Texas, USA, unveiled its Wii Performance course in 2009. Created by the university's Department of Health and Human Performance, the course incorporated several different Wii games including *Wii Fit* (2007), *EA Sports Active* (2009) and *Wii Sports Resort* (Nintendo, 2009). Students received a credit towards their degree for the class, which was designed to teach the practice of posture and centre-of-balance as well as the basic principles of maintaining a healthy body weight through proper nutrition.

BEST-SELLING Wii U GAME

Party game *Nintendo Land* (Nintendo, 2012) had sold some 2.21 million units as of 8 August 2013. Nintendo Land is a fictional amusement park containing 12 attractions that form mini-games featuring Nintendo legends such as Mario, Luigi and Zelda.

171

HIGHEST SCORE ON *WARIOWARE: SMOOTH MOVES*

Thanapat Voraphaphun (Thailand) scored 121 points on *WarioWare: Smooth Moves* in Bangkok, Thailand, on 17 May 2013. *Smooth Moves* is the fifth game in the *WarioWare* series of party puzzlers, which each contain a number of short games with mini-narratives.

ADMIT ONE

MOVIE GAMES

The perception of videogames based on films tends to be that they are rush-released to coincide with a movie of the same name. But that's not entirely fair to the genre, as Dan Morgan finds out as he takes a look at 30 years of film spin-offs.

THE RIGHTS STUFF

Videogame companies started trying to obtain movie licences in the 1970s. When Atari failed to gain the rights to Steven Spielberg's shark-attack blockbuster *Jaws*, they released a game called *Shark Jaws* (Atari, 1975) instead and bit back with a poster displaying the word "JAWS" in huge letters below small type for the word "SHARK".

RAIDERS OF THE BIG SCREEN

Atari's 1982 version of the Spielberg-directed *Raiders of the Lost Ark* was the **first videogame based on an official movie licence**. The game required two of the Atari 2600's single-button joysticks to fully control Indiana Jones – one stick for movement and object control, the other to select and drop inventory.

E.T. GO HOME

In order to hit the 1982 Christmas market, *E.T.: The Extra Terrestrial* (Atari), based on Spielberg's story of a boy and his alien chum, was made in just five weeks. Often cited as one of the worst ever videogames, *E.T.* was seen as a prime example of the poor-quality titles that fuelled the great videogame crash of 1983 (*see pp.82–83*).

172

1975

1982

1982

CREAM OF THE CROP

Chronicles of Riddick: Escape from Butcher Bay (Starbreeze, 2004) scores 88.72% on GameRankings. Praised for its visuals, it confidently merged action and stealth. Another popular tie-in was *Spider-Man 2* (Treyarch, 2004). Some attacked its repetitive missions, but many adored the feeling of swinging around the city just as in the movie.

LICENCE TO THRILL

GoldenEye 007 (Rare, 1997) was a good enough shooter to stand on its own without the Bond name to sell it. It is the **most critically acclaimed film spin-off game** with a 94.59% GameRankings score on the N64. The same *GoldenEye 007* is the **most successful film spin-off game** (as of June 2013), with more than 8.09 million copies sold.

2004

2012

FORCEFUL FRANCHISE

Star Wars boasts the **most games based on a licenced franchise**, with 296 titles across 44 platforms as of July 2013. The **biggest-selling *Star Wars* game** is *LEGO® Star Wars: The Complete Saga* (Traveller's Tales, 2007), shifting 13.37 million copies. The 2012 *Angry Birds Star Wars* (Rovio Entertainment, *above*) shows how the series continues to inspire.

2006

XBOX

ENTER THE MATRIX

2003

HARSH WORDS

Scarface: The World is Yours (Radical Entertainment, 2006) had a *GTA*-style open world and matching notoriety, with the **most swearing in a game** – the f-word appears 5,688 times in 31,000 dialogue lines. There's bad and there's *bad*: *Fight Club* (Genuine, 2004) failed, with the Gaming Age website commenting on its "layering of sheer badness".

NEVER-ENDING STORY

Some games have strayed from the original story. *Enter the Matrix* (Shiny Entertainment, 2003) ran parallel to *The Matrix Reloaded* (USA, 2003) and featured exclusive film footage. The Sega Mega Drive's *Jurassic Park* (BlueSky Software, 1993) allowed gamers to either *be* hero Dr Grant or hunt him down playing a Velociraptor dinosaur.

An exclusive GWR interview with Howard Scott Warshaw (*right, with Steven Spielberg*), who designed and programmed *Raiders of the Lost Ark* and *E.T.: The Extra Terrestrial*, and Martin Hollis, who directed *GoldenEye 007*.

What freedom did you have?
HSW: I had total control. I followed my vision in both games and was supported by Atari in doing so.
MH: An astonishing amount. We saw *GoldenEye* being filmed and the licence allowed us to use any villains or gadgets from the Bond series.

How much did you consider the film in making the game?
MH: The game follows the locations of the film but we put Bond into all of them so it's faithful in a dreamlike way. We also looked at both the Bond universe as a whole, and at Hong Kong action cinema.

What was the hardest part?
HSW: I had 10 months to make *Raiders* and five weeks for *E.T.* I like climbing mountains but five weeks isn't so much a mountain as a sheer cliff!
MH: Honestly, I feel it's easier to make a game out of a film than to make an original game with original IP.

What was your proudest moment?
HSW: When I showed *Raiders* to Spielberg, he said, "It's just like a movie!" That was the proudest moment I had.

SOCIAL, MOBILE & INSTANT

HIGHEST SCORE ON *THE WORLD'S BIGGEST* PAC-MAN

On 23 August 2011, Stephen Kish (UK), achieved a high score of 5,555,552. Stephen played on *The World's Biggest PAC-Man* (Soap Creative, 2011), an online version of the classic arcade title. Want to play? Go to worldsbiggest pacman.com.

As of 21 August 2013, the game holds the record for the **largest PAC-Man videogame** owing to its 4,014,144,000 pixels.

CONTENTS

SOCIAL NETWORK GAMES

LOWDOWN

With Google+ removing its games in 2013, Facebook is now the only major global social network to include gaming apps. In January 2013, a non-Zynga game reached the top of the Facebook chart for the very first time: *FarmVille 2* (2012) was eclipsed by the phenomenally popular *Candy Crush Saga* (King, 2012), which grew so quickly that it crashed the algorithm on AppData, a site that monitors the popularity of Facebook apps.

176

NAME THE GAME

Psychopathic Rock Islander Vaas Montenegro is the poster boy for this open-world FPS.

MOST PLAYED SOCIAL MUSIC GAME

SongPop (FreshPlanet, 2012) is the most popular music game on Facebook, with more than 85 million individual players between May 2012 and July 2013. Gameplay is simple: players hear short song clips and must guess the name of the track before their opponent. According to FreshPlanet, the average time it takes a player to guess a song is 2.7 seconds. Facebook founder Mark Zuckerberg said that "*SongPop* is one of the most fun Facebook games I've played in a while." The game is also available as an Apple and Android app.

MOST MAU FOR A GAME

As of 10 September 2013, the Facebook version of *Candy Crush Saga* (King, 2012) had a phenomenal 133.6 million monthly active users (MAU). The second most popular game by MAU is also a King title, *Pet Rescue Saga* (2012), on 41.09 million. *Candy Crush Saga*'s MAU also makes it the **most popular Facebook app** overall, beating the likes of Spotify and Pinterest to the accolade. The game is also on the Apple App Store and Google Play.

MOST FIVE-STAR RATINGS FOR A FACEBOOK GAME

As of 4 September 2013, police investigation sim *Criminal Case* (Pretty Simple, 2013) had been awarded 998,076 five-star ratings. Its overall rating is 4.4. By comparison, *Candy Crush Saga*, which is also rated 4.4, had 824,042 five-star ratings. Adventure and hidden-object title *Criminal Case* has been a real success story for Pretty Simple, the Paris-based indie developers who were only founded in 2010. In their hit game, which is available exclusively through Facebook, social gamers are invited to join the police force of the fictional Grimsborough in solving nefarious crimes. *Criminal Case* has more than 25 million MAU.

TOP TEN — MOST POPULAR FACEBOOK GAME DEVELOPERS

Developer	Monthly Active Users
King (UK)	249,491,185
Zynga (USA)	121,826,000
Microsoft (USA)	75,475,969
Social Point (Spain)	49,491,588
6waves (Hong Kong)	48,883,788
Wooga (Germany)	38,168,850
Pretty Simple (France)	29,898,736
Telaxo (France)	27,538,355
Yahoo! (USA)	26,873,214
Peak Games (Turkey)	22,955,650

Source: appdata.com, as of 11 September 2013 (monthly active users)

MOST POPULAR RPG ON FACEBOOK

The No.1 role-playing title on Facebook is *Dragon City* (Social Point, 2012). As of 5 September 2013, it had more than 25 million MAU, and the mobile version of the game has been downloaded nearly 5 million times. Some 5 million people also play the game every day. As with most of the successful social network games, *Dragon City* keeps it simple: the basic aim is to breed and raise dragons to earn gold with which food can be bought to feed more dragons and, in turn, earn more gold.

New Dragon Market

BO:OM!

Facebook may be the undisputed global leader, but it isn't the only social network showcasing games. Friendster, which came before both Myspace and Facebook, has become a games hub (the site's motto is "Living the Game"), while another early network, hi5, also re-positioned itself as a gaming community, in 2010.

FIRST ALBUM TO DEBUT IN A SOCIAL GAME

Fans of pop diva Lady Gaga got their first taste of her second album, *Born This Way*, on *FarmVille* (Zynga, 2009). In May 2011, a week before the album's release, Gaga and Zynga launched a special mod of the then most popular Facebook game, known as *GagaVille*. It contained various quests to unlock individual album tracks. Eventually, the whole album could be unlocked and heard within *GagaVille*. *Born This Way* had sold 6 million copies by September 2013.

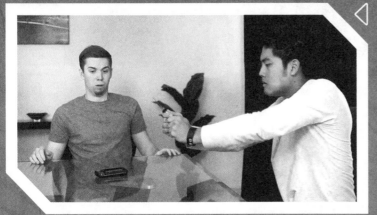

MOST WATCHED SPOOF GAME-BASED MOVIE TRAILER

On 11 June 2013, a trailer for a fictional movie based on *Candy Crush Saga* was uploaded to YouTube and by 5 September 2013, it had been watched 7,022,159 times. "Candy Crush The Movie (Official Fake Trailer)" was created by "nigahiga" aka Ryan Higa of Las Vegas, Nevada, USA, and featured jokes about the addictive nature of the game, along with nods to *Angry Birds* (Rovio, 2009), *FarmVille* and *Fruit Ninja* (Halfbrick Studios, 2010), and a cameo by Mario. For more on YouTube, see p.195.

APP GAMES

LOWDOWN

Videogames have been brought to the masses via apps on tablets and smartphones. And, according to data analyst Onavo, arcade is the **most popular iPhone game genre**. On 23 May 2013 they reported that 66% of gamers were playing arcade titles such as Sega's *Sonic Dash* (2013). It is Sega who are the **most prolific arcade game publisher**, with more than 530 arcade titles across all platforms since 1981.

NAME THE GAME
Cloud Strife is a blue-eyed soldier for the Shinra Company.

MOST CRITICALLY ACCLAIMED iOS GAME
With a GameRankings rating of 93%, *Jetpack Joyride* (Halfbrick Studios, 2011) was the best-rated iOS game as of 21 June 2013.

The **worst-rated iOS game** is *Final Fantasy: All the Bravest* (Square Enix, 2013), with a rating of just 23.21% as of 21 June 2013.

MOST EXPENSIVE IN-APP PURCHASE
The "Apathy Bear" in *Gun Bros* (Glu, 2010) was the most expensive in-app item as of 16 April 2013. The machine gun fires 300 rounds/min, causing 4,000 "damage" per hit, and at a costly 3,999 War Bucks is a difficult weapon to buy. Gamers wanting to quickly increase their arsenal can purchase Buck packs for £69.99 ($107), making the real cost of the "Apathy Bear" a hefty £395 ($600).

TOP TEN — MOST POPULAR ANDROID APP DEVELOPERS

Developer	Entries
Electronic Arts (USA) including: *Need for Speed; Monopoly; FIFA*	16
Gameloft (France) including: *Asphalt; Modern Combat; Dark Knight Rises*	13
SEGA (Japan) including: *Football Manager; Crazy Taxi; Virtua Tennis*	11
Disney (USA) including: *Wreck-it Ralph; Temple Run; Toy Story*	9
Rovio (Finland) including: *Tiny Thief; Angry Birds; Amazing Alex*	5
Zynga (USA) including: *Draw Something; Scramble with Friends*	
Crescent Moon Games (USA) including: *Ravensword; Slingshot Racing; Aralon*	4
Full Fat (UK) including: *Flick Golf!; Flick Soccer!; Flick Nations Rugby*	
Full Fat (UK) including: *Flick Golf!; Flick Soccer!; Flick Nations Rugby*	
Take-Two Interactive (USA) including *Grand Theft Auto; Max Payne; NBA*	

Source: data drawn from play.google.com, as of 22 July 2013 (number of entries in the top 250 best-selling games)

LARGEST MOBILE PHONE GAMING PARTY

On 5 April 2013, 510 participants from Team Airtel Karnataka (India) took part in a mobile phone gaming party in Mangalore, India. The **largest handheld console gaming party**, organized by Gamestop (USA) at the Mandalay Bay Resort and Casino in Las Vegas, Nevada, USA, consisted of 1,019 participants on 28 August 2011.

MOST REVIEWED WORD GAME

Words with Friends (Zynga, 2009–present) has been reviewed 1,438,229 times on Google play and iTunes as of 22 July 2013. It is also the **most popular word puzzle mobile game** with an estimated 3.8 million daily active users as of 22 July 2013. *Words with Friends Free* was the **most downloaded free iPhone game** as of May 2013.

MOST POPULAR iPAD GAME SERIES

As of May 2013, the most downloaded iPad gaming franchise is *Angry Birds* (Rovio, 2009). *Angry Birds HD* is the **most downloaded paid-for iPad game** ever, and the second most downloaded iPad app overall. The **most downloaded Android game** ever is also *Angry Birds*, with installations of more than 100 million as of 22 July 2013.

FASTEST-SELLING APP STRATEGY GAME

Just nine days was needed for *Plants vs. Zombies* (PopCap, 2010) to reach 300,000 downloads following its launch in February 2010. As an Electronic Arts subsidiary, PopCap contributed to EA's record for the **most successful App Store publisher**. EA featured six times in Apple's Top 25 paid-for iPhone apps list, released in May 2013 – more than any other company. However, it was Rovio that topped the list with *Angry Birds* (2009) – the **best-selling paid-for iPhone app**.

FIRST AR iPHONE GAME

Fairy Trails's (Freeverse) release on 26 September 2009 blazed a trail for iPhone Augmented Reality (AR). Using the smartphone's camera and compass, players can generate virtual fairies and butterflies within the real world. Tapping on the iPhone catches them in "jars" and the more captured, the more power gained.

HIGHEST SCORE ON iOS...

- **Flower Warfare (Thruster Apps, 2012):** 150,193 points, "tristeng", 9 July 2013
- **Fruit Ninja (Halfbrick Studios, 2011):** 1,616 points, "zaheerchand", 24 May 2013
- **MrPimple (Sobredosis Games, 2012):** 4,783 points, "silvio.sabba", 2 December 2012
- **Temple Run (Imangi Studios, 2011):** 67,702,984 points, "thymufasa707", 10 July 2012
- **Tiny Wings (Andreas Illiger, 2011):** 339,076 points, "saraporcheddu", 3 June 2013

LOWDOWN

While brand new blockbusters grab the headlines, a host of updated versions of classic games from the 1970s, '80s and '90s have found a new audience through apps, social networks and free2play sites. These are the simple, addictive games that kickstarted the gaming industry. It is fitting, therefore, that the **first game for Android phones** was *PAC-Man* (Namco Bandai), released on 23 September 2008.

180

NAME THE GAME
Son of Adam and Elain, Marcus Fenix follows his father into the army.

FIRST PERFECT SCORE ON *GALAGA* ON iPHONE

The highest score that can be earned in the "Score Attack" mode of *Galaga* for iPhone – which is part of the *Galaga 30th Collection* (Namco Bandai, 2011) – is 999,999,999 points. "Trancematrix" was the first player to achieve this, reaching the perfect score on 8 December 2012. Namco's *Galaga* arcade machine was released in 1981.

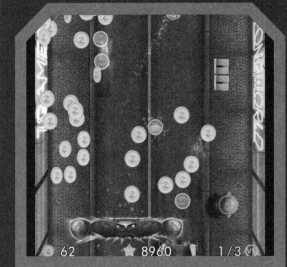

HIGHEST SCORE ON *PONG WORLD*

As of 29 June 2013, the highest score on the iOS version of *Pong World* (zGames, 2012) is 102,480 points, racked up by "Arthur.2000" on 4 December 2012. *Pong World* is the **first *Pong* game for smartphones and tablets**, and it offers a new, more detailed twist on the classic arcade smash.

BOOST

SPACE INNOVATORS

In 1981, legendary arcade release *Space Invaders* (Taito, 1978) became the **first arcade game debated in British Parliament** when the UK's Labour Party MP George Foulkes tabled a bill to have it banned for what he described as a connection to child "deviancy". It was also the **first game to feature animated aliens**. Decades after its heyday during the Golden Age of arcades, *Space Invaders* finally altered its basic, famous gameplay function: the **first *Space Invaders* game with vertical movement** was Taito's *Space Invaders Infinity Gene* (below), released for iOS on 27 July 2009. In all previous iterations of the game, players could only move the cannon left and right. For more of *Space Invaders'* other notable firsts, see p.94.

FIRST *SPACE INVADERS* GAME WITH MUSIC-GENERATED LEVELS

Seminal shooter *Space Invaders* (Taito) started out as an arcade game in 1978. The iOS version of *Space Invaders Infinity Gene* is the first in the series to feature levels generated by music tracks. The game's "Music Mode" allows you to choose any song on your iPhone or iPod Touch, then play a unique level designed to match the music.

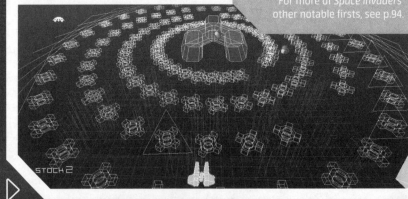

HIGHEST SCORE ON *PAC-MAN* FOR iOS

App Center user "[N.S.F] Lynx [BH]" notched up 3,361,200 points on *PAC-Man for iOS* (Namco Bandai, 2008) on 17 May 2011. The **highest score on *PAC-Man Championship Edition DX*** (Namco Bandai, 2010) is 519,200 points, by Olliver Kirby (USA) on 19 March 2013. Namco says that the original has been played more than 10 billion times.

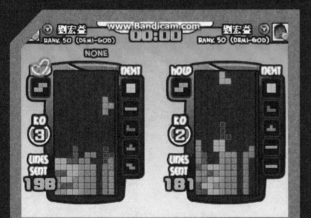

MOST WINS IN *TETRIS BATTLE*

As of 29 June 2013, the most wins in *Tetris Battle* was achieved by gamer Joe Lin, who has played the game 20,294 times and won on an incredible 16,449 occasions. *Tetris Battle* is a modern spin on the classic puzzle game *Tetris* (Alexey Pajitnov, 1985).

TOP TEN — BEST-SELLING ARCADE MACHINES

Machine	Units
PAC-Man (Namco, 1980)	400,000
Space Invaders (Taito Corporation, 1978)	360,000
Street Fighter II (Capcom, 1991)	200,000
Donkey Kong (Nintendo, 1981)	132,000
Ms. PAC-Man (Bally Midway, 1981)	125,000
Asteroids (Atari, 1979)	100,000
Defender (Williams Electronics, 1981)	60,000
Centipede (Atari, 1981)	55,988
Galaxian (Namco, 1979)	40,000
StarHorse2 (Sega, 2005)	38,600

Source: various sources combined; figures are approximate units sold

HIGHEST SCORE ON *FROGGER FREE*

The highest score ever achieved on *Frogger Free* (Konami, 2011) for iOS is 207,196 points earned by "Michael:V" on 5 September 2012. The aim on this modern version of the arcade game *Frogger* (Konami, 1981) is to help frogs cross busy roads and rivers. The **highest score on *Frogger*** is 970,440 points on 15 July 2012 by 45-year-old Michael Smith, who says he hopes to reach one million points.

LOWDOWN

Social network, smartphone and tablet games continue to flourish, making up 18% of the total gaming market in 2013, according to analysts Newzoo. While Zynga once ruled, in the summer of 2013 King usurped them as the most popular Facebook developer. In a sign of the increasing overlap between app games and social network titles, Facebook announced a new partnership with developers to publish and promote mobile games.

182

NAME THE GAME Private David Montes, a soldier killed by a shot to the head, is renowned for his profanities.

HIGHEST-GROSSING SMARTPHONE GAME

While *Candy Crush Saga* may be all the rage in the UK and USA, the most successful smartphone game in Japan – and the world – is *Puzzle & Dragons* (GungHo Online Entertainment, 2012). The Think Gaming website estimates that this grosses more than $2 million (£1.2 million) per day. By June 2013, the game had been installed 13 million times – a figure equal to 10% of Japan's total population.

FIRST TV GAMESHOW BASED ON A GAME

In April 2013, British broadcaster Channel 4 announced plans to launch a new television series based on popular Pictionary-style app *Draw Something* (OMGPop, 2012). Titled *Draw It!*, the Friday night programme is the first TV gameshow based on a videogame. Hosted by British comedian Mel Giedroyc (*above*), the show features two teams battling it out for the £5,000 ($7,800) prize money over three rounds of drawing contests.

FIRST GAME TO FEATURE PLAYER-CREATED ADVERTS

From May 2012, companies looking to advertise in *Draw Something* could buy words for the list of drawing choices players are given. KFC, NHL and Nike were three of the corporations to buy advertising words.

Despite the release of *Draw Something 2* earlier in the year, a drop in popularity led Zynga to shut down its OMGPop division in September 2013.

FIRST AUGMENTED REALITY TRADING CARDS BASED ON AN ONLINE GAME

In June 2013, sticker manufacturer Panini launched trading cards based on online game *Bin Weevils* (Bin Weevils Ltd, 2007). They incorporate augmented reality (AR) technology, meaning that the cards appear to come to life when looked at through a smartphone or tablet. Similar technology was used in Sony's *The Eye of Judgment* (2007), although effects had to be triggered by the bundled camera peripheral, the PlayStation Eye.

TOP TEN

HIGHEST-RATED PLAYERS ON *ASPHALT 8: AIRBORNE*

Brandon D'Souza	1,683
Rahul Patil	1,666
Anon	1,645
Anon	1,633
Ha Jun J	1,629
Duc KaKa	1,618
Driver 3151	1,617
Khang Ngo	1,612
Driver 8173	1,610
Thach Le	1,606

Source: in-game leaderboard, as of 24 September 2013

MOST LUCRATIVE GAME DOWNLOAD

Brandon Ashmore of Ohio, USA, got more than he expected when he installed word-association game *Say the Same Thing* (Space Inch, 2013) on 16 May 2013. It turned out to be the 50 billionth download of an app from the App Store. To celebrate, Apple awarded Ashmore a $10,000 (£6,400) gift card – not a bad earner, considering that the game is free.

LONGEST CHART-TOPPING RUN FOR A NINTENDO DS GAME

Moshi Monsters (Mind Candy, 2007) is one of the most popular online games, with a registered userbase of 80 million players worldwide. Spin-off title *Moshi Monsters: Moshling Zoo* (Mind Candy) was also a huge hit. Released on 11 November 2011, it spent 23 consecutive weeks at the top of the DS chart between 12 November 2011 and 23 June 2012 – the **most consecutive weeks at No.1 in the Nintendo DS game chart**. As of 22 August 2013, it had sold 1.33 million units.

183

BO:OM!

It has been a difficult year for Zynga. In July 2013, it gave up on its plan to move into games that use real money and focused instead on rebuilding user numbers for social gaming; having stood at 39 million in 2012, daily average users fell by 45% in 2013. Some 18% of the workforce – 520 jobs – were shed in June 2013.

GAMING MARATHONS

Ultra-gamers think differently. It isn't enough to set a high score. They keep going long after everyone else has gone to bed – and sometimes after everyone has got up again the next day. Lucian Randall meets gamers with an appetite for controller destruction.

NEED FOR RECORDS

Kenny Drews and Florian Fleissuer (both Germany) played *Need for Speed: Most Wanted* (EA, 2005) for 33 hours in Langenhagen, Hanover, Germany, from 31 May to 1 June 2013. Taking centre stage at a car exhibition for their attempt, the driving duo set the **longest marathon on a racing game**.

`33:00:00`

MARATHON KING

GWR marathons inspired Okan Kaya (Australia) to achieve the **longest videogame marathon on an FPS**. He played *Call of Duty: Black Ops II* (Treyarch, 2012) for 135 hr 15 min 10 sec, setting the overall record for **longest videogame marathon** in the process, in Waterloo, New South Wales, Australia, on 13–19 November 2012. "There were times when it felt very repetitive," he admits of the five-day-plus endurance feat. "On the third day I felt sick due to lack of sleep and felt I couldn't do the attempt but luckily I had my friends, family and 4Cabling staff to support me."

`135:15:10`

FLOOR FILLERS

Carrie Swidecki (USA), the star of our Party Time photoshoot (*see pp.162–63*), played *Just Dance 4* (Ubisoft, 2012) for 49 hr 3 min 22 sec in Bakersfield, California, USA, from 15 to 17 June 2013 – the **longest marathon on a dance game**. Her passion for dance games and setting records has led to her becoming an ambassador for "exergaming": "I never imagined I would be changing physical education, talking to politicians of the benefits of exergaming and demonstrating or setting world records. All while breaking boundaries for women in the gaming community, which is dominated by men and the youth." Carrie's enthusiasm can be infectious: "Exergaming encompasses everything I love in this world: dancing, sports, music, graphics, gaming and education."

`49:03:22`

LEAGUE OF THEIR OWN

Showing pluck – and puck – James Evans (*right*) and Bruce Ashton (*left*) played *NHL 10* (EA, 2009) for 24 hr 2 min on 30–31 July 2011, the **longest marathon on an NHL game**. Fresh from an energetic Guinness World Records photoshoot (*see pp.60–61*), James tells us: "As with many Canadians, we have a huge love for the game of hockey so we began thinking of how we could do something that was unique and was about hockey." As the organizer of the attempt, James found that the hardest part was trying to stay on top of everything. "The requirements for submitting evidence are very detailed so I was always trying to double-check the videos, camera, and, in the few seconds before we entered another game, I'd be taking down all the stats."

`24:02:00`

FIGHT STAR

Anthony "AJ" Lysiak (USA, *left*) played *Street Fighter X Tekken* (Capcom, 2012) in Garrettsville, Ohio, USA, for 48 hours exactly on 4–6 May 2012 – the **longest fighting game marathon**.

`48:00:00`

SUPERLATIVE SINGER

Julian Hill (UK, *right*) is a fan of Take That, and started and ended the **longest marathon on a karaoke game** on *SingStar* (London Studio, 2007) with the songs by the group. Raising money for Great Ormond Street Hospital, Julian took requests and finished after 24 hr 21 min 25 sec with "Rule the World".

`24:21:25`

THE GUITAR'S THE STAR

Charity is often the inspiration for a marathon. Patrick Young (USA) raised funds for the American Heart Association while setting the **longest marathon on *Guitar Hero***. His epic fret twiddle, from 23 to 26 February 2012, lasted 72 hr 17 min in Atlanta, Georgia, USA. Patrick said that the attempt was far from straightforward, despite the time he put into endurance training. "Day 3 was particularly bad," he recalls. "It was a very cold morning and no one knew how to turn the heat back on. We were huddled next to a small oscillating heater for several hours."

`72:17:00`

MARATHON TIPS

Guinness World Records marathon record holders give exclusive advice on making a successful attempt:
- **Okan Kaya:** "Plan a schedule for meals, breaks and recovery sessions. Eat healthily and keep moving."
- **Carrie Swidecki:** "Training for a marathon record is not only physically challenging, but mentally as well. Your body is going to take a lot of impact and I ask anyone who is considering these kinds of world records to do your research and be safe."
- **James Evans:** "Make sure you have a committed and reliable volunteer team! We wouldn't have been successful without our team of volunteers who stayed up almost as long as we did... [And] if you can tie a charity into your event, the interest that a Guinness World Records attempt brings can only increase exposure and awareness for good causes."

If these stories have inspired you to have a go, find out how to set your own Guinness World Records title on pp.8–9. And for a full list of all our videogame marathon records, simply turn the page...

FEATURE ▷

LONGEST MARATHON ON...	TIME
Call of Duty: Black Ops II	135 hr 15 min 10 sec
Assassin's Creed: Brotherhood	109 hr
*Q*bert*	84 hr 48 min
Guitar Hero	72 hr 17 min
Joust	67 hr 30 min
LittleBigPlanet 2	50 hr 1 min
Grand Theft Auto (series)	50 hr
Mario games (various)	50 hr
Just Dance 4	49 hr 3 min 22 sec
The Elder Scrolls V: Skyrim	48 hr 14 min
FIFA 12	48 hr 5 min
Metal Gear (series)	48 hr
Street Fighter X Tekken	48 hr
Final Fantasy (series)	34 hr
Need for Speed: Most Wanted (2005)	33 hr
Solitaire Blitz	30 hr
Resident Evil (series)	27 hr 8 min
Rock Band	26 hr 40 min
SingStar	24 hr 21 min 25 sec
Dungeon Defenders	24 hr 10 min
Pro Evolution Soccer 2011	24 hr 10 min
Minecraft	24 hr 10 min
Rainbow Six: Shadow Vanguard	24 hr 10 min
Guitar Hero World Tour	24 hr 2 min
NHL	24 hr 2 min

★ The longest videogame marathon on any game ever

RECORD HOLDER	DATE	NOTES
Okan Kaya (Australia)	13–19 Nov 2012	★ ▲ shooters
Tony Desmet, Jesse Rebmann, Jeffrey Gamon (all Belgium)	18–22 Dec 2010	▲ action-adventure
George Leutz (USA)	14–18 Feb 2013	▲ arcade
Patrick Young (USA)	23–26 Feb 2012	▲ rhythm
James Vollandt (USA)	5–8 Jul 1985	▲ platformer
David Dino, Lauren Guiliano, Sean Crowley (all USA)	17–19 Jan 2011	
Jeff Cork (USA)	6–8 Aug 2011	
Dan Ryckert (USA)	6–8 Aug 2011	
Carrie Swidecki (USA)	15–17 Jun 2013	▲ dance
Jeff Nation, JJ Locke, Casey Coffman, George Vogl, Jeff Sagedal, aka "The Great Falls Gamers" (all USA)	6–8 May 2012	▲ RPG
Jordan Bloemen, Scott Francis Winder (both Canada)	6–8 Aug 2012	▲ sports
Ben Reeves (USA)	6–8 Aug 2011	▲ stealth
Anthony "AJ" Lysiak (USA)	4–6 May 2012	▲ fighting
Philip Kollar (USA)	6–7 Aug 2011	▲ JRPG
Kenny Drews, Florian Fleissuer (both Germany)	31 May–1 Jun 2013	▲ racing
Laura Rich (UK), Kathleen Henkel (USA)	26–27 Jun 2012	▲ casual
Tim Turi (USA)	6–7 Aug 2011	▲ survival-horror
Sean "Phr34k" Feica (Canada)	26–27 Jul 2008	
Julian Hill (UK)	13–14 Apr 2012	▲ karaoke
Hanns Peter Glock (Austria)	19–20 Aug 2011	
Paul Dahlhoff (Germany)	19–20 Aug 2011	
Martin Fornleitner (Austria)	19–20 Aug 2011	▲ strategy
Stefan Reichspfarrer (Austria)	19–20 Aug 2011	
Guitar: Simo Piispanen; Bass: Aku Valmu; Vocals: Jaakko Kokkonen; Drums: Simo-Matti Liimatainen (all Finland)	21 Feb 2009	
James Evans, Bruce Ashton (both Canada)	30–31 Jul 2011	

▲ These marathons are also the longest within their genre

TOP 50 GAMES

Rank	Game		%
=50	Just Dance (Ubisoft, 2009–present)	›	0.29%
=50	Hitman (IO Interactive, 2000–present)	›	0.29%
=48	NBA 2K (Visual Concepts, 1999–present)	›	0.33%
=48	Gran Turismo (Polyphony Digital, 1997–present)	›	0.33%
=43	World of Tanks (Wargaming.net, 2010–present)	›	0.36%
=43	Red Dead Redemption (Rockstar, 2010)	›	0.36%
=43	Mortal Kombat (Midway/NetherRealm, 1992–present)	›	0.36%
=43	Crash Bandicoot (Various, 1996–2010)	›	0.36%
=43	LEGO (Traveller's Tales, 1997–present)	›	0.36%
42	LittleBigPlanet (Media Molecule, 2008–present)	›	0.39%
=40	WWE (Yuke's, 2000–present)	›	0.42%
=40	Saints Row (Volition, Inc., 2006–present)	›	0.42%
=36	Super Smash Bros. (HAL Laboratory, 1999–present)	›	0.46%
=36	Portal (Valve, 2007–present)	›	0.46%
=36	PAC-Man (Namco, 1980–present)	›	0.46%
=36	Half-Life (Valve, 1998–present)	›	0.46%
35	Mass Effect (BioWare, 2007–present)	›	0.49%
34	Gears of War (Epic Games, 2006–present)	›	0.52%
=32	Batman: Arkham Asylum & City (Rocksteady, 2009–2011)	›	0.55%
=32	DotA (Valve, 2005–present)	›	0.55%
31	Fallout (Various, 1997–present)	›	0.59%
=28	Uncharted (Naughty Dog, 2007–present)	›	0.62%
=28	Resident Evil (Capcom, 1996–present)	›	0.62%
=28	BioShock (Irrational Games, 2007–present)	›	0.62%
27	Far Cry (Crytek/Ubisoft, 2004–present)	›	0.65%
26	God of War (SCE Santa Monica, 2005–present)	›	0.69%
25	Pro Evolution Soccer (Konami, 2001–present)	›	0.72%
24	The Witcher (CD Projekt RED, 2007–present)	›	0.75%
=21	World of Warcraft (Blizzard, 2004–present)	›	0.78%
=21	The Last of Us (Naughty Dog, 2013)	›	0.78%
=21	Kingdom Hearts (Square/Square Enix, 2002–present)	›	0.78%
20	Counter-Strike (Valve, 1999–present)	›	0.81%
=17	Sonic the Hedgehog (Sega/Sonic Team, 1991–present)	›	0.88%
=17	Metal Gear (Konami/Kojima, 1987–present)	›	0.88%
=17	Borderlands (Gearbox Software, 2009–present)	›	0.88%
16	League of Legends (Riot Games, 2009)	›	1.01%
15	Mario Kart (Nintendo, 1992–present)	›	1.14%
14	Need for Speed (Various, 1994–present)	›	1.44%
13	Final Fantasy (Square/Square Enix, 1987–present)	›	1.53%
12	Angry Birds (Rovio, 2009–present)	›	1.89%
11	Pokémon (Game Freak, 1996–present)	›	1.93%
10	The Elder Scrolls (Bethesda, 1994–present)	›	2.19%
9	Battlefield (DICE, 2002–present)	›	2.25%
8	Assassin's Creed (Ubisoft, 2007–present)	›	3.00%
7	FIFA (EA, 1993–present)	›	3.04%
6	The Legend of Zelda (Nintendo, 1986–present)	›	3.30%
5	Halo (Bungie/343 Industries, 2001–present)	›	3.49%
4	Grand Theft Auto (Rockstar, 1997–present)	›	4.78%

Thousands of votes were cast in our 2013 reader poll at guinnessworld records.com/gamers to determine the most popular gaming franchise ever. Your tastes are clearly diverse, as more than 600 different games received votes. Turn the page to find out which three franchises the readers of *Gamer's Edition* love the most.

We received votes from 127 countries around the world, from Afghanistan to Zimbabwe. This chart shows the 27 countries with the most voters:

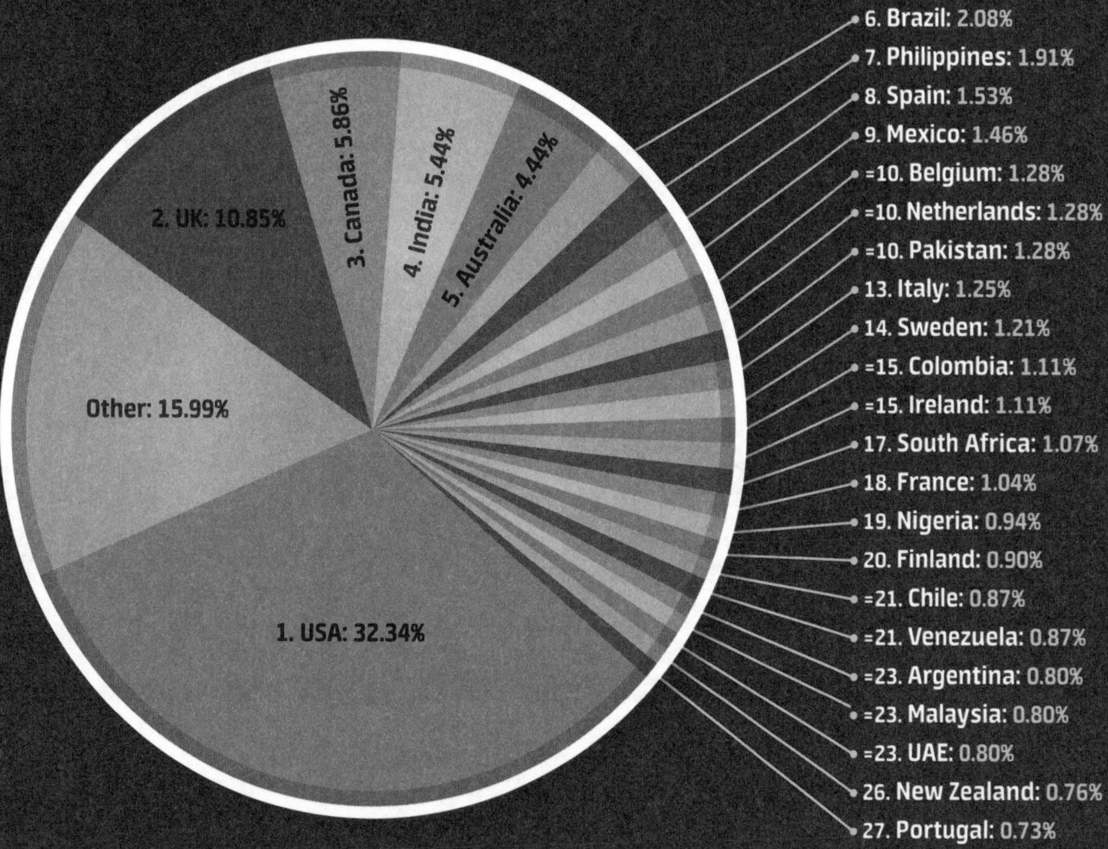

- 6. Brazil: 2.08%
- 7. Philippines: 1.91%
- 8. Spain: 1.53%
- 9. Mexico: 1.46%
- =10. Belgium: 1.28%
- =10. Netherlands: 1.28%
- =10. Pakistan: 1.28%
- 13. Italy: 1.25%
- 14. Sweden: 1.21%
- =15. Colombia: 1.11%
- =15. Ireland: 1.11%
- 17. South Africa: 1.07%
- 18. France: 1.04%
- 19. Nigeria: 0.94%
- 20. Finland: 0.90%
- =21. Chile: 0.87%
- =21. Venezuela: 0.87%
- =23. Argentina: 0.80%
- =23. Malaysia: 0.80%
- =23. UAE: 0.80%
- 26. New Zealand: 0.76%
- 27. Portugal: 0.73%

2. UK: 10.85%
3. Canada: 5.86%
4. India: 5.44%
5. Australia: 4.44%
Other: 15.99%
1. USA: 32.34%

The votes cast across your top 50 games fall into the following genres:

%	Genre
34.83%	SHOOTERS
21.89%	ACTION-ADVENTURE
9.68%	PLATFORMERS
9.39%	RPGs
9.06%	STRATEGY & SIMULATION
5.10%	SPORTS
3.63%	RACING
2.94%	PUZZLES
1.56%	FIGHTING
0.98%	MMORPGs
0.57%	SOCIAL, MOBILE & INSTANT
0.37%	PARTY TIME

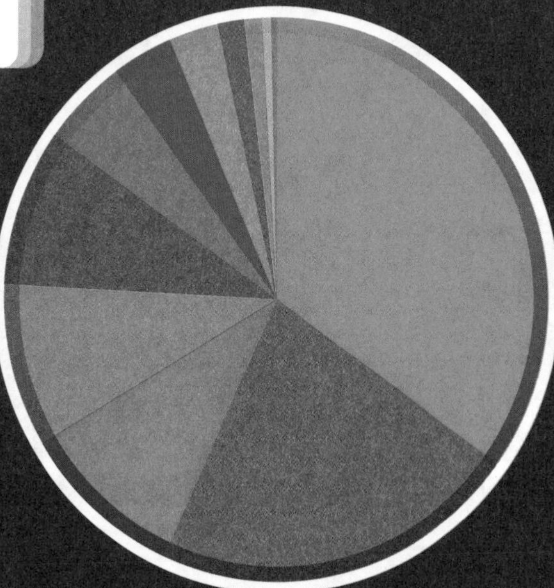

TOP 50 GAMES

3

MINECRAFT

It's no surprise that the block-builder is in your top three, considering its phenomenal success since debuting in 2009. This mammoth open-worlder is constantly updating itself both on PC and the Xbox 360, ensuring that its addictive gameplay keeps on growing.

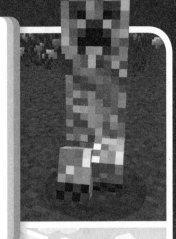

2

MARIO BROS.

The legendary Princess-saving plumber's first *Mario Bros.* outing with brother Luigi was in 1983. Thirty years and several games later, he's still doing the business and the *Bros.* games are by far your favourite platformer franchise. The most recent release, 2012's *New Super Mario Bros. U* (pictured left), is the fourth title in the *New Super Mario Bros.* series.

3	Minecraft (Mojang/4J Studios, 2011–present)
2	Mario Bros. & Super Mario Bros. (Nintendo, 1983–present)
1	Call of Duty (Infinity Ward/Treyarch, 2003–present)

1

CALL OF DUTY

The *CoD* games won our poll by a landslide, proving that – in the year of their 10th anniversary – these military shooters are still firing on all cylinders. *Black Ops II* (2012) was easily your favourite *CoD* game, although most of the titles got a look-in. The latest game in the series, *Ghosts*, is pictured left and top left.

> 5.39%

> 6.10%

> 18.15%

GAME CHANGERS

From the innovators who come up with the ideas to the executives who green-light them, Charlie Peacock profiles some of the most powerful and original thinkers in gaming. These are the men and women behind the games you play and the platforms you play them on.

THE STRATEGIST
> Andrew House

This is the man who unveiled the PS4 at E3 2013 and stole Microsoft's thunder (*see pp.18–21*) to rapturous cheers. House, the president and CEO of Sony Computer Entertainment, hails from Wales, UK, studied at Oxford University and in 1990 joined Sony, where he has stayed ever since. He worked on the launch of the original PlayStation in 1995, and then on the North American releases of the PS2 and PSP. Under his leadership, Sony fired the decisive first shots in the latest battle of the console wars and the launch of the PS4 is firmly under his command.

THE INVENTOR
> Shigeru Miyamoto

192

Creating Mario, the **most prolific character in videogames** (*see p.88–89*), might be enough for most people. The Italian plumber was key in transforming Nintendo into one of the most successful publishers, but Japanese gaming guru Shigeru Miyamoto has been responsible for much more. He was Nintendo's first staff artist, drafted into game design as the only available employee. Miyamoto went on to head up Nintendo Entertainment Analysis & Development (EAD), the company's development wing, and created such flagship series as *The Legend of Zelda* (1986–present; *see pp.40–41*). He is also the brains behind several Wii titles, including *Wii Fit* (2007).

THE MAVERICKS
> Sam & Dan Houser

Briton Sam Houser (*far right*) was a head honcho at the interactive arm of BMG Records when he acquired the original *Grand Theft Auto* (1997; *see pp.30–31*), a top-down driving game he liked for the tabloid-baiting innovation that players could use their cars for mowing down pedestrians. Alongside brother Dan, he founded Rockstar Games in the USA in 1998, and the company has gone on to develop consistently innovative games such as *Red Dead Redemption* (2010) and the *Max Payne* series (2001–13). They made it into *Time* magazine's list of the world's 100 most influential people in 2009.

THE RESCUER
> Don Mattrick

Having overseen such classic EA series as *The Sims* (2000–13) and *FIFA* (1993–2013), Canadian Don Mattrick headed up Microsoft's Interactive Entertainment Business from 2007 to 2013, presiding over all aspects of Xbox and PC gaming. Xbox turned a profit on his watch after years of damaging losses, helped by the success of the Kinect, which Mattrick championed. He left Microsoft to become CEO of struggling mobile and online games publisher Zynga in July 2013, and immediately began a significant re-structuring.

THE PIONEER
> Hideo Kojima

Metal Gear (Konami, 1987; *see pp.38–39*) was the first major game created by director, producer, designer and writer Hideo Kojima, but he had to wait until 1998 for a global hit with stealth genre pioneer *Metal Gear Solid*. With dozens of titles under his belt, Kojima began heading up his own studio, Kojima Productions, in 2005. Konami recognized him further by making him vice-president of digital entertainment.

THE PEOPLE'S PRESIDENT
> Satoru Iwata

Programmer-turned-boss Satoru Iwata joined Nintendo in 2000, after working at subsidiary company HAL Laboratory for 17 years. Iwata became president and CEO of Nintendo in 2002. He oversaw the development and launch of the Wii, the **best-selling seventh-generation console** (*see pp.14–17*), but he was also the man who signed off the Wii U, whose sales have been comparatively disappointing. But Iwata, who took a 50% pay cut in 2011, steadfastly refuses to fire any of his staff, stating that "I sincerely doubt employees who fear that they may be laid off will be able to develop software titles that could impress people around the world."

THE INDIE KID
> Gabe Newell

Valve is the "gamer's gaming company". PC fans say that whatever consoles do, Valve has already done it – and better. Under colourful co-founder and MD Gabe Newell, Valve has released some of the most celebrated PC games of all time, from *Half-Life* (1998) to *Portal* (2007). Valve was also the first with a cloud-based platform for digital downloads in the form of Steam, and Newell has championed indie developers through the Steam Greenlight scheme. Like Bill Gates, Newell dropped out of Harvard. He spent 13 years working at Microsoft.

THE PRODUCER
> Jade Raymond

Jade Raymond (Canada) produced the first title in the *Assassin's Creed* series (2007–present; *see pp.32–33*). She also produced *The Sims Online* in 2002, and, most recently, headed up a team of 600 working on *Tom Clancy's Splinter Cell: Blacklist* (2013). An avid gamer in her spare time, she is a trailblazing figure in an industry where 88% of developers are male. Raymond has been the Managing Director of Ubisoft Toronto since its inception in 2009.

193

THE BIG CHEESE
> Bobby Kotick

There are few people in the world with more influence on which games get to consumers than Bobby Kotick. The 2008 merger between Activision and Vivendi Games – the owners of Blizzard, who developed *World of Warcraft* (1994–2013) and *StarCraft* (1998–2013) – meant that Kotick became CEO of Activision Blizzard, the largest games publisher after Nintendo. He has been a controversial figure in the industry for a perceived "production-line attitude" to game creation, yet whatever opinion anyone has of him, successes such as the 2007 relaunch of *Call of Duty* have only served to raise his profile. Alongside his role at Activision Blizzard, Kotick is also a director at The Coca-Cola Company.

THE TASTEMAKERS
> Mike Krahulik & Jerry Holkins

Holkins and Krahulik met at high school in the mid-1990s and found they shared a love for games and comics. They launched *Penny Arcade*, a satirical online comic about gaming, in 1998, and 15 years on, it is published three times a week and has a readership of some 3.5 million. So great is the pair's influence that a few words from either one can make or break a game. In 2003, Holkins and Krahulik launched a charity, Child's Play, which distributes games to sick children, and in 2004 they started the Penny Arcade Expo (PAX), a regular convention attended by more than 70,000 gamers.

BEST OF ONLINE

MOST LIKES ON A FACEBOOK GAMING PAGE

1	Texas HoldEm Poker	70,152,018
2	Candy Crush Saga	43,457,538
3	FarmVille	39,240,437
4	PlayStation	34,922,988
5	CityVille	33,492,611
6	Criminal Case	30,999,704
7	Angry Birds	24,968,198
8	Xbox	22,115,212
9	EA SPORTS FIFA	20,871,206
10	Mafia Wars	18,671,260

Source: pagedatapro.com, as of 2 September 2013

MOST FOLLOWERS ON A GAMING TWITTER ACCOUNT

1	PlayStation, @PlayStation	2,470,369
2	Microsoft, @Microsoft	2,377,198
3	Xbox, @Xbox	1,827,151
4	Veronica Belmont, @Veronica	1,676,939
5	Electronic Arts, @EA	1,509,370
6	Call of Duty, @CallofDuty	1,417,531
7	Markus Persson, @notch	1,338,639
8	Frag Dolls, @FragDolls	1,278,543
9	Rockstar Games, @RockstarGames	1,258,909
10	EA SPORTS FIFA, @EASPORTSFIFA	1,023,638

Source: twitter.com, as of 2 September 2013

Social media is a big part of gaming, whether it be sharing scores, looking for tips or getting the news first. Here we look at some of the biggest social networks for videogamers.

MOST WATCHED GAMING VIDEOS ON YOUTUBE

1	"'Revenge' – A Minecraft Parody of Usher's DJ Got Us Fallin' in Love – Crafted Using Noteblocks", CaptainSparklez, 19 August 2011	112,456,020
2	"Angry Birds & the Mighty Eagle", RovioMobile, 10 September 2010	99,131,980
3	"Angry Birds Cinematic Trailer", RovioMobile, 3 February 2010	96,881,352
4	"Angry Birds Rio Trailer", RovioMobile, 27 January 2011	92,197,501
5	"Cars 2 HD Gameplay Compilation", DarkZeroTV, 7 August 2011	74,354,785
6	"Official Minecraft Trailer", TeamMojang, 6 December 2011	70,466,547
7	"'TNT' – A Minecraft Parody of Taio Cruz's Dynamite – Crafted Using Note Blocks", CaptainSparklez, 26 February 2011	69,998,774
8	"Baby Bathing Game for little kids Gameplay", GameplaysTv, 16 January 2011	67,214,765
9	"'Fallen Kingdom' – A Minecraft Parody of Coldplay's Viva la Vida (Music Video)", CaptainSparklez, 1 April 2012	63,193,611
10	"Dumb Ways to Die", DumbWays2Die, 14 November 2012	57,833,084

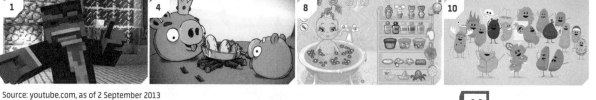

Source: youtube.com, as of 2 September 2013

MOST WATCHED REPLAY VIDEOS ON TWITCH

1	"Hotshot gets baited"	TSM_TheOddOne	League of Legends on SoloMid	368,463
2	"5 man lvl1 turret dive."	wickd	League of Legends on Evil Geniuses	305,888
3	"REACTION TO GOLD (Alvin Cheong Youtube)"	Hipmotop	League of Legends	280,148
4	"Nurse Akali cosplay ^_^"	Gemieee	League of Legends	277,686
5	"Dyrus moment of the year"	TSM_Dyrus	League of Legends on SoloMid	270,734
6	"Mid Veigar! Mid... gar... MIDGAR! FFVII!"	TaraBabcock	League of Legends on AdvancedGamers	252,318
7	"Siv HD gives Sovitia Scientific Makeover"	SivHD	League of Legends	227,418
8	"Super AMUMU – Bug?"	zafichan	League of Legends	225,845
9	"Xpecial - Thresh OP"	TSM_Xpecial	League of Legends on SoloMid	223,453
10	"HotshotGG and Friends take on Team Siren"	TSM_TheOddOne	League of Legends on SoloMid	222,686

Source: twitch.tv, as of 2 September 2013 (name of video / user / subject / views)

BEST OF THE BAFTAs

GAMES WITH MOST NOMINATIONS 2003-13

1	Uncharted 2: Among Thieves	10
=2	Batman: Arkham City Call of Duty: Modern Warfare 2 L.A. Noire	9
=5	Batman: Arkham Asylum Grand Theft Auto: Vice City Journey LocoRoco Tom Clancy's Ghost Recon Advanced Warfighter	8
=10	Assassin's Creed II Assassin's Creed: Brotherhood Call of Duty 4: Modern Warfare Call of Duty: Black Ops Grand Theft Auto IV Half-Life 2 Heavy Rain Uncharted 3: Drake's Deception The Walking Dead Wii Sports	7
=20	Burnout 3: Takedown The Elder Scrolls V: Skyrim EyeToy: Play Far Cry 3 Gears of War LittleBigPlanet (PS3) LittleBigPlanet 2 Mass Effect 2 Portal 2 We Love Katamari	6

Uncharted 2:
Among Thieves

Batman: Arkham City

Grand Theft Auto: Vice City

GAMES WITH MOST WINS 2003-13

=1	Grand Theft Auto: Vice City Half-Life 2 Wii Sports	6
4	Journey	5
5	Uncharted 2: Among Thieves	4
=6	Battlefield 3 Burnout 3: Takedown Call of Duty 4: Modern Warfare Heavy Rain	3
=10	Advance Wars 2: Black Hole Rising Batman: Arkham Asylum Batman: Arkham City Crackdown Dead Space EyeToy: Play FIFA 10 God of War II LittleBigPlanet 2 LocoRoco Ōkami Portal 2 Shadow of the Colossus Tom Clancy's Ghost Recon Advanced Warfighter The Unfinished Swan The Walking Dead	2

In 2003, the British Academy of Film and Television Arts awards (BAFTAs) began celebrating the best in gaming. The 9th British Academy Games Awards ceremony took place in March 2013.

BAFTA WINNERS AND NOMINEES 2013

CATEGORY	WINNER	NOMINEES
Action	Far Cry 3	Hitman: Absolution, Call of Duty: Black Ops II, Halo 4, Mass Effect 3, Borderlands 2
Artistic Achievement	Journey	The Room, Halo 4, Dear Esther, Borderlands 2, Far Cry 3
Audio Achievement	Journey	Far Cry 3, Beat Sneak Bandit, Halo 4, Assassin's Creed III, Dear Esther
Best Game	Dishonored	Far Cry 3, FIFA 13, Journey, Mass Effect, The Walking Dead
British Game	The Room	Need for Speed: Most Wanted, Forza Horizon, Dear Esther, Super Hexagon, LEGO: The Lord of the Rings
Debut Game	The Unfinished Swan	Deadlight, Forza Horizon, Dear Esther, The Room, Proteus
Family	LEGO Batman 2: DC Super Heroes	Minecraft: Xbox 360 Edition, Just Dance 4, Skylanders: Giants, Clay Jam, LEGO: The Lord of the Rings
Game Design	Journey	Dishonored, Far Cry 3, XCOM: Enemy Unknown, Borderlands 2, The Walking Dead
Game Innovation	The Unfinished Swan	Fez, Call of Duty: Black Ops II, Wonderbook: Book of Spells, Journey, Kinect Sesame Street TV
Mobile & Handheld	The Walking Dead	LittleBigPlanet PS Vita, The Room, New Star Soccer, Incoboto, Super Monsters Ate My Condo!!
Online – Browser	SongPop	The Settlers Online, Merlin: The Game, RuneScape, Amateur Surgeon Hospital, Dick & Dom's Hoopla!
Online – Multiplayer	Journey	Assassin's Creed III, Call of Duty: Black Ops II, Need for Speed: Most Wanted, Halo 4, Borderlands 2
Original Music	Journey	Diablo III, Assassin's Creed III, Thomas Was Alone, The Unfinished Swan, The Walking Dead
Performer	Danny Wallace (Thomas Was Alone)	Nolan North (Uncharted: Golden Abyss), Melissa Hutchison (The Walking Dead), Dave Fennoy (The Walking Dead), Adrian Hough (Assassin's Creed III), Nigel Carrington (Dear Esther)
Sports/Fitness	New Star Soccer	Forza Horizon, F1 2012, FIFA 13, Nike+ Kinect Training, Trials Evolution
Story	The Walking Dead	Journey, Far Cry 3, Thomas Was Alone, Mass Effect 3, Dishonored
Strategy	XCOM: Enemy Unknown	Dark Souls: Prepare to Die, Diablo III, Great Big War Game, Total War: Shogun 2 – Fall of the Samurai, Football Manager 2013

Far Cry 3

Dishonored

XCOM: Enemy Unknown

BEST OF KICKSTARTER

MOST FUNDED VIDEOGAME PROJECTS

1	"OUYA: A New Kind of Video Game Console"	OUYA (USA)	console	$8,596,474
2	"Torment: Tides of Numenera"	inXile entertainment (USA)	RPG	$4,188,927
3	"Project Eternity" (*below left*)	Obsidian Entertainment (USA)	RPG	$3,986,929
4	"Double Fine Adventure"	Double Fine and 2 Player (USA)	adventure game	$3,336,371
5	"Wasteland 2"	inXile entertainment (USA)	RPG	$2,933,252
6	"Homestuck Adventure Game"	MS Paint Adventures (USA)	adventure game	$2,485,506
7	"HEX MMO Trading Card Game"	Cryptozoic Entertainment (USA)	MMOTCG	$2,278,255
8	"Camelot Unchained"	City State Entertainment (USA)	MMORPG	$2,232,933
9	"Planetary Annihilation - A Next Generation RTS"	Uber Entertainment Inc. (USA)	RTS game	$2,229,344
10	"Star Citizen" (*below right*)	Cloud Imperium Games (USA)	RTS game	$2,134,374

3

10

MOST FUNDED PROJECTS OVERALL

1	"Pebble: E-Paper Watch for iPhone and Android"	Pebble Technology (USA)	watch	$10,266,845
2	"OUYA: A New Kind of Video Game Console"	OUYA (USA)	console	$8,596,474
3	"The Veronica Mars Movie Project"	Rob Thomas (USA)	movie	$5,702,153
4	"Torment: Tides of Numenera"	inXile entertainment (USA)	RPG	$4,188,927
5	"Project Eternity"	Obsidian Entertainment (USA)	RPG	$3,986,929
6	"Reaper Miniatures Bones: An Evolution Of Gaming Miniatures"	Reaper Miniatures (USA)	miniature figures	$3,429,235
7	"Double Fine Adventure"	Double Fine and 2 Player (USA)	adventure game	$3,336,371
8	"WISH I WAS HERE"	Zach Braff (USA)	movie	$3,105,473
9	"FORM 1: An affordable, professional 3D printer"	Formlabs (USA)	printer	$2,945,885
10	"Wasteland 2"	inXile entertainment (USA)	RPG	$2,933,252

HIGHEST PERCENTAGE PLEDGED FOR VIDEOGAME PROJECTS

	NAME	MAKER	TYPE	REQUIREMENT	PLEDGED	PERCENTAGE
1	"Energy Hook" (*below right*)	Happion Laboratories (USA)	action-adventure game	$1	$41,535	4,153,501%
2	"Build Your Own Arcade" (*below right*)	Archie (USA)	make-your-own kit	$25	$1,248	4,992%
3	"GAMEFUL, a Secret HQ for Worldchanging Game Developers"	Jane McGonigal (USA)	online forum	$2,000	$64,965	3,248%
4	"9 Year Old Builds Her First RPG... TRUTH & TROLLS!"	Susan Wilson (USA)	RPG	$829	$24,534	2,959%
5	"Super Drake Tracker 2000 EX"	Dan Teasdale (USA)	software	$550	$12,390	2,252%
6	"FTL: Faster Than Light"	Subset Games (China)	RTS game	$10,000	$200,542	2,005%
7	"Megatokyo Visual Novel Game"	Fred Gallagher (USA)	visual novel game	$20,000	$299,184	1,495%
8	"Girl Genius and the Rats of Mechanicsburg"	Stephen Beeman (USA)	action-adventure game	$7,500	$108,195	1,442%
9	"Resonance: Retro-Styled Adventure Game – contest entry fees and additional funding"	VinceTwelve (USA)	adventure game	$150	$2,080	1,386%
10	"Freedom Planet – High Speed Platform Game"	GalaxyTrail/Strife (Denmark)	platform game	$2,000	$25,472	1,273%

199

MOST FUNDED VIDEOGAME PROJECTS BY COUNTRY

1	USA	569		1	California	134
2	UK	54		2	New York	48
3	Canada	19		3	Texas	44
4	Denmark	7		4	Washington	41
=5	Australia	5		5	Massachusetts	26
=5	Spain	5		6	Illinois	25
7	Germany	4		7	Oregon	23
=8	Brazil	3		8	Florida	20
=8	China	3		9	Pennsylvania	19
=8	Japan	3		10	Michigan	15

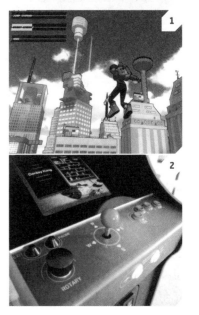

BEST OF 2012 & 2013

BEST-SELLING GAMES IN 2012

#	Game	Figures
1	*Call of Duty: Black Ops II* (Treyarch, 2012) on Xbox 360	10.86
2	*Call of Duty: Black Ops II* (Treyarch, 2012) on PS3	8.85
3	*Halo 4* (343 Industries, 2012) on Xbox 360	7.34
4	*Pokémon Black/White Version 2* (Game Freak, 2012) on DS	6.03
5	*FIFA 13* (EA Canada, 2012) on PS3	5.59
6	*Just Dance 4* (Ubisoft, 2012) on Wii	5.43
7	*New Super Mario Bros. 2* (Nintendo, 2012) on 3DS	5.04
8	*Kinect Adventures!* (Good Science Studio, 2010) on Xbox 360	4.56
9	*Assassin's Creed III* (Ubisoft, 2012) on PS3	4.37
10	*FIFA 13* (EA Canada, 2012) on Xbox 360	4.07

(figures in millions)

BEST-SELLING PLATFORMS IN 2012

#	Platform	Figures
1	Nintendo 3DS (Nintendo, 2011)	14.40
2	PS3 (Sony, 2006)	12.73
3	Xbox 360 (Microsoft, 2005)	11.09
4	Wii (Nintendo, 2006)	5.24
5	PlayStation Portable (Sony, 2004)	4.28
6	PlayStation Vita (Sony, 2011)	3.67
7	Nintendo DS (Nintendo, 2004)	3.01
8	Wii U (Nintendo, 2012)	2.24

(figures in millions)

MOST CRITICALLY ACCLAIMED GAMES RELEASED IN 2012

#	Game	Score
1	*Persona 4 Golden* (Atlus) on PS Vita	94.16%
2	*Journey* (Thatgamecompany) on PS3	92.56%
3	*Mass Effect 3* (BioWare) on Xbox 360	92.17%
4	*Xenoblade Chronicles* (Monolith Soft) on Wii	91.74%
5	*Mass Effect 3* (BioWare) on PS3	91.65%
6	*Trials Revolution* (RedLynx) on Xbox 360	91.52%
7	*Borderlands 2* (Gearbox Software) on PS3	90.50%
8	*Mark of the Ninja* (Klei Entertainment) on Xbox 360	90.43%
9	*Ōkami HD* (HexaDrive) on PS3	90.30%
10	*Borderlands 2* (Gearbox Software) on PC	90.10%

3

1

2

9

The best of 2012 and our 2013 snapshot includes sales figures of games and platforms from VGChartz up until 2 September 2013. GameRankings have provided us with a look at the critics' favourites of 2012 and 2013 so far.

BEST-SELLING GAMES IN 2013

1	The Last of Us (Naughty Dog, 2013) on PS3	3.10
2	Animal Crossing: New Leaf (Nintendo, 2013) on 3DS	2.69
3	Luigi's Mansion: Dark Moon (Next Level Games, 2013) on 3DS	2.44
4	Call of Duty: Black Ops II (Treyarch, 2012) on PS3	1.83
5	Call of Duty: Black Ops II (Treyarch, 2012) on Xbox 360	1.81
6	Tomb Raider (Crystal Dynamics, 2013) on PS3	1.42
7	Tomodachi Collection: Shin Seikatsu (Nintendo, 2013) on 3DS	1.39
8	BioShock Infinite (Irrational Games, 2013) on Xbox 360	1.35
9	God of War: Ascension (SCE, 2013) on PS3	1.34
10	New Super Mario Bros. 2 (Nintendo, 2012) on 3DS	1.25

BEST-SELLING PLATFORMS IN 2013

1	Nintendo 3DS (Nintendo, 2011)	5.65
2	PS3 (Sony, 2006)	5.09
3	Xbox 360 (Microsoft, 2005)	3.46
4	PlayStation Portable (Sony, 2004)	2.26
5	PlayStation Vita (Sony, 2011)	1.46
6	Wii (Nintendo, 2006)	1.25
7	Wii U (Nintendo, 2012)	1.21
8	Nintendo DS (Nintendo, 2004)	0.57

(figures in millions)

201

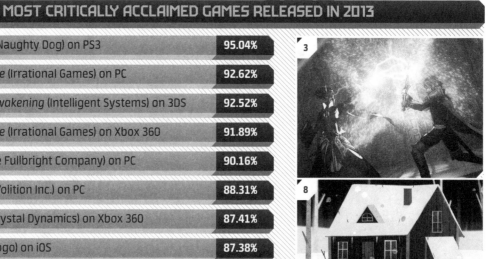

(figures in millions)

MOST CRITICALLY ACCLAIMED GAMES RELEASED IN 2013

1	The Last of Us (Naughty Dog) on PS3	95.04%
2	BioShock Infinite (Irrational Games) on PC	92.62%
3	Fire Emblem: Awakening (Intelligent Systems) on 3DS	92.52%
4	BioShock Infinite (Irrational Games) on Xbox 360	91.89%
5	Gone Home (The Fullbright Company) on PC	90.16%
6	Saints Row IV (Volition Inc.) on PC	88.31%
7	Tomb Raider (Crystal Dynamics) on Xbox 360	87.41%
8	Year Walk (Simogo) on iOS	87.38%
9	MLB 13: The Show (SCEA) on PS3	87.16%
10	Animal Crossing: New Leaf (Nintendo) on 3DS	87.09%

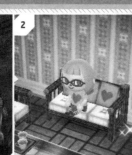

STATS ALL, FOLKS!

MOST CRITICALLY ACCLAIMED GAMES EVER

#	Game	Score
1	*Super Mario Galaxy* (Nintendo, 2007) on Wii	97.64%
2	*The Legend of Zelda: Ocarina of Time* (Nintendo, 1998) on N64	97.54%
3	*Super Mario Galaxy 2* (Nintendo, 2010) on Wii	97.35%
4	*Grand Theft Auto IV* (Rockstar North, 2008) on PS3	97.04%
5	*SoulCalibur* (Namco, 1999) on Dreamcast	96.94%
6	*Grand Theft Auto IV* (Rockstar North, 2008) on Xbox 360	96.67%
7	*Super Mario 64* (Nintendo, 1996) on N64	96.41%
8	*Uncharted 2: Among Thieves* (Naughty Dog, 2009) on PS3	96.38%
9	*The Orange Box* [compilation] (Valve, 2007) on Xbox 360	96.36%
10	*Metroid Prime* (Retro Studios/Nintendo, 2002) on GameCube	96.35%

Source: gamerankings.com, as of 9 September 2013

BEST-SELLING GAMES EVER

#	Game	Sales
1	*Wii Sports* (Nintendo, 2006) on Wii	81.50
2	*Super Mario Bros.* (Nintendo, 1985) on NES	40.24
3	*Mario Kart Wii* (Nintendo, 2008) on Wii	33.92
4	*Wii Sports Resort* (Nintendo, 2008) on Wii	31.86
5	*Pokémon Red/Green/Blue Version* (Game Freak, 1996) on Game Boy	31.37
6	*Tetris* (Nintendo, 1989) on Game Boy	30.26
7	*New Super Mario Bros.* (Nintendo, 2006) on DS	29.26
8	*Wii Play* (Nintendo, 2006) on Wii	28.74
9	*Duck Hunt* (Nintendo, 1984) on NES	28.31
10	*New Super Mario Bros. Wii* (Nintendo, 2006) on Wii	27.08

Source: vgchartz.com, as of 9 September 2013 (figures in millions)

GAME CRITICS AWARDS – BEST OF E3 2013

Tearaway

Watch Dogs

Fantasia: Music Evolved

Best of Show	*Titanfall (Respawn Entertainment) for PC, Xbox 360, Xbox One*
Best Original Game	*Titanfall (Respawn Entertainment) for PC, Xbox 360, Xbox One*
Best Console Game	*Titanfall (Respawn Entertainment) for Xbox 360, Xbox One*
Best Handheld/Mobile Game	*Tearaway (Media Molecule) for PS Vita*
Best PC Game	*Titanfall (Respawn Entertainment) for PC*
Best Hardware/Peripheral	*Oculus Rift (Oculus VR)*
Best Action Game	*Titanfall (Respawn Entertainment) for PC, Xbox 360, Xbox One*
Best Action/Adventure Game	*Watch Dogs (Ubisoft Montreal) for PC, PS3, PS4, Xbox 360, Xbox One, Wii U*
Best Role Playing Game	*The Elder Scrolls Online (ZeniMax Online) for PC, PS4, Xbox One*
Best Racing Game	*Need for Speed: Rivals (Ghost Games) for PC, PS3, PS4, Xbox 360, Xbox One*
Best Sports Game	*NHL 14 (EA Canada) for PS3, Xbox 360*
Best Strategy Game	*Total War: Rome II (The Creative Assembly) for PC*
Best Social/Casual Game	*Fantasia: Music Evolved (Harmonix) for Xbox 360, Xbox One*
Best Online Multiplayer	*Titanfall (Respawn Entertainment) for PC, Xbox 360, Xbox One*
Best Downloadable Game	*Transistor (Supergiant Games) for PC, PS4*

MOST RATED GAMES ON LOVEFILM

1	*Call of Duty 4: Modern Warfare* (Infinity Ward, 2007)	23,021
2	*Grand Theft Auto IV* (Rockstar North, 2008)	17,412
3	*Batman: Arkham Asylum* (Rocksteady Studios, 2009)	15,468
4	*Assassin's Creed* (Ubisoft, 2007)	15,363
5	*Star Wars: The Force Unleashed* (LucasArts, 2008)	14,170
6	*Assassin's Creed II* (Ubisoft, 2009)	13,720
7	*Call of Duty: World at War* (Treyarch, 2008)	12,788
8	*L.A. Noire* (Team Bondi, 2011)	11,861
9	*BioShock* (Irrational Games, 2007)	11,835
10	*Resident Evil 5* (Capcom, 2009)	11,464

Source: lovefilm.com, as of 27 June 2013 (service has now been discontinued)

LARGEST VIDEOGAME COLLECTION

He has more games and more consoles than you... or anyone else. Here Michael Thomasson reveals how his passion for collecting games began after the most unpromising start...

COUNT THEM ALL IN

The **largest collection of videogames** belongs to Michael Thomasson (USA). He has some 10,607 titles, as counted on 3 December 2012 in New York, USA. He also owns the gear to play the games – 104 console systems jostle for space with the obscure cult classics nestling next to the ranks of million-seller blockbusters.

Pictured with Michael are games for the Bandai's WonderSwan, Tiger's game.com, Bally Astrocade, Atari Jaguar, Watara's Supervision, Sony's PlayStation, Nintendo's Virtual Boy and Fairchild Channel F.

The most games Michael has for one console is 725 for the PS2, and it is Nintendo-manufactured consoles that have the highest representation in his collection, with a total of 4,110 games.

COLLECTING A FORTUNE

Michael started buying games in December 1982, but sold the lot when he went to college in 1988. When the Sega Genesis (or Mega Drive) was released the following year, he began to build a collection that is now more valuable than most people's houses.

■ **What was your first game?**
MT: My first game was *Cosmic Avenger* for the ColecoVision. It was a gift from my grandparents on Christmas Eve. I thought for sure that an actual ColecoVision would emerge the following day but it was the hot Christmas item and sold out everywhere. I looked at the *Cosmic Avenger* box and read the manual every day until the following Christmas (no luck on my birthday in April, either) when a ColecoVision unit did emerge.

■ **What got you started in collecting?**
MT: We went to hook up the ColecoVision, the *Donkey Kong* screen came up on the television and then a snow storm knocked the power out. I had to go to bed, and as soon as my head hit the pillow the power came back on and I lay there in bed listening to my big brother and sister play until I fell asleep. It was the best gift my parents gave me other than their love.

■ **What are your rarest items?**
MT: I have an Apple Pippin @World with a stack of games, perhaps the worst system of the 104 different units that I own. I also have a functioning Brown Box replica made by hand by Ralph Baer [inventor of the Brown Box, later the Magnavox Odyssey – *see p.14*], which he personalized and autographed.

■ **Which is your favourite item in your collection?**
MT: Definitely the ColecoVision. I still play that system the most, followed by the Xbox 360, Sega Dreamcast, Sega Genesis and the GCE Vectrex.

■ **How many of your games do you play?**
MT: I'll eventually play them all, although the thrill of the hunt has become more of the game, excuse the pun! I still have some Bally Astrocade games sealed from 1982 that I have yet to find the time to fire up... The NES is my least played unit, quite an oddity among retro gamers. It premiered following the crash [of 1983; *see pp.82–83*] and due to getting freedom in the form of wheels and discovering girls I hardly noticed that games had re-emerged.

■ **Do you collect anything else?**
MT: I used to be heavily into collecting comic books until I began college [and] couldn't afford to do both.

■ **Any advice for readers who want to collect?**
MT: It took me decades to acquire my collection, but I spent very little money doing it. Learn to barter. Wheel 'n' deal and do not be afraid to purchase duplicates. I'd purchase a collection from an individual, pick out what I needed and resell the extras to finance my next purchase. I estimate that my million-dollar collection was built with less than $5,000 [£3,200].

SHELF RESPECT

More than 30 shelves groan under the weight of Michael's games. The ranks of units – some custom-built – line up across the room in library-style rows and extend from floor to ceiling, leaving no bare walls. "Games are all in alphabetical order by system type," says Michael, "so I can locate any single game in the massive collection in a matter of seconds!"

QUIZ ANSWERS ▷

■ **How many games could you successfully name in the quiz throughout this book?
Check your answers here, tot up how many you got right and check your rating below.**

PAGE 18
Borderlands 2 (Gearbox Software, 2012)

PAGE 20
Left 4 Dead 2 (Valve, 2009)

PAGE 22
Double Dragon (Technōs Japan, 1987)

PAGE 24
Gran Turismo 5 (Polyphony Digital, 2010)

PAGE 30
Sonic the Hedgehog (Sonic Team, 1991)

PAGE 32
Infinity Blade II (ChAIR/ Epic Games, 2011)

PAGE 34
Bubble Safari (Zynga, 2012)

PAGE 36
Tropico 4 (Haemimont Games, 2011)

PAGE 38
BioShock Infinite (Irrational Games, 2013)

PAGE 40
SoulCalibur (Namco, 1998)

PAGE 42
Cut the Rope (ZeptoLab, 2010)

PAGE 48
Guitar Hero (Harmonix, 2005)

PAGE 50
Uncharted: Drake's Fortune (Naughty Dog, 2007)

PAGE 52
Darksiders II (Vigil Games, 2012)

PAGE 54
DotA 2 (Valve, 2013)

PAGE 56
World of Warcraft (Blizzard, 2004)

PAGE 62
Grand Theft Auto IV (Rockstar North, 2008)

PAGE 64
Call of Duty (Infinity Ward/Treyarch, 2003–present)

PAGE 66
Dark Souls (From Software, 2011)

PAGE 68
Resident Evil (Capcom, 1996–present)

PAGE 74
God of War (SCE, 2005)

PAGE 76
Tekken (Namco, 1994)

PAGE 78
Counter-Strike (Valve, 2000)

PAGE 80
Metal Gear (Konami, 1987)

PAGE 86
Skylanders (Toys for Bob/Vicarious Visions, 2011–present)

PAGE 88
The Sims (Maxis, 2000–present)

PAGE 90
Assassin's Creed III (Ubisoft, 2012)

PAGE 92
The World Ends with You (Square Enix, 2007)

PAGE 98
Plants vs. Zombies (PopCap Games, 2009)

PAGE 100
Halo (343 Industries/ Bungie, 2001–present)

PAGE 102
LittleBigPlanet (Media Molecule, 2008)

PAGE 104
Diablo III (Blizzard, 2012)

PAGE 110
Bayonetta (Platinum Games, 2009)

PAGE 112
Mirror's Edge (DICE, 2008)

PAGE 114
Street Fighter II (Capcom, 1991)

PAGE 116
Bad Piggies (Rovio, 2012)

PAGE 118
Portal (Valve, 2007)

PAGE 120
Dead or Alive (Team Ninja, 1997)

PAGE 126
Candy Crush Saga (King, 2012)

PAGE 128
Super Mario (Nintendo, 1985–present)

PAGE 130
Mortal Kombat (Midway, 1992)

PAGE 132
Red Dead Redemption (Rockstar, 2010)

PAGE 134
Temple Run 2 (Imangi Studios, 2013)

PAGE 140
Heavy Rain (Quantic Dream, 2010)

PAGE 142
Angry Birds (Rovio, 2009)

PAGE 144
Castlevania (Konami, 1986)

PAGE 150
Dishonored (Arkane Studios, 2012)

PAGE 152
Command & Conquer (Westwood Studios, 1995)

PAGE 154
Fez (Polytron Corporation, 2012)

PAGE 156
Half-Life (Valve, 1998)

PAGE 158
Mass Effect (BioWare, 2007)

PAGE 164
The Legend of Zelda (Nintendo, 1986– present)

PAGE 166
StarCraft (Blizzard, 1998)

PAGE 168
Metroid (Nintendo, 1986)

PAGE 170
The Walking Dead (Telltale Games, 2012)

PAGE 176
Far Cry 3 (Ubisoft, 2012)

PAGE 178
Final Fantasy VII (Square Enix, 1997)

PAGE 180
Gears of War (Epic Games, 2006)

PAGE 182
Battlefield 3 (DICE, 2011)

206

■ **How did you fare?
Are you a top dog, like
Tropico 4's El Presidente
(pictured right), or are
you at the bottom of
the heap, like Mario's
nemesis, Wario?**

0	Disappointing. Wario is your gaming equivalent.
1–10	A poor score. You're down with a *Minecraft* Creeper.
11–20	You're a Plant being over-run by a Zombie.
21–30	Decent, but more work needed. Think Luigi.
31–40	A cultured score – you're Ezio Auditore da Firenze.
41–50	A score as solid as Solid Snake himself.
51–55	You're awesome, like the Master Chief.
56–59	You rock it. El Presidente would be proud.

AI	Artificial Intelligence: in gaming this refers to computer-generated, human-like opponents that react realistically and challenge the skills of human players
alpha	the first phase of software testing, usually conducted exclusively by the developers
beta	phase of software testing that comes after alpha and is usually open for public use
combo	a series of actions performed in sequence, especially in fighting games
cutscene	non-playable sequence in a game used to advance the plot
DAU	Daily Average Users, often used to measure the popularity of Facebook games
DLC	downloadable content
FPS	first-person shooter, with its action shown from the player's point of view
fragfest	a multiplayer deathmatch
free2play	games that are free to play
glitch	a mistake/bug in the game's programming. Some can be exploited to boost speed-runs (*see definition*)
HDD	hard-disk drive
hit points/HP	a number in RPGs that determines how much damage a character can take before expiring. Each attack deducts a certain number of hit points in damage
isometric	a form of rendering objects in games so that they are viewed from a perspective that makes them seem 3D
JRPG	Japanese role-playing game
kill-to-death ratio	the number of enemies you eliminate divided by the number of lives you lose; also known as kill:death ratio
MAU	Monthly Average Users, often used to measure the popularity of Facebook games
MMO	any kind of massively multiplayer online game – includes (and is often used interchangeably with) MMORPG (*see definition*). These "massive" games feature persistent "worlds"
MMORPG	a type of MMO game that is specifically a role-playing game (RPG)
mod	modification made to a game by a fan or a developer, from the smallest in-game tweak to a complete new version of a game (such as *Counter-Strike*, a take on *Half-Life*)
NES	Nintendo Entertainment System, known as the Famicom in Japan. Its successor was the SNES (Super Nintendo Entertainment System), known as the Super Famicom in Japan
NPC	non-player character, controlled by the computer rather than the gamer
NTSC	National Television System Committee: the TV system used in North America
OS	operating system, such as Windows, Mac OS, iOS, Android or Linux – the software that runs the basic functions of a computer or device
PAL	Phase Alternating Line: the TV system used in Europe. Consoles are produced for both NTSC (*see definition*) and PAL territories
polygon	vast numbers can be used to build up 3D-looking graphics
port	the transfer of a game from one platform to another
PS	PlayStation. Can Include PS2, PS3, PSP (PlayStation Portable), PSN (PlayStation Network), PS Vita
RPG	role-playing game
RTS	real-time strategy
speed-run	a play-through of a whole game or a part of it, completed as quickly as possible
story mode	used in fighting games to describe the single-player fighting battles as a narrative unfolds, perhaps through linking cutscenes (*see definition*)
TCG	trading card game
TPS	third-person shooter, with the player character visible on screen
triple-A	major games developed for the mass market gaming platforms, with big marketing budgets; also known as AAA
twin-stick control	using two joysticks, one to control character movement and the other to control aim
XP	experience points – gained through battles and achieving goals. They help to raise the level of a character, often in an RPG

INDEX ▷

211

CONTRIBUTORS ▷

■ These are the men and women behind *Gamer's Edition 2014*. Pictured right is the GWR team, who plan and edit the book, find the pictures and put the whole thing together. Below you can meet our team of expert section writers.

MARTYN CARROLL (Action-adventure)
Martyn's first article on gaming was published in 1997 and he has since contributed to many sites and publications including *Games*™, *Micro Mart* and Eurogamer.net. He launched *Retro Gamer* in 2004.

■ **Favourite game ever?**
Jet Set Willy from 1984. One of the first games I ever played and still the most memorable.
■ **Most exciting gaming event of 2013?**
The release of *Grand Theft Auto V*. The last great game of this console generation.
■ **Game most played in 2013?**
The most recent *Tomb Raider*.

DAVID CROOKES (Sports)
David began his career on *Amstrad Action* in 1993, and now writes for *The Independent* newspaper and several magazines including *Games*™, *Retro Gamer* and *PLAY*. He was formerly news editor of N*Revolution.

■ **Favourite game ever?**
Uncharted 2: Among Thieves.
■ **Most exciting gaming event of 2013?**
The unveiling of the PlayStation 4.
■ **Game most played in 2013?**
The Last of Us.

LOUISE BLAIN (Hardware)
Previously a staff writer at *Official PlayStation Magazine*, Louise is a freelance games journalist who has written for various publications including *Official Nintendo Magazine* and *PSM3*. She also writes a monthly page for *GamesMaster*.

■ **Favourite game ever?**
Assassin's Creed II.
■ **Most exciting gaming event of 2013?**
BioShock Infinite still managed to surprise with an incredible world, astonishing visuals and a story that had us thinking – and arguing – long after the TV was turned off.
■ **Game most played in 2013?**
Animal Crossing: New Leaf.

ELLIE GIBSON (Social, Mobile & Instant)
Associate features editor at Eurogamer.net and a long-time fan of casual gaming, Ellie thought breaking her *FarmVille* habit was tough, but then she discovered *Candy Crush Saga*.

■ **Favourite game ever?**
Tomb Raider. I love the original games, but I really enjoyed playing the reboot and getting to know Lara all over again.
■ **Most exciting gaming event of 2013?**
The Last of Us: a brilliant, thoughtful and beautiful game. It represents how far we've come in this console generation.
■ **Game most played in 2013?**
Candy Crush Saga. It's horribly addictive.

MATTHEW EDWARDS (Fighting)
Matthew used to work at *GAME*™ and once won a *Street Fighter* tournament in a Cornish cinema. He has written for the likes of Eurogamer.net, *Games*™ and ONE Gamer. He also knows how to ride a motorbike... like, for reals.

■ **Favourite game ever?**
Landstalker: The Treasures of King Nole.
■ **Most exciting gaming event of 2013?**
Watching the 2013 Evolution Championship Series. The Justin Wong comeback against ChrisG was all kinds of hype!
■ **Game most played in 2013?**
Monster Hunter 3 Ultimate.

PHILIPPA WARR (Strategy & Simulation)
A freelance writer specializing in art, digital culture and videogames, Philippa has written for sites and publications including *Wired*, MTV, *PC Gamer*, AOL, The Huffington Post and Digital Spy.

■ **Favourite game ever?**
The *Mass Effect* series.
■ **Most exciting gaming event of 2013?**
The International 3 – the *DotA 2* tournament that took place in Seattle in August.
■ **Game most played in 2013?**
DotA 2.

BEN GRIFFIN (MMORPGs)
Ben is a freelance journalist and copywriter who has written about videogames, motoring and tech for Bit-Gamer, CNET, MSN Tech, Recombu Cars and Stuff.tv. His love affair with gaming began with the Sega Mega Drive (Genesis).

■ **Favourite game ever?**
Vectorman on the Mega Drive.
■ **Most exciting gaming event of 2013?**
The announcement of the Xbox One and PS4. Nothing drives innovation quite like a games console war.
■ **Game most played in 2013?**
Call of Duty: Black Ops II.

PHIL IWANIUK (Racing)
Phil is staff writer at *Official PlayStation Magazine* and a racing games obsessive. His love for all things fast and four-wheeled in games started with *F1 Race* on the Game Boy, and led him to play *Gran Turismo 5* for 24 hours straight.

■ **Favourite game ever?**
Half-Life.
■ **Most exciting gaming event of 2013?**
The PlayStation 4 announcement meeting in New York on 20 February.
■ **Game most played in 2013?**
NBA 2K13.

DAN WHITEHEAD (RPGs)
Dan has been playing games since 1982 and writing about them for over 20 years. He currently works for Eurogamer.net and has been a BAFTA judge for games. He keeps promising to get a grown-up job one of these days...

■ **Favourite game ever?**
Chaos on the ZX Spectrum from 1985.
■ **Most exciting gaming event of 2013?**
LEGO Marvel Super Heroes – two of my favourite things in the same game!
■ **Game most played in 2013?**
The Xbox 360 version of *Minecraft* – every time I think I've had enough, they release a new update!

ROB CAVE (Shooters)
Rob started his gaming life in the 1980s with a second-hand Binatone TV Master IV. He has contributed to a number of books on comics, including *1001 Comics You Must Read Before You Die*, and has worked on every *Gamer's Edition*.

■ **Favourite game ever?**
How could I ever choose just one? But I do have a range of old favourites and I bought my 360 just so I could play *BioShock*.
■ **Most exciting gaming event of 2013?**
The new consoles – not just the big two from Sony and Microsoft, but the Ouya and the somewhat unexpected 2DS.
■ **Game most played in 2013?**
BioShock Infinite.

RACHAEL FINN (Party Time)
Rachael is from London, UK, and makes a living working for Eurosport television. Her earliest game-related memory is of playing *Adventure*. Although now in her early 30s, she still gets that same child-like thrill from gaming.

■ **Favourite game ever?**
One from my childhood: the seminal *Super Mario Bros. 3.*
■ **Most exciting gaming event of 2013?**
The advent of eighth-generation consoles and the potential to sync mobile and in-home gaming with second-screen apps.
■ **Game most played in 2013?**
The TribeZ – a fun and highly addictive city-builder available on both iOS and Android.

MATTHEW BRADFORD (Puzzles)
Matt is a Canadian freelancer whose words have most recently been spotted on GamesRadar, Gaming World Wide, Twin Galaxies and in *Gamer's Edition 2013*. He can also be heard on the Video Game Outsiders podcast.

■ **Favourite game ever?**
If forced to pick one, I'd have to say *Final Fantasy VII.*
■ **Most exciting gaming event of 2013?**
Sony and Microsoft's reveals of the PlayStation 4 and Xbox One. No generation feels as important to the future of gaming – or even the way we play games – as this round.
■ **Game most played in 2013?**
The Last of Us. It has a way of hooking you in.

DAN MORGAN (Platformers)
A writer and sub-editor who has worked across a range of children's magazines as well as music, games and news publications, Dan has been gaming since he received a NES for Christmas at the tender age of four, and got hooked on *Mario*.

■ **Favourite game ever?**
Final Fantasy VII.
■ **Most exciting gaming event of 2013?**
The release of *Grand Theft Auto V.*
■ **Game most played in 2013?**
Sound Shapes.

RYAN GALE (Design)
Ryan has been a dedicated gamer since the days of the Mega Drive. He began as a designer on *Toxic* magazine before becoming an art editor for various publications including *Moshi Monsters* and gaming magazine *Megaton*.

■ **Favourite game ever?**
It was always *Streets of Rage 2* on the Mega Drive until I first played *Red Dead Redemption.*
■ **Most exciting gaming event of 2013?**
The release of *Grand Theft Auto V.*
■ **Game most played in 2013?**
Easily *Halo 4.*

STOP PRESS!

As our work on *Gamer's Edition 2014* draws to a close, here are some records that were approved just in time to make it on to the very last spread.

The console wars heated up in late summer 2013 with Sony announcing that the PS4 would launch on 15 November 2013 in the USA, Europe and South America. Microsoft is set to launch Xbox One just days later, on 22 November 2013. There is everything to play for with 2013's first two quarters of spending on gaming content reaching $2.88 billion (£1.79 billion) in the USA alone.

OLDEST SONG IN A GAME

On 29 August 2013 it was confirmed that the oldest song used in *SingStar* (2007–11) – and indeed any videogame – is "Auld Lang Syne". The popular celebration of new year is attributed to 18th-century Scottish poet Robert Burns. The lyrics were set to the tune of a traditional folk song, and the DLC game version was a rendition by Bing Crosby.

FASTEST VIDEOGAME TO GROSS $1 BILLION

According to VGChartz, *Grand Theft Auto V* (Rockstar, 2013) had reached $1 billion (£625 million) in sales by 20 September 2013 – just three days after its release. It smashed the 10-day record previously set by *The Avengers* movie (USA, 2012) to also become the **fastest entertainment property of any kind to gross $1 billion**. In turn, *GTA V* could be challenged by *Call of Duty: Ghosts*, due in late 2013.

FASTEST LAP OF "KALIMARI DESERT" ON MARIO KART 64

Dan Russell (Canada) zipped around Kalimari Desert – a track on the N64's *Mario Kart 64* (Nintendo, 1996) – in 36.73 seconds on 21 August 2013, as verified on the Guinness World Records Challengers website.

BEST-SELLING PSP GAME

By 6 September 2013, *Grand Theft Auto: Liberty City Stories* (Rockstar Games, 2005) had sold 7.51 million on the PSP.

FASTEST COMPLETION OF "DAM" ON GOLDENEYE 007

Adam Crosbie (UK) completed the "Dam" mission on the N64 game *GoldenEye 007* (Rare, 1997) in 118 seconds on 2 September 2013. The dam jump in the 1995 movie itself was over 220 m (759 ft), making it the **highest bungee jump from a structure in a film**.

MOST TOURNAMENT WINS BY A TEAM

Empire Arcadia (USA) had 1,411 documented gaming tournament wins by 3 August 2013, and celebrates a decade of gaming in 2014. The team's Job "Flocker" Figueroa (USA) had the **most viewed live competitive fighting game match** when he played Justin Wong (USA) of Evil Geniuses at the 2013 EVO competition in *Ultimate Marvel vs. Capcom 3*, with 144,848 concurrent views on 14 July 2013.

MOST POINTS ON *PINCH HITTER* (2007)

Roshan Ramachandra (India) achieved 120,608 points in Chintamani, Karnataka, India, on 7 September 2013.

MOST SUBSCRIBERS ON YOUTUBE

As of 12 September 2013, Felix Arvid Ulf Kjellberg (Sweden), better known by his YouTube channel name "PewDiePie", had 13,052,908 subscribers to his comedic gaming highlight channel. His inspired, motormouth commentaries, generally on horror games, have been viewed 2,399,788,285 times. Felix's most watched video is "FUNNY GAMING MONTAGE!" with 24,556,020 views.

MOST GOALS FROM THE 18-YARD LINE ON *FIFA 13* IN ONE MINUTE

On 26 August 2013, Shawn Alvarez (USA) scored nine goals from the 18-yard line in *FIFA 13* (EA, 2012). Shawn also holds the record for the **longest manual on *Skate 3*** (EA, 2010), keeping going for 12,832 m (42,100 ft) on 11 May 2013 on the Xbox 360.

FASTEST TIME TRIAL FOR "ANCIENT LAKE" ON *DIDDY KONG RACING*

David M Popke (USA) completed "Ancient Lake" on *Diddy Kong Racing* (Rare, 1997) in 47.58 seconds on 6 September 2013.

MOST POPULAR ULTIMATE MARVEL VS. CAPCOM 3 PLAYER

On 26 August 2013, a poll of the best three players on *Ultimate Marvel vs. Capcom 3* (2011) on the Capcom fansite Event Hubs revealed that Justin Wong (USA, *see Most tournament wins by a team, above*) scooped the No.1 spot with 844 votes.

HIGHEST SCORE ON *MISSILE COMMAND* AFTER 100 ROUNDS

We are happy to finally ratify the highest score on *Missile Command* (Atari, 1980) on "Tournament Settings" after 100 rounds of play, which is 1,147,395 points by Roy Daarstad Schildt (USA) at the Laser Blazer arcade in Los Angeles, California, USA, on 11 August 2008.

PICTURE CREDITS ▷

006	Ranald Mackechnie/GWR	102	Kayane.fr
	Ryan Schude/GWR	103	Yves Tennevin
	Ryan Schude/GWR	107	Paul Michael Hughes/GWR
	Kevin Scott Ramos/GWR		Curse.com
008	Paul Michael Hughes/GWR		SC2Earnings.com
010	Michael Bowles	116	Blizzard
	Jason Redmond/AP/PA	126	Time.com
011	Jemal Countess/Getty Images		Eugene Tanner
013	Juergen Schwarz/Getty Images	131	Sculpture Studios
	BAFTA	136	Ari Hollander and Howard Rose/UW
028	Ryan Schude/GWR		Hunter Hoffman/UW
051	Paul Michael Hughes/GWR		Pamel Redford/US Army
058	55design.co.uk	137	Kerbal
060	Kevin Scott Ramos/GWR		RSC Publishing/LOC
062	Clive Rose/Getty Images	144	© 2012 Open 4 Business Productions LLC
064	Ethan Miller/Getty Images	146	Steve Blum
065	Chris Park/AP/PA		Barry Brecheisen/Getty Images
069	Brian Ach/AP/PA	147	Ellen McLain
070	Ina Fassbender/Reuters		Steve Granitz/Getty Images
	Multiplay UK	148	Marina Borodjieva
	Ina Fassbender/Reuters	153	Paul Michael Hughes/GWR
	Ina Fassbender/Reuters	162	Ryan Schude/GWR
	Kevork Djansezian/Getty Images	166	Yui Mok/PA
071	Agencia EFE/Rex Features	171	Marisa Ramirez/UH
	Albert L Ortega/Getty Images	172	Dave Staugas
	Ina Fassbender/Reuters	174	Ranald Mackechnie/GWR
	Invision/Nintendo	182	Dave Bennett/Getty Images
072	Ranald Mackechnie/GWR	184	Ryan Schude/GWR
075	Särkänniemi Adventure Park	185	Kevin Scott Ramos/GWR
080	Bonhams	192	Robyn Beck/Getty Images
082	INTERFOTO/Alamy		Chris Lyons/*Time* magazine
	Joe Fox/Alamy		Kevork Djansezian/Getty Images
	Berekin/iStock	193	Jeff Kravitz/Getty Images
	AK2/iStock		Isaac Brekken/PA
083	Evan-Amos		Steven Simko
098	Penny Arcade	212	Paul Michael Hughes/GWR

216

ACKNOWLEDGEMENTS ▷

■ **Guinness World Records would like to thank the following for their help in the creation of the *Guinness World Records Gamer's Edition 2014*:**

Patrick Abrahart; Angry Birds Nest (angrybirdsnest.com/); m Armitage (Hide&Seek); a Ashton; Aylesbury Studios re Blum; Ren Cave;

Garth Chouteau (PopCap Games); Cyberscore; Paul Deacon (and everyone at 55design.co.uk); Gemma Doherty; James Evans; FMG, London; GameRankings; Games Press; Sean "DarthKnight" Grayson; Daniel Nye Griffiths (Forbes.com); Andy, Mandy, Sidney and Foster Grignon (Quake Labs); Hunter Hoffman (University of Washington);

Martin Hollis; Melanie Johnson; Stephen Kish; Leafs Ice Centre, West Dundee, Illinois; Neil Long (*Edge* magazine); Ciara Mackey; Sarah and Martin Mackey; Theresa Mackey; Sophia Metz (Meltdown); Cindy Morrison; Jon Rushby; Carrie Swidecki; Michael Thomasson; Twin Galaxies; Video Game Records; Gary Vincent; Howard Scott Warshaw; YouTube